Lecture Notes in Computer Science

Vol. 1: GI-Gesellschaft für Informatik e.V. 3. Jahrestagung, Hamburg, 8.–10. Oktober 1973. Herausgegeben im Auftrag der Gesellschaft für Informatik von W. Brauer. XI, 508 Seiten. 1973.

Vol. 2: GI-Gesellschaft für Informatik e.V. 1. Fachtagung über Automatentheorie und Formale Sprachen, Bonn, 9.–12. Juli 1973. Herausgegeben im Auftrag der Gesellschaft für Informatik von K.-H. Böhling und K. Indermark. VII, 322 Seiten. 1973.

Vol. 3: 5th Conference on Optimization Techniques, Part I. (Series: I.F.I.P. TC7 Optimization Conferences.) Edited by R. Conti and A. Ruberti. XIII, 565 pages. 1973.

Vol. 4: 5th Conference on Optimization Techniques, Part II. (Series: I.F.I.P. TC7 Optimization Conferences.) Edited by R. Conti and A. Ruberti. XIII, 389 pages. 1973.

Vol. 5: International Symposium on Theoretical Programming. Edited by A. Ershov and V. A. Nepomniaschy. VI, 407 pages. 1974.

Vol. 6: B. T. Smith, J. M. Boyle, J. J. Dongarra, B. S. Garbow, Y. Ikebe, V. C. Klema, and C. B. Moler, Matrix Eigensystem Routines – EISPACK Guide. XI, 551 pages. 2nd Edition 1974. 1976.

Vol. 7: 3. Fachtagung über Programmiersprachen, Kiel, 5.–7. März 1974. Herausgegeben von B. Schlender und W. Frielinghaus. VI, 225 Seiten. 1974.

Vol. 8: GI-NTG Fachtagung über Struktur und Betrieb von Rechensystemen, Braunschweig, 20.–22. März 1974. Herausgegeben im Auftrag der GI und der NTG von H.-O. Leilich. VI, 340 Seiten. 1974.

Vol. 9: GI-BIFOA Internationale Fachtagung: Informationszentren in Wirtschaft und Verwaltung. Köln, 17./18. Sept. 1973. Herausgegeben im Auftrag der GI und dem BIFOA von P. Schmitz. VI, 259 Seiten. 1974.

Vol. 10: Computing Methods in Applied Sciences and Engineering, Part 1. International Symposium, Versailles, December 17–21, 1973. Edited by R. Glowinski and J. L. Lions. X, 497 pages. 1974.

Vol. 11: Computing Methods in Applied Sciences and Engineering, Part 2. International Symposium, Versailles, December 17–21, 1973. Edited by R. Glowinski and J. L. Lions. X, 434 pages. 1974.

Vol. 12: GFK-GI-GMR Fachtagung Prozessrechner 1974. Karlsruhe, 10.–11. Juni 1974. Herausgegeben von G. Krüger und R. Friehmelt. XI, 620 Seiten. 1974.

Vol. 13: Rechnerstrukturen und Betriebsprogrammierung, Erlangen, 1970. (GI-Gesellschaft für Informatik e.V.) Herausgegeben von W. Händler und P. P. Spies. VII, 333 Seiten. 1974.

Vol. 14: Automata, Languages and Programming – 2nd Colloquium, University of Saarbrücken, July 29–August 2, 1974. Edited by J. Loeckx. VIII, 611 pages. 1974.

Vol. 15: L Systems. Edited by A. Salomaa and G. Rozenberg. VI, 338 pages. 1974.

Vol. 16: Operating Systems, International Symposium, Rocquencourt 1974. Edited by E. Gelenbe and C. Kaiser. VIII, 310 pages. 1974.

Vol. 17: Rechner-Gestützter Unterricht RGU '74, Fachtagung, Hamburg, 12.–14. August 1974, ACU-Arbeitskreis Computer-Unterstützter Unterricht. Herausgegeben im Auftrag der GI von K. Brunnstein, K. Haefner und W. Händler. X, 417 Seiten. 1974.

Vol. 18: K. Jensen and N. E. Wirth, PASCAL – User Manual and Report. VII, 170 pages. Corrected Reprint of the 2nd Edition 1976.

Vol. 19: Programming Symposium. Proceedings 1974. V, 425 pages. 1974.

Vol. 20: J. Engelfriet, Simple Program Schemes and Formal Languages. VII, 254 pages. 1974.

Vol. 21: Compiler Construction, An Advanced Course. Edited by F. L. Bauer and J. Eickel. XIV. 621 pages. 1974.

Vol. 22: Formal Aspects of Cognitive Processes. Proceedings 1972. Edited by T. Storer and D. Winter. V, 214 pages. 1975.

Vol. 23: Programming Methodology. 4th Informatik Sympo IBM Germany Wildbad, September 25–27, 1974. Edited by Hackl. VI, 501 pages. 1975.

Vol. 24: Parallel Processing. Proceedings 1974. Edited by T. VI, 433 pages. 1975.

Vol. 25: Category Theory Applied to Computation and Contr ceedings 1974. Edited by E. G. Manes. X, 245 pages. 1975.

Vol. 26: GI-4. Jahrestagung, Berlin, 9.–12. Oktober 1974. ausgegeben im Auftrag der GI von D. Siefkes. IX, 748 S 1975.

Vol. 27: Optimization Techniques. IFIP Technical Confer Novosibirsk, July 1–7, 1974. (Series: I.F.I.P. TC7 Optimiz Conferences.) Edited by G. I. Marchuk. VIII, 507 pages.

Vol. 28: Mathematical Foundations of Computer Science Symposium at Jadwisin near Warsaw, June 17–22, 1974. E by A. Blikle. VII, 484 pages. 1975.

Vol. 29: Interval Mathematics. Procedings 1975. Edited by K. VI, 331 pages. 1975.

Vol. 30: Software Engineering. An Advanced Course. Edit F. L. Bauer. (Formerly published 1973 as Lecture Notes in nomics and Mathematical Systems, Vol. 81) XII, 545 pages.

Vol. 31: S. H. Fuller, Analysis of Drum and Disk Storage Uni 283 pages. 1975.

Vol. 32: Mathematical Foundations of Computer Science Proceedings 1975. Edited by J. Bečvář. X, 476 pages. 1975.

Vol. 33: Automata Theory and Formal Languages, Kaisersla May 20–23, 1975. Edited by H. Brakhage on behalf of G 292 Seiten. 1975.

Vol. 34: GI – 5. Jahrestagung, Dortmund 8.–10. Oktober Herausgegeben im Auftrag der GI von J. Mühlbacher. X, 755 S 1975.

Vol. 35: W. Everling, Exercises in Computer Systems Ana (Formerly published 1972 as Lecture Notes in Economics Mathematical Systems, Vol. 65) VIII, 184 pages. 1975.

Vol. 36: S. A. Greibach, Theory of Program Structures: Sche Semantics, Verification. XV, 364 pages. 1975.

Vol. 37: C. Böhm, λ-Calculus and Computer Science Theory ceedings 1975. XII, 370 pages. 1975.

Vol. 38: P. Branquart, J.-P. Cardinael, J. Lewi, J.-P. Delesc M. Vanbegin. An Optimized Translation Process and Its Applic to ALGOL 68. IX, 334 pages. 1976.

Vol. 39: Data Base Systems. Proceedings 1975. Edited by H. Ha meier and W. Spruth. VI, 386 pages. 1976.

Vol. 40: Optimization Techniques. Modeling and Optimization Service of Man. Part 1. Proceedings 1975. Edited by J. Cea. 854 pages. 1976.

Vol. 41: Optimization Techniques. Modeling and Optimization Service of Man. Part 2. Proceedings 1975. Edited by J. Cea 852 pages. 1976.

Vol. 42: James E. Donahue, Complementary Definitions of gramming Language Semantics. VII, 172 pages. 1976.

Vol. 43: E. Specker und V. Strassen, Komplexität von Entscheidu problemen. Ein Seminar. V, 217 Seiten. 1976.

Vol. 44: ECI Conference 1976. Proceedings 1976. Edited Samelson. VIII, 322 pages. 1976.

Vol. 45: Mathematical Foundations of Computer Science 1 Proceedings 1976. Edited by A. Mazurkiewicz. XI, 601 pages.

Vol. 46: Language Hierarchies and Interfaces. Edited by F. L. B and K. Samelson. X, 428 pages. 1976.

Vol. 47: Methods of Algorithmic Language Implementation. E by A. Ershov and C. H. A. Koster. VIII, 351 pages. 1977.

Vol. 48: Theoretical Computer Science, Darmstadt, March 1 Edited by H. Tzschach, H. Waldschmidt and H. K.-G. Walte

Lecture Notes in Computer Science

Edited by G. Goos and J. Hartmanis

92

Robin Milner

A Calculus of Communicating Systems

Springer-Verlag
Berlin Heidelberg New York 1980

Author

Robin Milner
University of Edinburgh
Dept. of Computer Science
James Clerk Maxwell Building
The King's Buildings
Mayfield Road
Edinburgh EH9 3JZ
Great Britain

AMS Subject Classifications (1979): 68-02
CR Subject Classifications (1974): 4.30, 5.20, 5.22, 5.24

ISBN 3-540-10235-3 Springer-Verlag Berlin Heidelberg New York
ISBN 0-387-10235-3 Springer-Verlag New York Heidelberg Berlin

Library of Congress Cataloging in Publication Data. Milner, Robin. A calculus of communicating systems. (Lecture notes in computer science; 92) Bibliography: p. Includes index. 1. Machine theory. 2. Formal languages. I. Title. II. Series. QA267.M53. 511.3 80-21068

Printed in Germany

Printing and binding: Beltz Offsetdruck, Hemsbach/Bergstr.
2145/3140-543210

ACKNOWLEDGEMENTS

This work was mainly done during my six-month appointment, from August 1979 to January 1980, at the Computer Science department in Aarhus University, Denmark. Although much of the ground work had been done previously it was mainly in response to their encouragement (to make the theory more accessible and related to practice), and to their informed criticism, that the material reached a somewhat coherent form. I am deeply grateful to them and their students for allowing me to lecture once a week on what was, at first, a loosely connected set of ideas, and for the welcoming environment in which I was able to put the ideas in order. I also thank Edinburgh University for awarding me five months sabbatical leave subsequently, which helped me to complete the task in a reasonable time.

The calculus presented here grew out of work which was inspired by Dana Scott's theory of computation, though it has since diverged in some respects. At every stage I have been influenced by Gordon Plotkin; even where I cannot trace particular ideas to him I have been greatly illuminated by our discussions and by his chance remarks, and without them the outcome would certainly be less than it is. I would also like to thank others with whom I have worked: George Milne, with whom I worked out the Laws of Flow Algebra; Matthew Hennessy, with whom the notion of observation equivalence developed; and Tony Hoare, whose parallel work on different but strongly related ideas, expressed in his "Communicating Sequential Processes", has been a strong stimulus.

Many people have given detailed and helpful criticisms of the manuscript, and thus improved its final form. In particular I thank Michael Gordon and David MacQueen, who went through it all in detail in a Seminar at the Information Sciences Institute, University of California; this not only exposed some mistakes and obscurities but gave me more confidence in the parts they didn't criticise.

Finally, I am very thankful to Dorothy McKie and Gina Temple for their patience and skill in the long and involved task of typing.

CONTENTS

CHAPTER 0

Introduction

0.1 Purpose

These notes present a calculus of concurrent systems. The presentation is partly informal, and aimed at practice; we unfold the calculus through the medium of examples each of which illustrates first its expressive power, and second the techniques which it offers for verifying properties of a system.

A useful calculus, of computing systems as of anything else, must have a high level of articulacy in a full sense of the word implying not only richness in expression but also flexibility in manipulation. It should be possible to describe existing systems, to specify and program new systems, and to argue mathematically about them, all without leaving the notational framework of the calculus.

These are demanding criteria, and it may be impossible to meet them even for the full range of concurrent systems which are the proper concern of a computer scientist, let alone for systems in general. But the attempt must be made. We believe that our calculus succeeds at least to this extent: the same notations are used both in defining and in reasoning about systems, and - as our examples will show - it appears to be applicable not only to programs (e.g. operating systems or parts of them) but also to data structures and, at a certain level of abstraction, to hardware systems. For the latter however, we do not claim to reach the detailed level at which the correct functioning of a system depends on timing considerations.

Apart from articulacy, we aim at an underlying theory whose basis is a small well-knit collection of ideas and which justifies the manipulations of the calculus. This is as important as generality - perhaps even more important. Any theory will be superseded sooner or later; during its life, understanding it and assessing it are only possible and worthwhile if it is seen as a logical growth from rather few basic assumptions and concepts. We take this further in the next section, where we introduce our chosen conceptual basis.

One purpose of these notes is to provide material for a graduate course. With this in mind (indeed, the notes grew as a graduate course at Aarhus University in Autumn 1979) we have tried to find a good expository sequence, and have omitted some parts of the theory - which will appear in technical publications - in favour of case studies. There are plenty of exercises, and anyone who bases a course on the notes should be able to think of others; one pleasant feature of concurrent systems is the wealth and variety of small but non-trivial examples! We could have included many more examples in the text, and thereby given greater evidence for the fairly wide applicability of the calculus; but, since our main aim is to present it as a calculus, it seemed a good rule that every example program or system should be subjected to some proof or to some manipulation.

0.2 Character

Our calculus if founded on two central ideas. The first is observation; we aim to describe a concurrent system fully enough to determine exactly what behaviour will be seen or experienced by an external observer. Thus the approach is thoroughly extensional; two systems are indistinguishable if we cannot tell them apart without pulling them apart. We therefore give a formal definition of observation equivalence (in Chapter 7) and investigate its properties.

This by no means prevents us from studying the structure of systems. Every interesting concurrent system is built from independent agents which communicate, and synchronized communication is our second central idea. We regard a communication between two component agents as an indivisible action of the composite system, and the heart of our algebra of systems is concurrent composition, a binary operation which composes two independent agents, allowing them to communicate. It is as central for us as sequential composition is for sequential programming, and indeed subsumes the latter as a special case. Since for us a program or system description is just a term of the calculus, the structure of the program or system (its intension) is reflected in the structure of the term. Our manipulations often consist of transforming a term, yielding a term with different intension but identical behaviour (extension). Such transformations are familiar in sequential programming, where the extension may just be a mathematical function (the "input/output behaviour"); for concurrent systems however, it seems clear that functions are inadequate as extensions.

These two central ideas are really one. For we suppose that the only way to observe a system is to communicate with it, which makes the observer and system together a larger system. The other side of this coin is that to place two components in communication (i.e. to compose them) is just to let them observe each other. If observing and communicating are the same, it follows that one cannot observe a system without its participation. The analogy with quantum physics may or may not be superficial, but the approach is unifying and appears natural.

We call the calculus CCS (Calculus of Communicating Systems). The terms of CCS stand for behaviours (extensions) of systems and are subject to equational laws. This gives us an algebra, and we are in agreement with van Emde Boas and Janssen [EBJ] who argue that Frege's principle of compositionality of meaning requires an algebraic framework. But CCS is somewhat more than algebra; for example, derivatives and derivations of terms play an important part in describing the dynamics of behaviours.

The variety of systems which can be expressed and discussed in CCS is illustrated by the examples in the text: an agent for scheduling task performance by several other agents (Chapter 3); 'data flow' computations and a concurrent numerical algorithm (Chapter 4); memory devices and data structures (Chapter 8); semantic description of a parallel programming language (Chapter 9). In addition, G. Milne [Mln 3] modelled and verified a peripheral hardware device - a cardreader - using an earlier version of the present ideas.

After these remarks, the character of the calculus is best discovered by a quick look through Chapters 1-4, ignoring technical details. §0.5 (Outline) may also help, but the next two sections are not essential for a quick appraisal.

0.3 Related Work

At present, the most fully developed theory of concurrency is that of Petri and his colleagues. (See for example C.A. Petri, "Introduction to General Net Theory" [Pet], and H.J. Genrich, K. Lautenbach, P.S. Thiagarajan, "An Overview of Net Theory" [GLT].) It is important to contrast our calculus with Net Theory, in terms of underlying concepts.

For Net Theory, a (perhaps the) basic notion is the concurrency relation over the places (conditions) and transitions (events) of a system; if two events (say) are in this relation, it indicates that they are causally independent and may occur in either order or simultaneously. This relation is conspicuously absent in our theory, at least as a basic notion. When we compose two agents it is the synchronization of their mutual communications which determines the composite; we treat their independent actions as occurring in arbitrary order but not simultaneously. The reason is that we assume of our external observer that he can make only one observation at a time; this implies that he is blind to the possibility that the system can support two observations simultaneously, so this possibility is irrelevant to the extension of the system in our sense. This assumption is certainly open to (extensive!) debate, but gives our calculus a simplicity which would be absent otherwise. To answer the natural objection that it is unwieldy to consider all possible sequences (interleavings) of a set of causally independent events, we refer the reader to our case studies, for example in Chapters 3 and 8, to satisfy himself that our methods can avoid this unwieldiness almost completely.

On the other hand, Net Theory provides many strong analytic techniques; we must justify the proposal of another theory. The emphasis in our calculus is upon synthesis and upon extension; algebra appears to be a natural tool for expressing how systems are built, and in showing that a system meets its specification we are demanding properties of its extension. The activity of programming - more generally, of system synthesis - falls naturally into CCS, and we believe our approach to be more articulate in this respect than Net Theory, at least on present evidence. It remains for us to develop analytic techniques to match those of Net Theory, whose achievements will be a valuable guide.

As a bridge between Net Theory and programming languages for concurrency, we should mention the early work of Karp and Miller [KM] on parallel program schemata. This work bears a relation to Net Theory in yielding an analysis of properties of concurrent systems, such as deadlock and liveness; it also comes closer to programming (in the conventional sense), being a generalisation of the familiar notion of a sequential flow chart.

In recent proposals for concurrent programming languages there is a trend towards direct communication between components or modules, and away from communication through shared registers or variables. Examples are:

N. Wirth "MODULA: A language for modular multiprogramming", [Wir]; P. Brinch Hansen "Distributed Processes; a concurrent programming concept", [Bri 2]; C.A.R. Hoare "Communicating Sequential Processes", [Hoa 3]. Hoare's "monitors" [Hoa 2] gave a discipline for the administration of shared resources in concurrent programming. These papers have helped towards understanding the art of concurrent programming. Our calculus differs from all of them in two ways: first, it is not in the accepted sense an imperative language - there are no commands, only expressions; second, it has evolved as part of a mathematical study. In the author's view it is hard to do mathematics with imperative languages, though one may add mathematics (or logic) to them to get a proof methodology, as in the well-known "assertion" method or Hoare's axiomatic method.

One of the main encumbrances to proof in imperative languages is the presence of a more-or-less global memory (the assignable variables). This was recognized by Hoare in "Communicating Sequential Processes"; although CSP is imperative Hoare avoids one aspect of global memory which makes concurrent programs hard to analyse, by forbidding any member of a set of concurrent programs to alter the value of a variable mentioned by another member. This significant step brings CSP quite close to our calculus, the more so because the treatment of communication is similar and expressed in similar notation. Indeed, algorithms can often be translated easily from one to the other, and it is reasonable to hope that a semantics and proof theory for CSP can be developed from CCS. Hoare, in his paper and more recently, gives encouraging evidence for the expressiveness of CSP.

We now turn to two models based on non-synchronized communication. One, with strong expressive power, is Hewitt's Actor Systems; a recent reference is [HAL]. Here the communication discipline is that each message sent by an actor will, after finite time, arrive at its destination actor ; no structure over waiting messages (e.g. ordering by send-time) is imposed. This, together with the dynamic creation of actors, yields an interesting programming method. However, it seems to the author that the fluidity of structure in the model, and the need to handle the collection of waiting messages, poses difficulties for a tractable extensional theory.

Another non-synchronized model, deliberately less expressive, was first studied by Kahn and reported by him and MacQueen [KMQ]. Here the intercommunication of agents is via unbounded buffers and queues, the whole being determinate. Problems have arisen in extending it to non-determinate systems, but many non-trivial algorithms find their best expression in this medium, and it is an example of applicative (i.e. non-imperative) programming which yields to extensional treatment by the semantic techniques of Scott. Moreover, Wadge [Wad] has recently shown how simple calculations can demonstrate the liveness of such systems.

A lucid comparative account of three approaches - Hewitt, Kahn/MacQueen and Milner - is given in [MQ].

In Chapter 9 of these notes we show how one type of concurrent language - where communication is via shared variables - may be derived from or expressed in terms of CCS. This provides some evidence that our calculus is rich in expression, but we certainly do not claim to be able to derive every language for concurrency.

A rather different style of presenting a concurrent system is exemplified by the path expressions of Campbell and Habermann [CaH]. Here the active parts of the system are defined separately from the constraints (e.g. the path expressions) which dictate how they must synchronize. More recent work by Lauer, Shields and others - mainly at Newcastle - shows that this model indeed yields to mathematical analysis. A very different example of this separation is the elegant work of Maggiolo-Schettini et al [MWW]; here the constraints are presented negatively, by stating what conjunctions of states (of separate component agents) may not occur. This approach has an advantage for systems whose components are largely independent (the authors call it "loose coupling"), since then only few constraints need to be expressed.

This section has shown the surprising variety of possible treatments of concurrent systems. It is nothing like a comprehensive survey, and the author is aware that important work has not been mentioned, but it will serve to provide some perspective on the work presented here.

0.4 Evolution

This work evolved from an attempt to treat communication mathematically. In Milner : "Processes: a mathematical model of computing agents" [Mil 1] a model of interacting agents was constructed, using Scott's theory of domains. This was refined and grew more algebraic in G. Milne and Milner: "Concurrent Processes and their syntax" [MM]. At this point we proposed no programming language, but were able to prove properties of defined concurrent behaviours. For example, Milne in his Ph.D. Thesis "A mathematical model of concurrent computation" [Mln] proved partial correctness of a piece of hardware, a card-reader, built from four separate components as detailed in its hardware description. Our model at this stage drew upon Plotkin's and Smyth's Powerdomain constructions, [Plo 1, Smy]. which extended Scott's theory to admit non-determinism. Part of our algebra is studied in depth in [Mil 2].

At this point there were two crucial developments. First - as we had hoped - our behaviour definitions looked considerably like programs, and the resemblance was increased by merely improving notation. The result, essentially the language of CCS, is reported in [Mil 3] and was partly prompted by discussions with Hoare and Scott. (For completeness, two other papers [Mil 4,5] by the author are included in the reference list. Each gives a slightly different perspective from [Mil 3], and different examples.) The second development was to realise that the resulting language has many interpretations; and that the Powerdomain model, and variants of it, may not be the correct ones. A criterion was needed, to reject the wrong interpretations. For this purpose, we turned to <u>observation equivalence</u>; two behaviour expressions should have the same interpretation in the model iff in all contexts they are indistinguishable by observation.

It now turns out that a definition of observation equivalence (for which admittedly there are a few alternatives) <u>determines</u> a model, up to isomorphism, and moreover yields algebraic laws which are of practical use in arguing about behaviours. We have strong hope for a set of laws which are in some sense complete; in fact the laws given in Chapters 5 and 7 have been shown complete for a simplified class of finite (terminating) behaviours. In this case, "complete" means that if two behaviour expressions are observation-equivalent in all contexts then they may be proved equal by the laws; this completeness is shown in [HM].

0.5 Outline

In Chapter 1 we discuss informally the idea of experimenting on, or observing, a non-deterministic agent; this leads to the notion of synchronisation tree (ST) as the behaviour of an agent. Chapter 2 discusses mutual experiment, or communication, between agents, and develops an algebra of STs. In Chapter 3 we do a small case-study (a scheduling system) and prove something about it, anticipating the formal definition of observation equivalence and its properties to be dealt with fully in Chapter 7.

Chapter 4 enriches our communications - up to now they have been just synchronizations - to allow the passing of values from one agent to another, and illustrates the greater expressive power in two more examples; one is akin to Data Flow, and the other is a concurrent algorithm for finding a zero of a continuous function. The notion of derivative of a behaviour is introduced, and used in the second example.

In Chapter 5 we define CCS formally, giving its dynamics in terms of derivations (derivative sequences). This yields our strong congruence relation, under which two programs are congruent iff they have essentially the same derivations, and we establish several laws obeyed by the congruence. In Chapter 6 we present communication trees (CTs, a generalisation of STs) as a model which obeys these laws; this model is not necessary for the further development, but meant as an aid to understanding.

Chapter 7 is the core of the theory; observation equivalence is treated in depth, and from it we gain our main congruence relation, observation congruence, under which two programs are congruent iff they cannot be distinguished by observation in any context. Having derived some properties of the congruence, we use them in Chapter 8 to prove the correct behaviour of two further systems, both to do with data structures.

In Chapters 9 and 10 we look at some derived Algebras. One takes the form of an imperative concurrent programming language, with assignment statements, "cobegin-coend" statements, and procedures. In effect, we show how to translate this language directly into CCS. The other is a restriction of CCS in which determinacy is guaranteed, and we indicate how proofs about such programs can be simpler than in the general case.

Finally, in Chapter 11 we try to evaluate what has been achieved, and indicate directions for future research.

CHAPTER 1

Experimenting on nondeterministic machines

1.1 Traditional equivalence of finite state acceptors

Take a pair S,T of nondeterministic acceptors over the alphabet $\Sigma = \{a,b,c,d\}$:

S

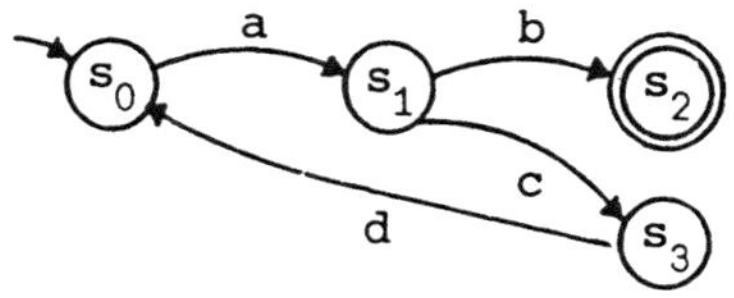

T

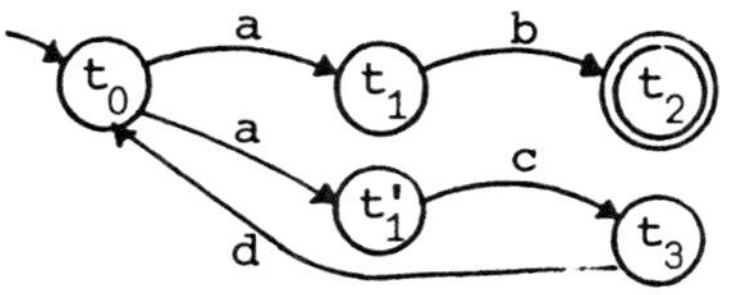

The accepting states of S and T are s_2 and t_2 respectively; in non-deterministic acceptors we can always make do, as here, with a single 'dead' accepting state.

A standard argument that S and T are equivalent, meaning that they accept the same language (set of strings), runs as follows. Taking s_i (resp t_i) to represent the language accepted starting from state s_i (resp t_i), we get a set of equations for S , and for T :

$s_0 = as_1$	$t_0 = at_1 + at_1'$
$s_1 = bs_2 + cs_3$	$t_1 = bt_2$
$s_2 = \varepsilon$	$t_1' = ct_3$
$s_3 = ds_0$	$t_2 = \varepsilon$
	$t_3 = dt_0$

Here as usual + stands for union of languages, ε for the language $\{\varepsilon\}$ containing only the empty string, and we can think of the symbol a standing for a function over languages: $as = a(s) = \{a\sigma;\ \sigma \in s\}$.

Now by simple substitution we deduce

$$s_0 = a(b\varepsilon + cds_0) .$$

By applying the distributive law $a(s + s') = as + as'$ we deduce

$$s_0 = ab\varepsilon + acds_0 ,$$

and we can go further, using a standard rule for solving such equations known as Arden's rule, to get

$$s_0 = (acd)^*abc \ .$$

For T it is even simpler; we get directly (without using distributivity)

$$t_0 = abc + acdt_0$$

and the unique solvability of such equations tells us that $s_0 = t_0$, so S and T are equivalent acceptors.

But are they equivalent, in all useful senses?

1.2 Experimenting upon acceptors

Think differently about an acceptor over $\{a,b,c,d\}$. It is a black box, whose behaviour you want to investigate by asking it to accept symbols one at a time. So each box has four buttons, one for each symbol:

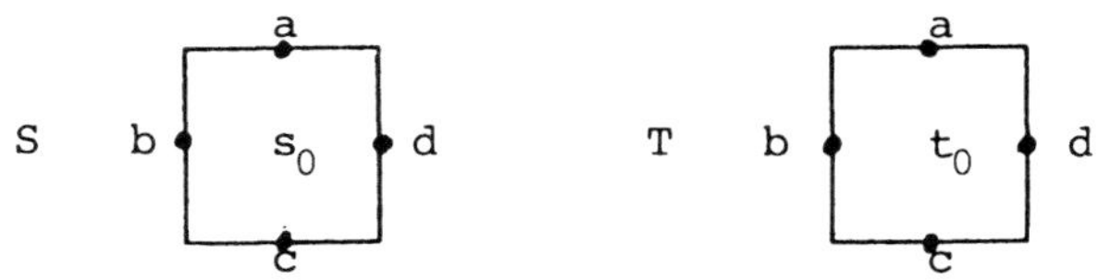

There are four atomic experiments you can do, one for each symbol. Doing an a-experiment on S (secretly in state s_0 , but you don't know that) consists in trying to press the a-button, with two possible outcomes in general:

(i) Failure - the button is locked;

(ii) Success - the button is unlocked, and goes down (and secretly a state transition occurs).

In fact we cannot distinguish between S and T , in their initial states, by any single atomic experiment; the a-experiment succeeds in each case, and the other three fail.

After a successful a-experiment on each machine, which may yield

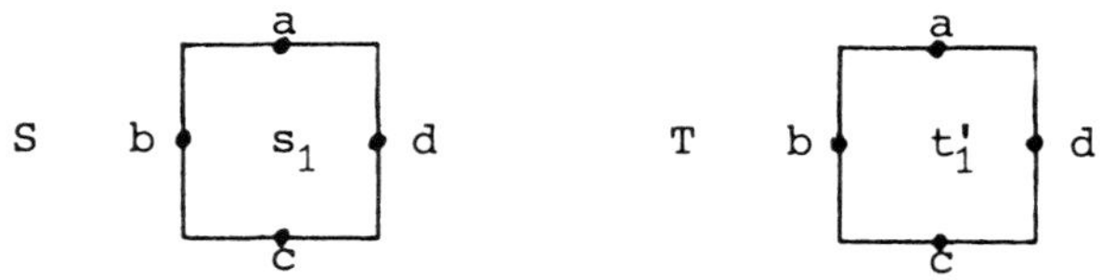

we may try another atomic experiment, in our aim to see if the machines are equivalent or not. Clearly a b-experiment now succeeds for S and fails for T , though the other three experiments fail to distinguish them. After trying the b-experiment, then, can we conclude that S and T are <u>not</u> equivalent?

No, because S's response to the a-experiment could have been different (for all we know) and locked the b-button, while T's response could have been different (for all we know - and it could indeed!) and unlocked the b-button. Following this argument further, we may feel forced to admit that <u>no</u> finite amount of experiment could prove to us that S and T are, or are not, equivalent!

But suppose

(i) It is the <u>weather</u> at any moment which determines the choice of transition (in case of ambiguity, e.g. T at t_0 under an a-experiment) ;

(ii) The weather has only finitely many states - at least as far as choice-resolution is concerned ;

(iii) We can control the weather .

For some machines these assumptions are not so outrageous; for example, one of two pulses may always arrive first <u>within</u> a certain temperature range, and <u>outside</u> this range the other may always arrive first. (At the boundary of the range we have the well-known <u>glitch</u> problem, which we shall ignore here.)

Now, by conducting an a-experiment on S and T under <u>all</u> weather conditions (always in their start states, which we have to assume are recoverable), we can find that S's b-button is always unlocked, but that T's b-button is sometimes locked, and we can conclude that <u>the machines are not equivalent</u>.

Is this sense of equivalence, in which S and T are not equivalent, a meaningful one? We shall find that we can make it precise and shall adopt it - partly because it yields a nice theory, partly because it is a finer (smaller) equivalence relation than the standard one (which we can always recover by introducing the distributive law used in §1.1), but more for the following reason. Imagine that the b-buttons on S and T are hidden. Then <u>in all weathers</u> every successful experiment upon S unlocks some visible button:

<u>S (with b hidden) is not deadlockable</u>,

while <u>in some weathers</u>, and after some experiments, all of T's visible buttons will be locked:

<u>T (with b hidden) is deadlockable</u>.

We wish to think of a nondeterministic choice in such machines as being resolved irreversibly, at a particular moment, by information flowing into the system from an unseen source; if a deadlock can thus arise in one machine but not in another, we do not regard them as behaviourally equivalent.

1.3 Behaviour as a tree

Because we reject the distributive law $a(x + y) = ax + ay$, we can no longer take languages (sets of strings) as the behaviours of our machines. We proceed to an alternative. From now on we will use NIL instead of ε to stand for a behaviour which can do nothing (= admits no experiment) ; we shall also use Greek letters for our symbols - i.e. names of buttons - so you should consider $\alpha,\beta,\gamma,\delta$ as replacements for a,b,c,d in our simple example.

First, take the transition graph for S and unfold it into a tree with states as node labels and symbols as arc labels:

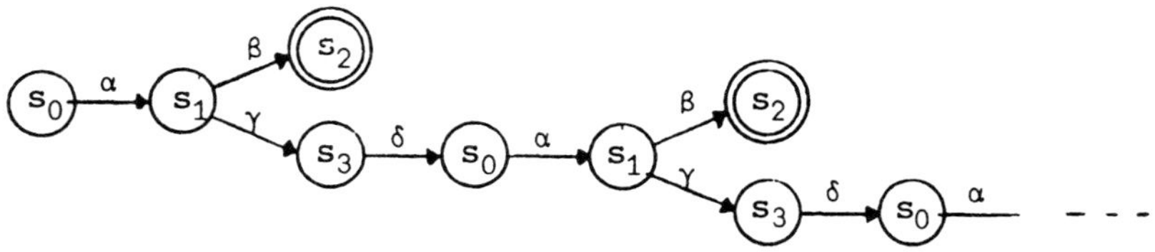

Because state names are present we have lost no information; the state transition graph can be recovered from such a tree. But the experimenter cannot see the state - he can only see the transitions. This leads us to drop the node labels, and take the infinite tree

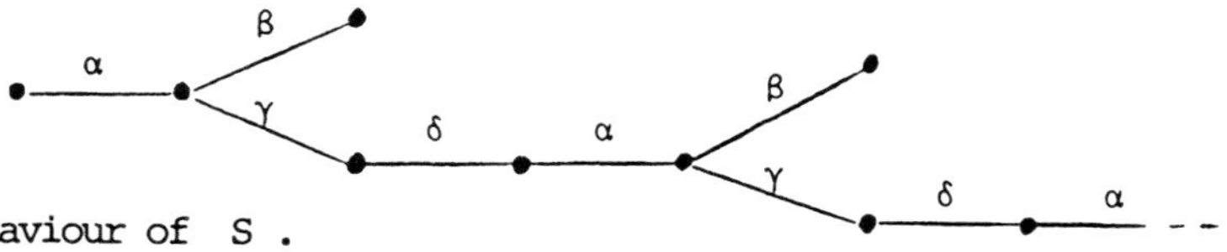

as the behaviour of S .

<u>Definition</u> A <u>label</u> is a member of a given (fixed) label set Λ .

We are using $\alpha,\beta,\gamma,\ldots$ to stand for labels. (The use of the word 'label' in place of 'symbol' will be further motivated later.)

<u>Definition</u> A <u>sort</u> is a subset of Λ .

We shall usually use L,M,N,.. to stand for sorts. We shall also often use the word <u>agent</u> in place of 'machine' or 'acceptor', so

'S is an acceptor over the alphabet Σ'

becomes

'S is an agent of sort L' .

<u>Definition</u> A <u>Rigid Synchronization Tree</u> (RST) of sort L is a rooted, unordered, finitely branching tree each of whose arcs is labelled by a member of L .

Thus the tree in the last diagram is an RST of sort $\{\alpha, \beta, \gamma, \delta\}$. (It is also an RST of any larger sort.)

Why 'rigid'? Because it is the behaviour of a rigid agent - one which can make no transition except that corresponding to an atomic experiment. We shall soon meet other transitions.

Why 'synchronization'? Because we shall later see how the communication of two agents can be represented in forming their joint tree from their separate trees. Then the joint tree will <u>not</u> be rigid, in general, since intercommunication between component agents is not observable.

Notice that <u>finite</u> RSTs can be represented as expressions:

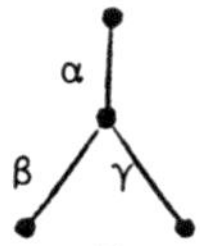

is $\alpha(\beta NIL + \gamma NIL)$

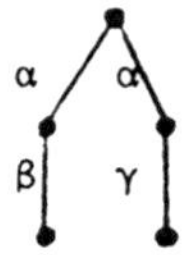

is $\alpha\beta NIL + \alpha\gamma NIL$

and usually there is more than one natural expression:

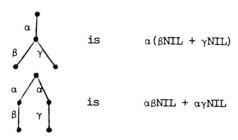

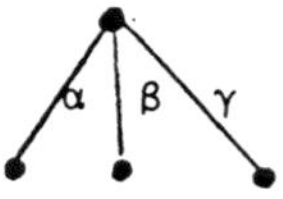

is $\alpha NIL + (\beta NIL + \gamma NIL)$, or
$(\alpha NIL + \beta NIL) + \gamma NIL$.

Indeed, + is both commutative and associative, since we declared RSTs to be unordered trees - and NIL is easily seen to be a zero for summation. To justify these remarks we now define the algebra of RSTs.

1.4 Algebra of RSTs

Ignoring sorts for a moment, we have an elementary algebra over RSTs, whose operations are:

NIL (nullary operation)

NIL is the tree • ;

+ (binary operation)

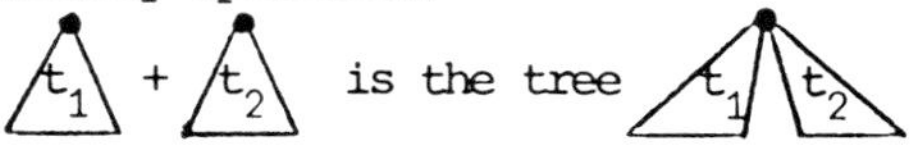

(identify roots) ;

λ (unary operation, for each $\lambda \in \Lambda$)

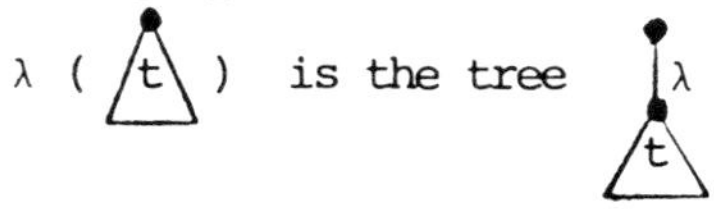

.

They obey the following laws, as you can easily see:

Associativity	$x + (y + z) = (x + y) + z$
Commutativity	$x + y = y + x$
Nullity	$x + \text{NIL} = x$

In fact, these laws are complete: any true equation between RST expressions can be deduced from them.

If we consider sorts, and let RST_L be the set of RSTs of sort L, then NIL is of sort L for any L :

$$\text{NIL} \in \text{RST}_L \, .$$

Further, + takes trees of sort L,M respectively to a tree of sort $L \cup M$:

$$+ \in \text{RST}_L \times \text{RST}_M \to \text{RST}_{L \cup M} \, ,$$

and λ takes a tree of sort L to a tree of sort $L \cup \{\lambda\}$:

$$\lambda \in \text{RST}_L \to \text{RST}_{L \cup \{\lambda\}} \, .$$

We shall usually forget about sorts for the present, but there are times later when they will be essential.

Consider now solving recursive equations over RSTs. We wish the equations for our agent S of §1.1

$$s_0 = \alpha s_1 \qquad s_1 = \beta s_2 + \gamma s_3$$
$$s_2 = \text{NIL} \qquad s_3 = \delta s_0$$

to define the (infinite) behaviour of S as an RST of sort $\{\alpha,\beta,\gamma,\delta\}$.

This set of equations has a unique solution for the variables $s_0, \ldots, s_3$; you can see this by the fact that the entire tree can be developed top-down to any depth:

s_0 = 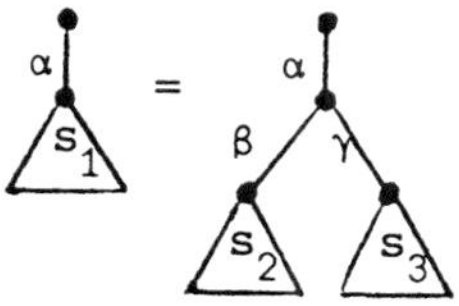 = ... and so on.

Warning. Not every set of recursive equations has a unique solution; consider the simple equation

$$s = s$$

which is satisfied by any RST (or anything else, for that matter). Again, some sets of equations define no RST at all. Consider the equation

$$s = s + \alpha\text{NIL} \quad ;$$

a solution would have to be infinitely branching at the root. Even if we allowed infinitely branching RSTs, so that

s_0 = 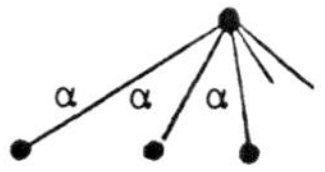 . . . → ∞

would be a solution, it would not be unique since $s_0 + t$ would also be a solution for any t . We defer this problem to Chapter 5.

Exercise 1.1 Can you find a condition on a set of equations

$$\begin{aligned} s_0 &= \ldots \\ s_1 &= \ldots \\ &\ldots \\ s_n &= \ldots \end{aligned}$$

(with RST expressions involving $s_0, \ldots, s_n$ on the right-hand sides)

which ensures that it possesses a unique solution in RSTs? (Hint: consider cycles of ε-transitions in transition graphs.)

1.5 Unobservable actions

Under the conventional definition, a nondeterministic acceptor may have transitions labelled by ε , the null string. Consider R , a modification of our S of §1.1 (reverting briefly to Roman alphabet):

R

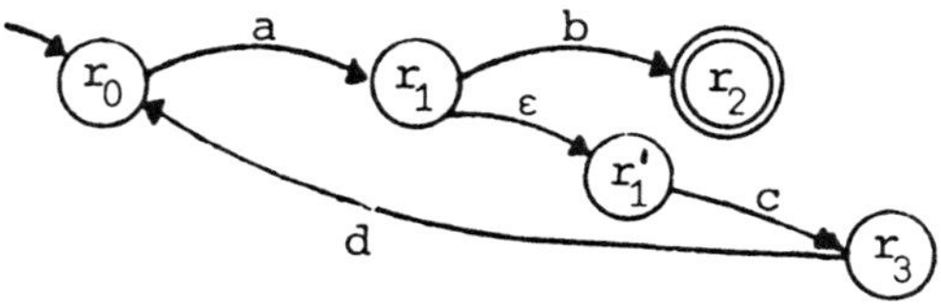

(The loop formed by the d-transition is irrelevant to our comparison.) In the conventional sense, R and S are equivalent. But what does the ε-transition mean, in our more mechanistic interpretation? It means that R in state r_1 (i.e. after the a-button has been pressed) <u>may</u> at any time move silently to state r_1', and that if a b-experiment is never attempted it <u>will</u> do so.

Thus, if we attempt a b-experiment on R, after the successful a-experiment, there are some weather conditions in which we find the b-button permanently locked; if on the other hand we attempt a c-experiment (after the a-experiment) we shall in <u>all</u> weather conditions find the c-button eventually unlocked (eventually, because although R may take a little time to decide on its ε-transition, it will do so since no b-experiment is attempted).

<u>Exercise 1.2</u> Use this as the basis of an argument that <u>no pair of R, S and T</u> are equivalent. A rigorous basis for the argument will be given later.

Let us return to our Greek alphabet, and ask how we should write the equations specifying R's behaviour. We choose the symbol τ in place of ε (to avoid confusion with the null string), and use it as a new unary operation upon behaviours. The equations determining the behaviours $r_0,\ldots,r_3$ are:

$$r_0 = \alpha r_1 \qquad r_1 = \beta r_2 + \tau r_1' \qquad r_1' = \gamma r_3$$
$$r_2 = \mathrm{NIL} \qquad r_3 = \delta r_0$$

We are assuming that $\tau \notin \Lambda$ (the fixed label set).

<u>Definition</u> A <u>Synchronization Tree</u> (ST) of sort L is a rooted, unordered, finitely branching tree each of whose arcs is labelled by a member of $L\cup\{\tau\}$.

Thus a <u>rigid</u> ST (an RST) is just an ST with no arcs labelled τ; it is the behaviour of an agent which can make no silent transitions.

Since we are taking the unary operation τ over STs to be given by

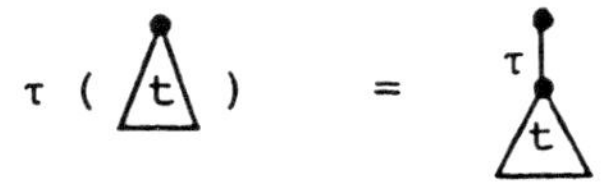

we can of course deduce the ST-behaviour of R. It is

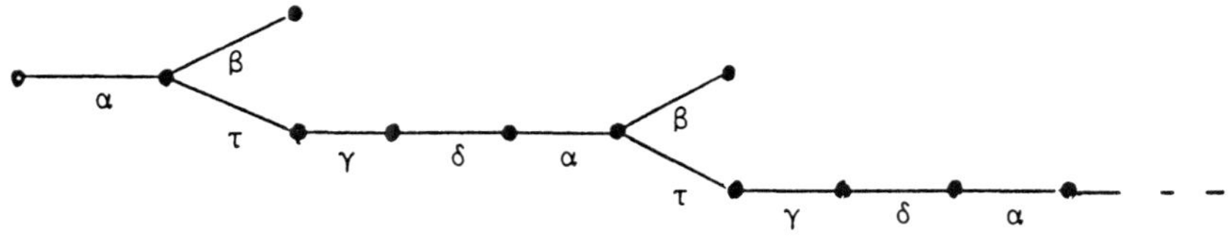

STs are a simple and useful notion of behaviour. They are just the unfoldings of behaviour equations, which in turn follow directly from transition graphs. Of course in this way different transition graphs can yield the same ST, from which we can be certain that they are indistinguishable by experiment.

Exercise 1.3 Convince yourself that the transition graphs

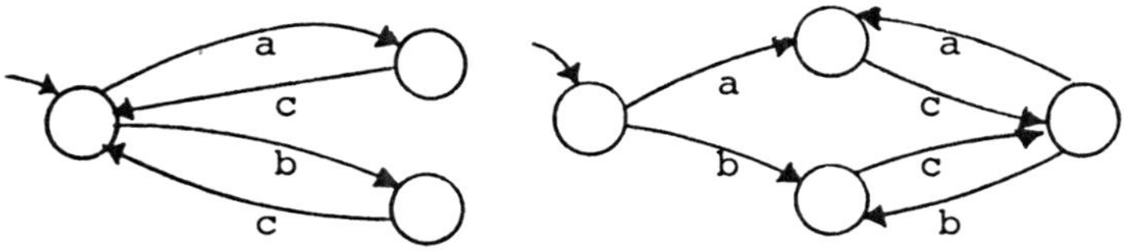

have the same unfolding.

However, different STs (or transition graphs yielding different STs) may be indistinguishable by experiment. This is true even for RSTs; consider the simple pair

each of which admits a single α-experiment and then nothing else.

But it is even more true in the case of unobservable actions. Later we shall study an equivalence relation, observation equivalence, over STs, which can (for finite STs) be axiomatized by a finite set of equations added to those given in §1.4 above. To get a foretaste of the equivalence consider the following exercise.

Exercise 1.4 Examine each of the following pairs of simple STs and try to decide by informal argument, as in Exercise 1.2 above, which are observation equivalent (i.e. indistinguishable by experiment). You may reasonably conclude that four pairs are equivalent, or that six pairs are equivalent, but you should also find that the notion of equivalence is not yet precise. The point of this exercise is that it is not trivial to capture our informal arguments by a precise notion.

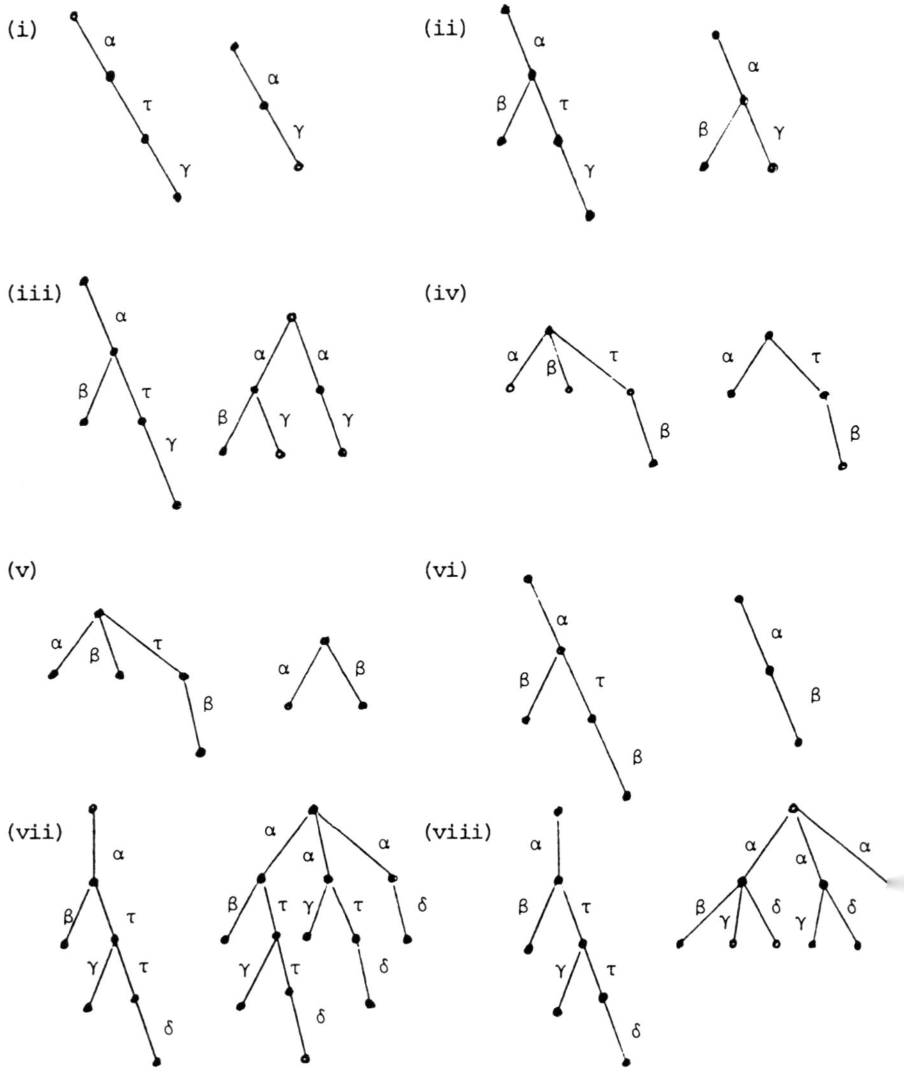

Can you think of some equational axioms of observation equivalence?

Chapter 2

Synchronization

2.1 Mutual experimentation

The success of an α-experiment enables the machine to proceed (to offer further experiments); it also allows the observer to proceed (to attempt further experiments). This suggests an obvious symmetry; we would like to represent the observer as a machine, then to represent the composite observer/machine as a machine, then to understand how *this* machine behaves for a new observer.

How should two machines interact?

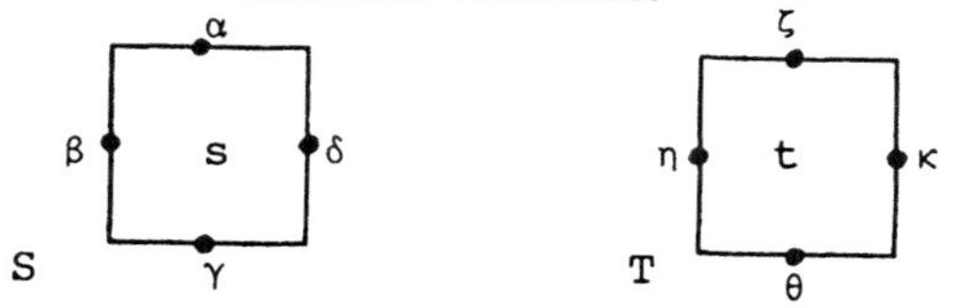

We must say which experiments offered by S may combine with or (*complement*) which experiments of T to yield an interaction. Rather than set up a label correspondence (e.g. $\alpha \leftrightarrow \zeta$, $\delta \leftrightarrow \eta$) for each machine combination, we introduce a little structure on our label set Λ.

We assume a fixed set Δ of *names*. We use $\alpha, \beta, \gamma, \ldots$ to stand for names.

We assume a set $\bar{\Delta}$ of *co-names*, disjoint from Δ and in bijection with it; the bijection is $(\bar{\ })$:

$$\alpha(\in\Delta) \mapsto \bar{\alpha}(\in\bar{\Delta})$$

and we call $\bar{\alpha}$ the *co-name* of α. Using $(\bar{\ })$ also for the inverse bijection, we have $\bar{\bar{\alpha}} = \alpha$.

Now we assume $\Lambda = \Delta \cup \bar{\Delta}$ to be our set of *labels*. We shall use λ to range over Λ. We call λ and $\bar{\lambda}$ *complementary* labels.

The function $(\bar{\ })$ is now a bijection over Λ. We extend it to subsets of Λ; in particular for any *sort* L, $\bar{L} = \{\bar{\lambda};\ \lambda\in L\}$.

We shall sometimes need the function

$$\text{name}(\alpha) = \text{name}(\bar{\alpha}) = \alpha$$

which we extend to sorts by defining

$$\text{names}(L) = \{\text{name}(\lambda);\ \lambda \in L\}.$$

Now consider the pair of machines

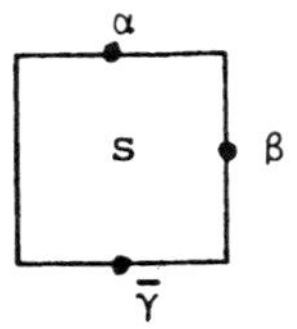

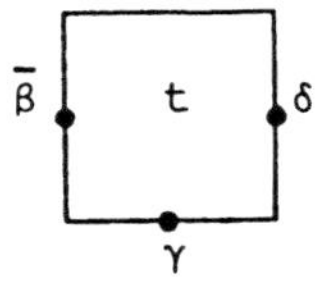

$S: \{\alpha, \beta, \bar{\gamma}\}$ $T: \{\bar{\beta}, \gamma, \delta\}$

The natural candidate, perhaps, for the combined machine $S \| T$ may be pictured thus:

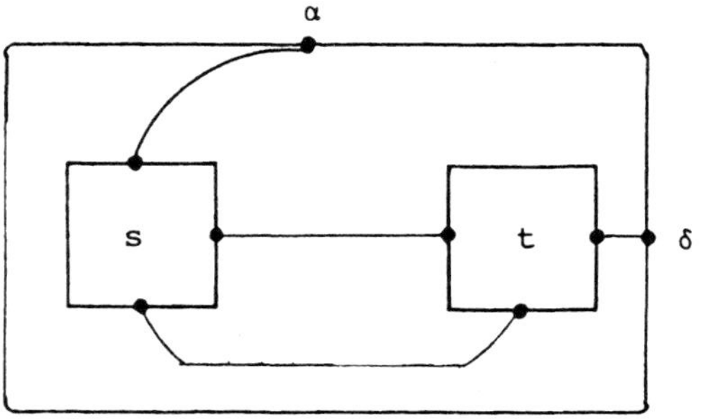

or:

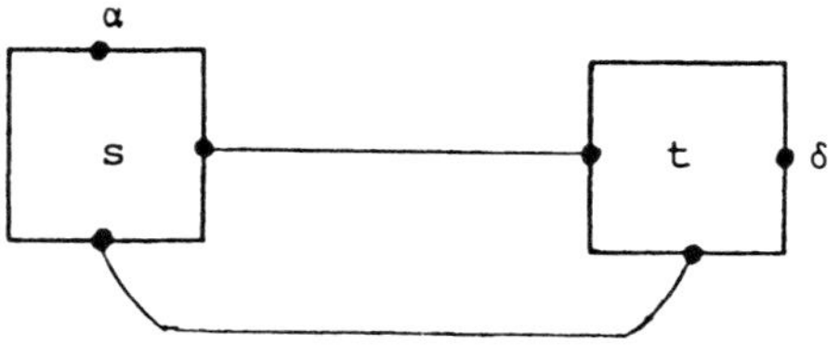

The intuition is that complementary ports, one in each machine, are linked and hidden (labels removed), since these links represent <u>mutual</u> observation, while other ports still support <u>external</u> observation.

But under this scheme there are two disadvantages. First, consider

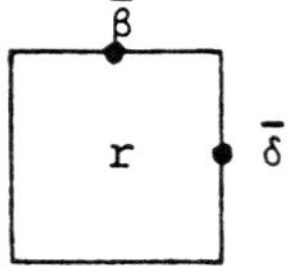

$R: \{\bar{\beta}, \bar{\delta}\}$

We can form $R \| (S \| T)$ and $(R \| S) \| T$:

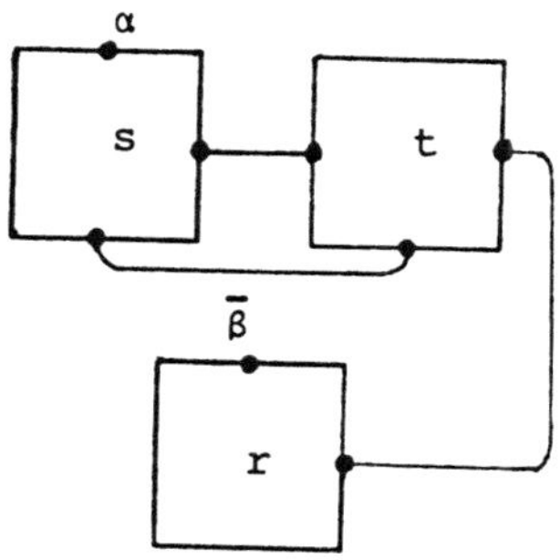

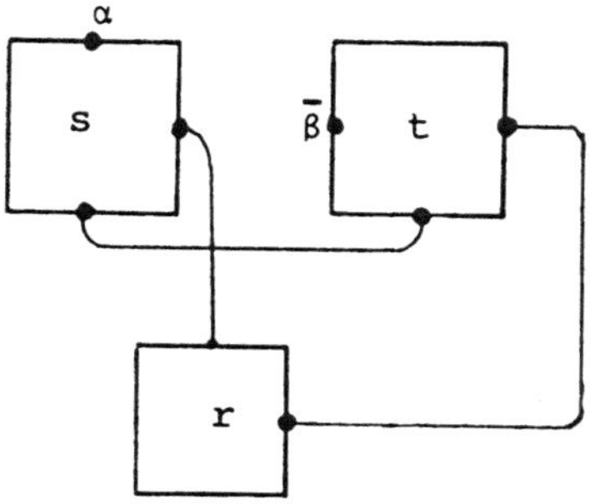

each of sort $\{\alpha,\bar{\beta}\}$ but clearly different. S's offers of β-experiments are observed by T in the first case, but by R in the second case. So $\|$ is not associative.

Second, it is useful to allow that S's β-experiment-offers (or β-capabilities as we shall sometimes call them) may be observed by either R or T (that is, each β-experiment on S may be done by either R or T, but not both); this makes S into a resource shared by R and T.

The solution is to factor combination into two separate operations: one to link ports, the other to hide them. We shall use the word composition for the first of these operations, and the second we shall call restriction.

2.2 Composition, restriction and relabelling

The composite $R|S$ of our two machines R and S may be pictured

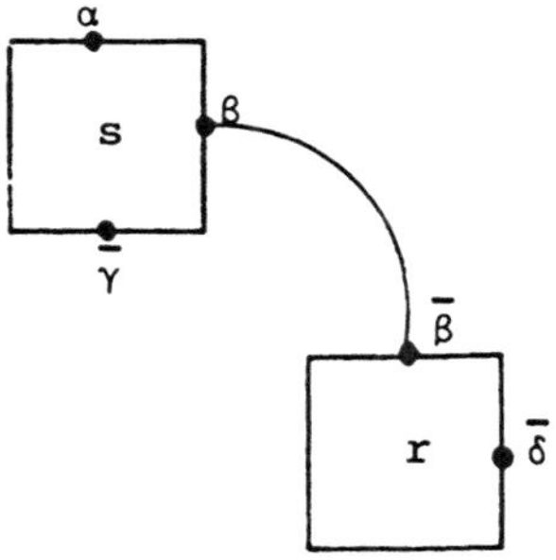

while for $(R|S)|T$ we get

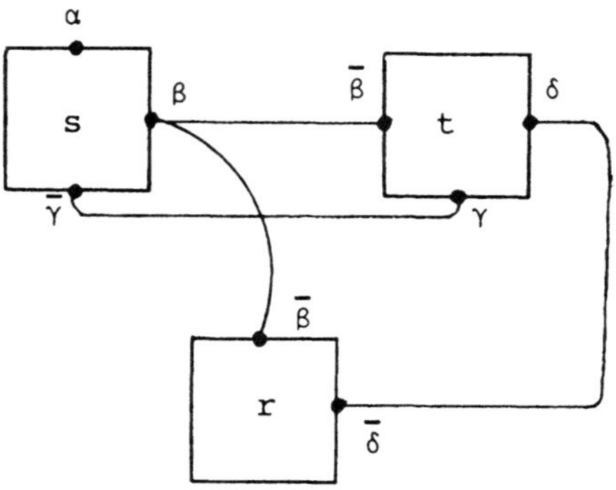

That is, for each λ, in forming $U|V$ we link every port labelled λ in U to every port labelled $\bar{\lambda}$ in V.

<u>Exercise 2.1</u> From $R|(S|T)$ as a picture, and convince yourself by other examples that - on pictures - composition is an associative and commutative operation.

Before defining composition of <u>behaviours</u>, let us look at two other operations on <u>pictures</u>.

For each $\alpha \in \Delta$, we define a postfixed <u>restriction</u> operation $\backslash\alpha$, which on pictures just means "hide the ports labelled α or $\bar{\alpha}$", i.e. it drops the labels α and $\bar{\alpha}$ from pictures, thus reducing their sort.

$(R|S)\backslash\beta$

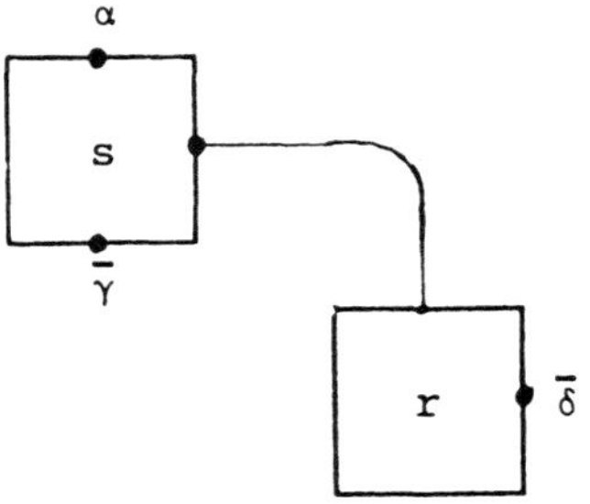

$(= R\|S)$

$((R|S)|T)\backslash\beta\backslash\gamma\backslash\delta$

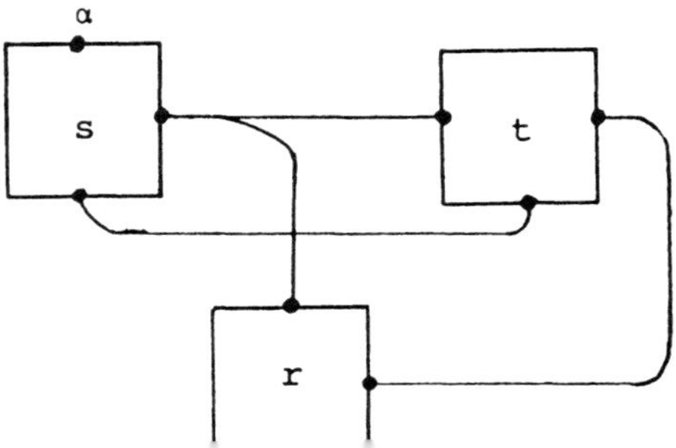

Exercise 2.2 Which of the following are identical as pictures?

(i) $((R|S)|T)\backslash\beta\backslash\gamma\backslash\delta$ (v) $(R|(S|T)\backslash\delta)\backslash\beta\backslash\gamma$

(ii) $((R|S)\backslash\beta|T)\backslash\gamma\backslash\delta$ (vi) $(R|(S|T)\backslash\gamma)\backslash\beta\backslash\delta$

(iii) $((R|S)\backslash\gamma|T)\backslash\beta\backslash\delta$ (vii) $((R|T)\backslash\delta|S)\backslash\beta\backslash\gamma$

(iv) $((R\backslash\gamma|S)|T)\backslash\beta\backslash\delta$ (viii) $((R|T)\backslash\delta|S\backslash\delta)\backslash\beta\backslash\gamma$

Note: $\backslash\alpha$ binds tighter than $|$, so that $U|V\backslash\alpha$ means $U|(V\backslash\alpha)$.

Besides its use with composition, the restriction operation by itself corresponds to a simple, rather concrete, action:- that of hiding or 'internalising' certain ports of a machine. Compare the remarks on hiding the b-buttons of two machines, at the end of §1.2.

Note that we can define $S\|T$, where $S:L$ and $T:M$, by $S\|T = (S|T)\backslash\alpha_1\ldots\backslash\alpha_n$ where $\{\alpha_1,\ldots,\alpha_n\}$ = names $(L\cap\bar{M})$.

We shall henceforth abandon the use of upper case letters for machines. There is a fine distinction between the ideas of (i) a machine which may move through states but remains the same machine (a physical notion) and (ii) a machine-state pair, i.e. a way of specifying a behaviour with a definite start (a more mathematical notion, exemplified by the normal definition of Finite-state Acceptor as consisting of a state set, a transition relation, a set of accepting states and a start state). Our lower case letters correspond to the latter idea - indeed, they denote the specified behaviours (here as STs), and it is these which are the domain of our algebra; we shall soon see what $r|s$ etc. mean as behaviours.

We also have another use for upper case letters; we say that $S:L \to M$ (where L,M are sorts) is a relabelling from L to M if

(i) it is a bijection;

(ii) it respects complements
(i.e. $\overline{S(\alpha)} = S(\bar{\alpha})$ for $\alpha,\bar{\alpha}\in L$).

We define the postfixed relabelling operation $[S]$, over (pictures of) machines of sort L, as simply replacing each label $\lambda\in L$ by $S(\lambda)$. Thus for r,t as above we have

$r|t$ =

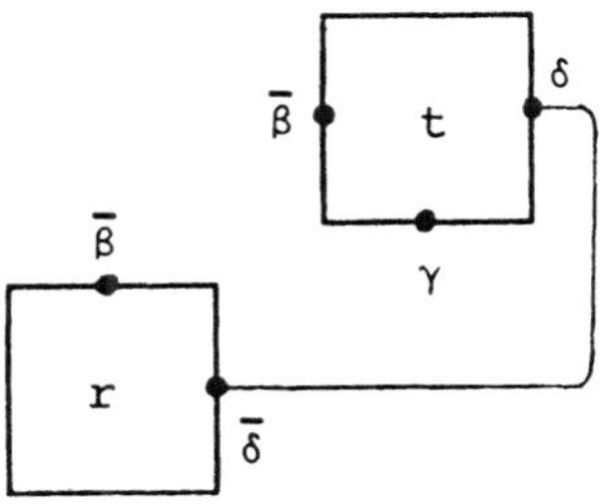

and $S: \{\bar{\beta},\gamma,\delta,\bar{\delta}\} \to \{\delta,\gamma,\varepsilon,\bar{\varepsilon}\}$, given by

$S(\bar{\beta}) = \delta,\ \ S(\gamma) = \gamma,\ \ S(\delta) = \varepsilon,\ \ S(\bar{\delta}) = \bar{\varepsilon}$

is a relabelling; we then have

$(r|t)[S] =$

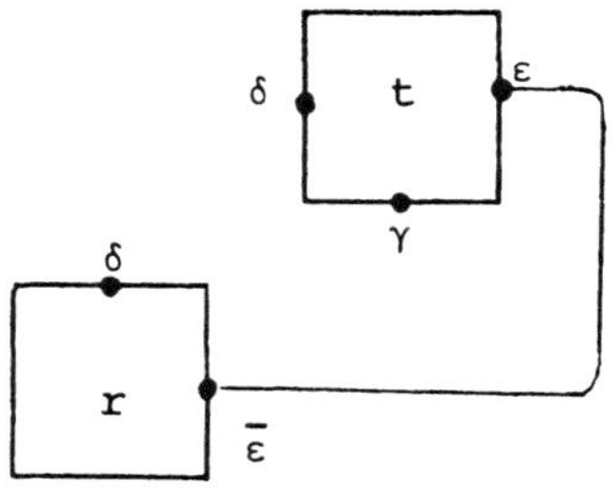

We shall use convenient abbreviations in writing relabellings explicitly. Thus

$$\lambda_1/\alpha_1,\ldots,\lambda_n/\alpha_n \quad \text{or} \quad \lambda_1\lambda_2\ldots\lambda_n/\alpha_1\alpha_2\ldots\alpha_n$$

(where $\alpha_1,\ldots,\alpha_n$ are distinct names, and $\lambda_1,\ldots,\lambda_n$ are labels with distinct names) stands for the relabelling $S:L \to M$ given by

(i) $S(\alpha_i) = \lambda_i$ if $\alpha_i \in L$

(ii) $S(\bar{\alpha}_i) = \bar{\lambda}_i$ if $\bar{\alpha}_i \in L$

(iii) $S(\lambda) = \lambda$ if name $(\lambda) \notin \{\alpha_1,\ldots,\alpha_n\}$

provided that the function so defined <u>is</u> a relabelling. So in place of $(r|t)[S]$ above, we write

$$(r|t)[\bar{\delta}/\beta,\ \varepsilon/\delta] \quad \text{or} \quad (r|t)[\bar{\delta}\varepsilon/\beta\delta].$$

When we see the laws of the Flow Algebra (laws for the Composition, Restriction and Relabelling operations) in Theorem 5.5, we shall see that relabelling distributes over composition, so that we have

$$(r|t)[\bar{\delta}/\beta,\ \varepsilon/\delta] = r[\bar{\delta}/\beta,\ \varepsilon/\delta]\,|\,t[\bar{\delta}/\beta,\ \varepsilon/\delta]$$

(as you can readily check) - even though in strict formality $\bar{\delta}/\beta,\ \varepsilon/\delta$ stands for a different relabelling in each case, because r,t and $r|t$ possess different sorts.

2.3 Extending the Algebra of Synchronization Trees

We must now add our three new operations to the algebra of STs, using intuition about the operational meaning of these trees. In future we continue to use λ to range over Λ, and use μ,ν to range over $\Lambda\cup\{\tau\}$.

<u>Composition</u> $\mid : ST_L \times ST_M \to ST_{L \cup M}$

Consider two STs

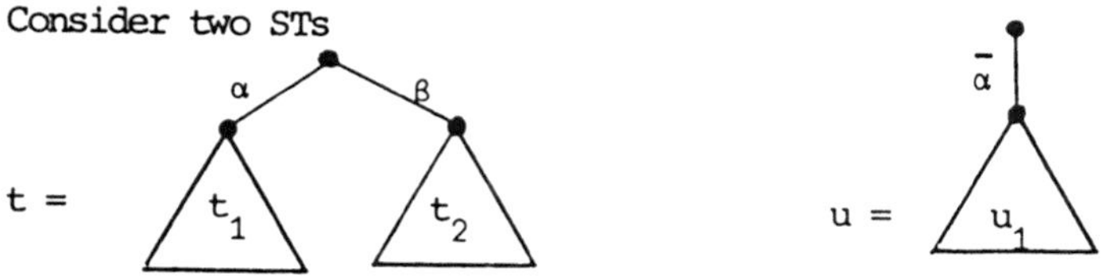

For their composite, four actions are possible. $t|u$ admits an α-experiment (because t does), so one branch of $t|u$ will be

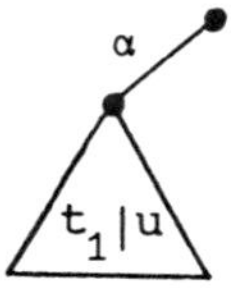

This branch represents independent action by one component, and similar branches exist for a β-experiment on t and an $\bar{\alpha}$-experiment on u. None of these three branches represents interaction between t and u; but there <u>is</u> a possible interaction, since u's $\bar{\alpha}$-offer complements t's α-offer. Since this action is internal (not observable) we use τ and represent it in the composite tree by a branch

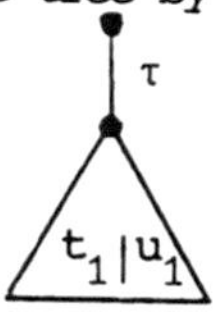

Putting all the branches together yields

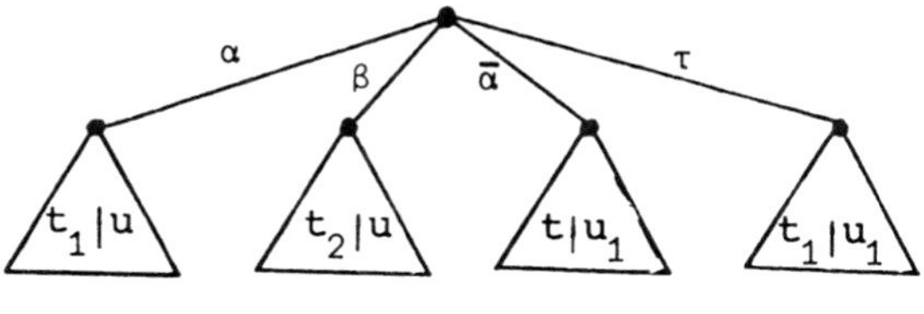

Now composition of t and u has been defined in terms of composition of their sons; clearly this amounts to a recursive definition of $|$. More precisely, since every tree may be written in the form

$$t = \sum_{1 \le i \le m} \mu_i t_i \ , \qquad \mu_i \in \Lambda \cup \{\tau\}$$

(with $m=0$ if $t = NIL$), we may define composition as follws:

<u>Definition</u> If $t = \sum_i \mu_i t_i$ and $u = \sum_j \nu_j u_j$, then

$$t|u = \sum_i \mu_i (t_i|u) + \sum_j \nu_j (t|u_j) + \sum_{\mu_i = \bar{\nu}_j} \tau (t_i|u_j) \ .$$

Exercise 2.3 (Consider only finite STs).

(i) Prove by induction on the depth of t that $t|NIL = t$.

(ii) Work out $t|u$ for $t =$ 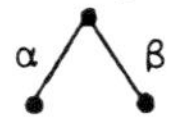 and $u =$ ; choose some other examples.

(iii) Prove by induction on the sum of the depths of trees that $t|u = u|t$ and $t|(u|v) = (t|u)|v$.

We should criticize two aspects (at least) of our definition. Considering our first example of ST composition, it can well be argued that the form we gave for $t|u$ fails to represent the possible concurrent activity of t and u - for example, we may think that a β-experiment on t can be performed simultaneously with an $\bar{\alpha}$-experiment on u, while (looking at your result for Exercise 2.3(ii) also) the ST for $t|u$ merely indicates that the two experiments may be performed in either order. Indeed, STs in no way represent true concurrency.

Two not completely convincing defences can be given. First, STs are simple, and tractability in a model has great advantages; second, in so far as we wish a 'behaviour-object' to tell us how a system may appear to an observer who is only capable of one experiment at a time, we find it possible to ignore true concurrency. You are urged to consider this question in greater depth.

The second aspect for criticism is the introduction of τ to represent successful 'mutual observations'. If we had no need for it in defining $|$, we could leave it out of our theory altogether.

Again, there are two defences, but this time convincing ones. First, consider replacing the third term in the recursive definition of $t|u$ - namely the term $\sum_{\mu_i=\bar{\nu}_j} \tau(t_i|u_j)$ - by just $\sum_{\mu_i=\bar{\nu}_j} (t_i|u_j)$;

intuitively, an internal action just vanishes. It turns out that $|$ is no longer an associative operation, which conflicts strongly with our assumption that the joint behaviour of three agents should in no way depend upon the order in which we wire them together before they do anything!

Exercise 2.4 With this new definition work out $t|(u|v)$ and $(t|u)|v$

for $t =$ 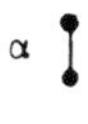, $u =$ 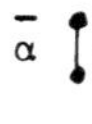, $v =$  to justify the above assertion.

The second defence is that we must somehow express, in the ST $(t|u)\backslash\alpha$ when $t = \alpha\bigwedge\beta$, $u = \,|\bar{\alpha}$, the possibility that communication between t and u can prevent any β-experiment.

Exercise 2.5 Under the normal definition of $|$, and of $\backslash\alpha$ (see below), work out that

$$(t|u)\backslash\alpha = \tau\bigwedge\beta$$

in this case.

This ST does indeed represent possible prevention of a β-experiment, and unless we leave STs (and derived models) altogether it is hard to see how such deadlock phenomena can be represented without τ.

Restriction $\backslash\alpha : ST_L \to ST_{L-\{\alpha,\bar{\alpha}\}}$ $(\alpha\in\Delta)$

We wish to deny all α- and $\bar{\alpha}$-experiments, so that $t\backslash\alpha$ is formed by pruning away all branches and sub-branches labelled α or $\bar{\alpha}$. Considering

t = 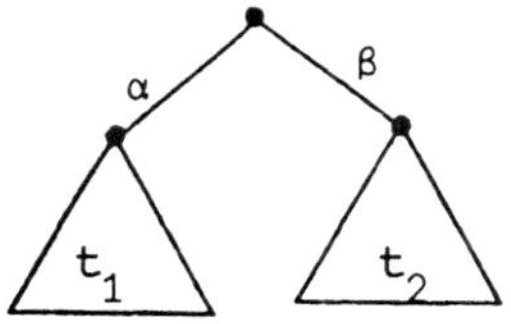

u = 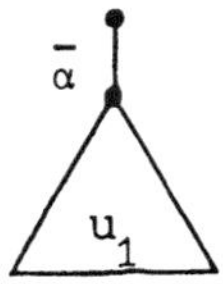

again, we see that

$(t|u)\backslash\alpha =$ 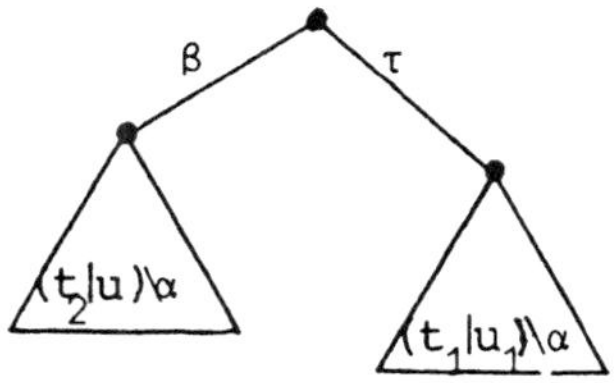

More formally, for $t = \sum_i \mu_i t_i$ we have

Definition $t\backslash\alpha = \sum_{\mu_i\notin\{\alpha,\bar{\alpha}\}} \mu_i(t_i\backslash\alpha)$

An obvious alternative to the restriction operation would be to define $\backslash\lambda$ for each member λ of Λ by

$$t\backslash\lambda = \sum_{\mu_i\neq\lambda} \mu_i(t_i\backslash\lambda) \ ;$$

in other words, we might choose to restrict names and co-names independently, instead of both at once. This would, of course, have a correspondingly different effect on pictures. The reason for our choice is in fact to do with the algebra of pictures (Flow Algebra) under $|$, $\backslash\alpha$ and $[S]$; it has a particularly simple algebraic theory [MM, Mil 2], which we have not found for the suggested alternative.

<u>Relabelling</u> $[S]$: $ST_L \to ST_M$ $(S{:}L \to M$ a relabelling)

This operation is as simple on STs as it is on pictures; it just applies the relabelling S to all labels in the tree. More formally, for $t = \sum_i \mu_i t_i$ we have

<u>Definition</u> $t[S] = \sum_i S(\mu_i)(t_i[S])$

where we now adopt the convention that $S(\tau) = \tau$ for any relabelling S.

An important (though not the only) use of relabelling is in cases where we have several instances of a single agent r in a system, but each with different labelling, so that under composition they are properly linked. We have only to define several 'copies'

$$r_i = r[S_i]$$

of the generic agent r, and then compose the r_i.

One might have allowed more general relabellings, using many-one functions over Λ (so that differently labelled ports come to bear the same label) or even relations in place of functions (so that one port could 'split' into two differently labelled ports). Suffice it to say that this creates problems in the axiomatization of Flow Algebra. The present choice allows plenty of scope.

2.4 <u>A simple example: binary semaphores</u>

A binary semaphore s, of sort $\{\bar\pi, \bar\phi\}$, may be pictured

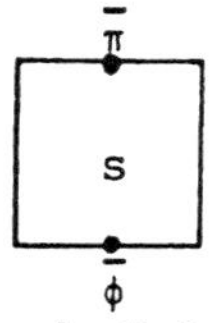

To gain the semaphore (Dijkstra's P Operation) we must perform a $\bar\pi$-experiment; we release it (the V operation) by a $\bar\phi$-experiment. Clearly

$$s = \bar\pi\ \bar\phi\ s$$

expresses the appropriate behaviour (a long thin ST!). Imagine a generic agent p, whose critical section we represent by a sequence $<\alpha,\beta>$ of atomic actions (experiments upon a resource, say), and whose non-critical section we ignore:

$$p = \pi\alpha\beta\phi p\ .$$

We wish to place several instances of p

$$p_i = p[S_i] = \pi\alpha_i\beta_i\phi p_i \qquad (\text{where } S_i = \alpha_i\beta_i/\alpha\beta)$$

in communication with s, and derive the composite ST. Consider just two copies of p $(i = 1,2)$ and form

$$q = (p_1|p_2|s)\backslash\pi\backslash\phi$$

which may be pictured as shown:

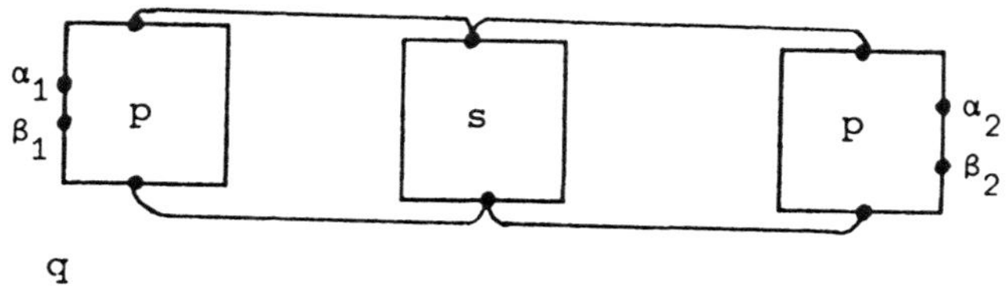

We easily derive an equation for the composite ST q, using the Expansion Theorem - given in §2.5 - repeatedly. You should read that section with reference to the expansion which follows:

$$\begin{aligned} q &= (\pi\alpha_1\beta_1\phi p_1|\pi\alpha_2\beta_2\phi p_2|\bar{\pi}\bar{\phi}s)\backslash\pi\backslash\phi \\ &= \tau((\alpha_1\beta_1\phi p_1|p_2|\bar{\phi}s)\backslash\pi\backslash\phi) + \tau((p_1|\alpha_2\beta_2\phi p_2|\bar{\phi}s)\backslash\pi\backslash\phi \\ &= \tau\alpha_1\beta_1((\phi p_1|p_2|\bar{\phi}s)\backslash\pi\backslash\phi) + \tau\alpha_2\beta_2((p_1|\phi p_2|\bar{\phi}s)\backslash\pi\backslash\phi) \\ &= \tau\alpha_1\beta_1\tau((p_1|p_2|s)\backslash\pi\backslash\phi) + \tau\alpha_2\beta_2\tau((p_1|p_2|s)\backslash\pi\backslash\phi) \\ &= \tau\alpha_1\beta_1\tau q + \tau\alpha_2\beta_2\tau q\ . \end{aligned}$$

So q is the ST given recursively by

$q =$

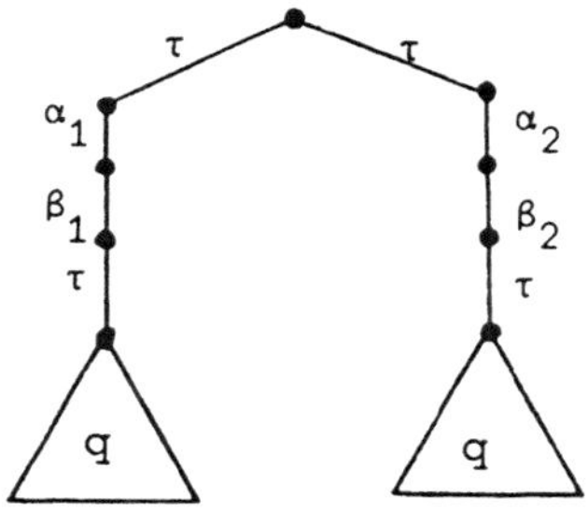

and exactly expresses the fact that the critical sections of p_1 and p_2 can never overlap in time, i.e. a sequence like $\alpha_1\alpha_2\beta_1\ldots$ is not possible.

In fact, an n-bounded semaphore $(n \geq 1)$ can be constructed as

$$s_n = \underbrace{s|s|\ldots|s}_{n \text{ times}} \quad ;$$

this is an example of composition which effects no linkage, but will yield a multi-way linkage with 'user' agents.

The 2-bounded semaphore s_2, with 3 users, can be pictured

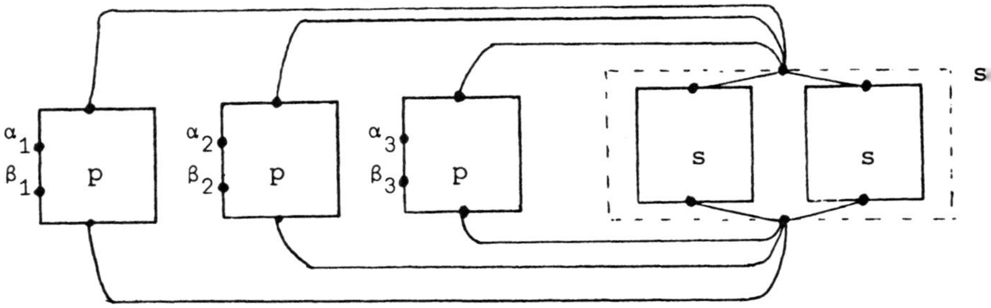

Diagram for $(p_1|p_2|p_3|s_2)\backslash\pi\backslash\phi$

(s_2's border, and its two collector nodes, are fictitious; they are just used here to avoid drawing 12 links in the picture).

<u>Exercise 2.6</u> As practice in using the Expansion Theorem, develop the expression $q = (p_1|p_2|p_3|s|s)\backslash\pi\backslash\phi$, and draw part of the ST to convince yourself that at most two critical sections can be simultaneously active. Can you even derive a set of mutually recursive behaviour equations, for which q is the solution? It's a bit lengthy, but possible. The development is shorter if you take $\alpha_1=\alpha_2=\alpha_3=\alpha$, $\beta_1=\beta_2=\beta_3=\beta$; i.e. deal with $(p|p|p|s|s)\backslash\pi\backslash\phi$ instead; then the ST will not distinguish the critical sections of each copy of p, but you should be able to show that at any point in time the excess of α's over β's performed lies in the range $[0,2]$.

2.5 The ST Expansion Theorem

We consider trees expressed in the form

$$t = \sum_{1 \le i \le n} \mu_i t_i \ .$$

For a set $\{\alpha_1, \dots, \alpha_k\} = A$ of names, we abbreviate $\backslash\alpha_1\backslash\alpha_2 \dots \backslash\alpha_k$ by $\backslash A$.

Theorem 2.1 (The Expansion Theorem)

Let $t = (t_1 | t_2 | \dots | t_m)\backslash A$, where each t_i is a sum as above. Then

$$t = \sum\{\mu((t_1 | \dots | t_i' | \dots | t_m)\backslash A);\ 1 \le i \le m,\ \mu t_i' \text{ a summand of } t_i,\ \text{name}(\mu) \notin A\}$$
$$+ \sum\{\tau((t_1 | \dots | t_i' | \dots | t_j' | \dots | t_m)\backslash A);\ 1 \le i < j \le m,\ \lambda t_i' \text{ a summand of } t_i,\ \bar{\lambda} t_j' \text{ a summand of } t_j\}$$

Proof Omitted; it uses properties of the Flow operations $|$, $\backslash\alpha$ and $[S]$, and can be done by induction on m. ⊠

The theorem states that each branch of t corresponds either to an unrestricted action of some t_i, or to an internal communication between t_i and t_j $(i < j)$. For example consider

$$((\alpha t + \beta t') | (\bar{\alpha} u + \gamma u') | (\bar{\beta} v + \bar{\gamma} v'))\backslash\alpha\backslash\beta;$$

the theorem gives us

$$\gamma(((\alpha t + \beta t') | u' | (\bar{\beta} v + \bar{\gamma} v'))\backslash\alpha\backslash\beta)$$
$$+ \bar{\gamma}(((\alpha t + \beta t') | (\bar{\alpha} u + \gamma u') | v')\backslash\alpha\backslash\beta) \qquad \text{(unrestricted actions)}$$
$$+ \tau((t | u | (\bar{\beta} v + \bar{\gamma} v'))\backslash\alpha\backslash\beta) \qquad (\alpha\text{-communication})$$
$$+ \tau((t' | (\bar{\alpha} u + \gamma u') | v)\backslash\alpha\backslash\beta) \qquad (\beta\text{-communication})$$
$$+ \tau(((\alpha t + \beta t') | u' | v')\backslash\alpha\backslash\beta) \qquad (\gamma\text{-communication})$$

<u>Exercise 2.7</u> A lot can be done using compositions of two kinds of element

<u>Cycler</u>

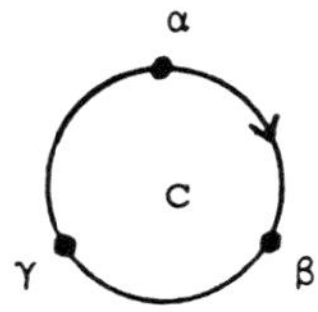

$c = \alpha\beta\gamma c$

<u>Disjoiner</u>

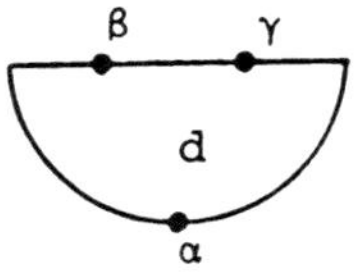

$d = \alpha(\beta d + \gamma d)$

(i) Write the behaviour of

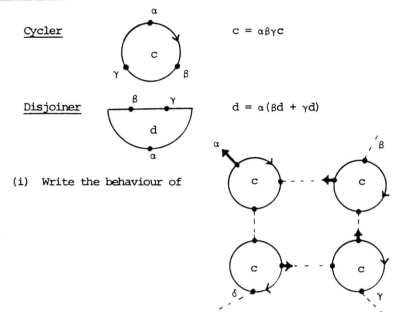

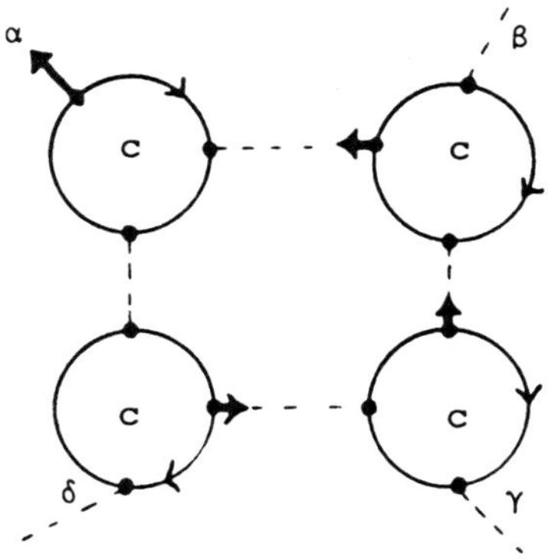

as a restricted composition of relabellings of c. (The little arrows represent the port at which each copy of c offers its first experiment; the progress of the system can be simulated by "swinging arrows" try it). Expand the behaviour, to get a recursive definition of an ST which doesn't involve composition, restriction or relabelling.

(ii) Design a system (using c only) to behave as the ST

$s = \alpha(\tau\beta\tau s + \tau\gamma\tau s)$.

Is this equivalent to d?

CHAPTER 3

A case study in synchronization, and proof techniques

3.1 A scheduling problem

Suppose that a set $\{p_i \ ; \ 1 \le i \le n\}$ of agents all wish to perform a certain task repeatedly, and we wish to design a scheduler to ensure that they perform it in rotation, starting with p_1. (This example was used in [Mil 5].)

More precisely, the p_i are to <u>start</u> their performance of the task in rotation; we do not impose the restriction that their performances should exclude each other in time (this could be done using a semaphore) but we do impose the restriction that each p_i should be prevented from initiating the task twice without completing his first initiation. (p_i may try this unintentionally, because of bad programming for example.)

Suppose that p_i requests initiation at label α_i, and signals completion at β_i $(1 \le i \le n)$. Then our scheduler Sch of sort $\bar{A} \cup \bar{B}$, where $A = \{\alpha_i \ ; \ 1 \le i \le n\}$ and $B = \{\beta_i \ ; \ 1 \le i \le n\}$, must impose two constraints on any signal sequence $\in (A \cup B)^\omega$:

(i) When all occurrences of β_i $(1 \le i \le n)$ are deleted, it becomes

$$(\alpha_1 \alpha_2 \ \ldots . \alpha_n)^\omega \ ;$$

(ii) For each i, when all occurrences of $\alpha_j, \beta_j \ (j \ne i)$ are deleted, it becomes

$$(\alpha_i \beta_i)^\omega \ .$$

We could write a behaviour description for Sch directly, but prefer to build it as a ring of elementary identical components, called cyclers.

<u>Generic cycler c</u> :

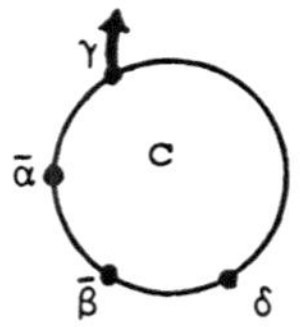

Scheduler Sch :

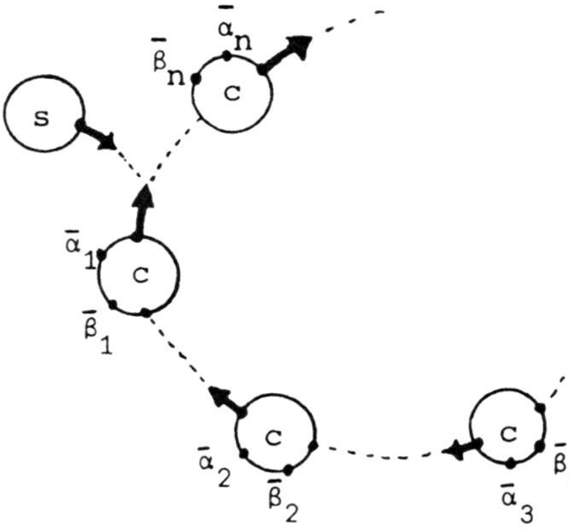

using also a 'start button',

Starter s :

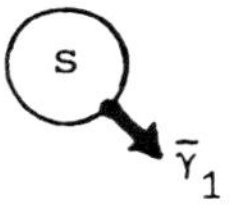

In building the net we have instantiated c by

$$c_i = c[\alpha_i/\alpha,\ \beta_i/\beta,\ \gamma_i/\gamma\ ,\ \bar{\gamma}_{i+1}/\delta]$$

for $1 \leq i \leq n$, where addition on subscripts is modulo n , so that

$$Sch = (s \mid c_1 \mid \cdots \mid c_n)\backslash\gamma_1 \cdots \backslash\gamma_n$$

What are the behaviours s and c ? The starter is there just to enable c_1 at γ_1 and die, so

$$s = \bar{\gamma}_1\ NIL$$

As for the cycler, it appears that he should cycle endlessly as follows:

(i) Be enabled by predecessor at γ ;
(ii) Receive initiation request at $\bar{\alpha}$;
(iii) Receive termination signal at $\bar{\beta}$ and enable successor at δ , in either order.

So we define

$$\boxed{c = \gamma\bar{\alpha}(\bar{\beta}\delta c + \delta\bar{\beta}c)}$$

and this determines Sch completely. But does it work? Informally we can convince ourselves that it does, by arrow-swinging. More formally, there are two possibilities:

<u>Method 1</u> Show as directly as possible that constraints (i) and (ii) are met. For the first constraint, this may be expressed as absorbing (i.e. permitting) all $\bar{\beta}_i$ communications, and showing that the result is observationally equivalent to

$$(\bar{\alpha}_1\bar{\alpha}_2\ldots\bar{\alpha}_n)^{\omega}$$

Let us make this precise by adopting the convention that if s is any non-empty label sequence, then s^{ω} is the behaviour given by

$$s^{\omega} = s(s^{\omega}).$$

Then what we want to prove, for the first constraint, is

(i) $\mathrm{Sch} \,\|\, (\beta_1{}^{\omega}|\ldots|\beta_n{}^{\omega}) \;\approx\; (\bar{\alpha}_1\bar{\alpha}_2\ldots\bar{\alpha}_n)^{\omega}$

(where $\approx$ is observational equivalence, which we define formally in §3.3). Using the notation

$$\prod\{q_i \;;\; i\in I\} \quad\text{or}\quad \prod_{i\in I} q_i$$

for multiple composition, we can rewrite (i) as

$$\mathrm{Sch} \,\|\, \prod_{1\le j\le n} \beta_j{}^{\omega} \;\approx\; (\bar{\alpha}_1\ldots\bar{\alpha}_n)^{\omega}\,.$$

The required equivalence for the second constraint is

(ii) $\mathrm{Sch} \,\|\, (\prod_{j\ne i} \alpha_j{}^{\omega} \,|\, \prod_{j\ne i} \beta_j{}^{\omega}) \;\approx\; (\bar{\alpha}_i\bar{\beta}_i)^{\omega}$ for each i , $1\le i\le n$.

<u>Method 2</u> We can <u>specify</u> the behaviour of the complete scheduler by a single parameterized behaviour equation, in the following way. Observe that the scheduler has to keep two pieces of information:

(a) An integer i $(1\le i\le n)$ indicating whose turn it is to initiate next.

(b) A subset X of $[1,n]$ indicating which agents are currently performing the task.

If Spec(i,X) represents the required behaviour of the scheduler for parameter values i and X , then we can specify the scheduler by

$$\mathrm{Spec}(i,X) = \sum_{j\in X} \bar{\beta}_j \, \mathrm{Spec}(i, X-\{j\}) \qquad (i \in X)$$

$$\mathrm{Spec}(i,X) = \bar{\alpha}_i \, \mathrm{Spec}(i+1, X\cup\{i\}) + \sum_{j\in X} \bar{\beta}_j \, \mathrm{Spec}(i, X-\{j\}) \qquad (i \notin X)$$

These equations say that if p_i is not performing he can initiate, and in any case any $p_j (j \in X)$ can signal completion. For this method we only have to prove one observation equivalence:

$$\mathrm{Sch} \approx \mathrm{Spec}(1,\emptyset)$$

In §3.4 we give part of a proof using Method 1, which may be preferred since it directly represents the constraints as specified. Method 2 is possible, but a little harder.

Exercise 3.1 Can you 'build' the cycler defined here, using six copies of the cycler c of Exercise 2.7? It is not hard, but the sense in which the construction behaves like the present cycler needs careful study. This is dealt with in §3.3.

Exercise 3.2 Build a scheduler which imposes a third constraint on a signal sequence $\in (A \cup B)^{\omega}$:

(iii) When all occurrences of α_i $(1 \le i \le n)$ are deleted, it becomes $(\beta_1\beta_2 \cdots \beta_n)^{\omega}$.

This constraint says that the p_i must also terminate their tasks in cyclic order.

Note: These exercises are playing to some extent, but they may have some significance for building asynchronous hardware from components. This remains to be seen.

We shall now divert to compare our behaviours with Petri Nets, informally, using the scheduler as an example. Readers unfamiliar with Net Theory may skip the next section.

3.2 Building the scheduler as a Petri Net

We will use Petri nets in which the events or transitions are labelled by members of $\Lambda \cup \{\tau\}$. In fact, we shall just omit the τ labels.

A net c , for our cycler, is as follows, where circles stand for places and bars for transitions:

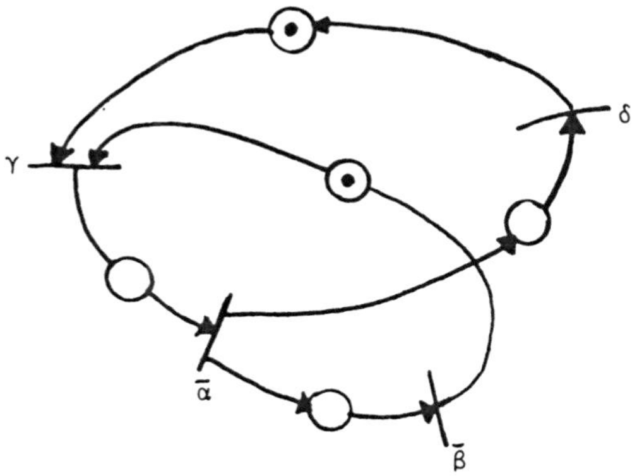

With the initial marking as shown, the net is clearly live in the usual sense. But in our interpretation a λ-labelled event is merely potential; it needs cooperation with an event which bears a complementary label, or with an observer performing a λ-experiment.

The flow operations $|$, $\backslash\alpha$ and $[S]$ can be satisfactorily defined over a class of nets (as Mogens Nielsen has shown) in such a way as to yield a Flow Algebra. Here, however, it will be enough to use only [S] - the obvious relabelling operation - and the derived operation $\|$; if n_1 and n_2 are nets of sort L and M and if $\{\alpha_1,\ldots,\alpha_k\}$ = names $(L \cap \bar{M})$, then

$$n_1 \| n_2 \quad = \quad (n_1 | n_2)\backslash\alpha_1 \cdots \backslash\alpha_k$$

may be described as follows:

Identify the event labelled α_i (resp $\bar{\alpha}_i$) in n_1 with the event labelled $\bar{\alpha}_i$ (resp α_i) in n_2 , for each i , and then drop the labels $\alpha_1,\ldots,\alpha_k$ and their complements.

[<u>Note</u>: This needs more careful phrasing if we allow that n_1 may <u>not have</u> a λ-event even though $\lambda \in L$. Also, in general we must take care of the possibility that n_1 - for example - may have <u>two or more</u> λ-events.

However, if we start with nets n of sort L having exactly one event labelled $\lambda \in L$, and confine the use of composition to pairs $n_1 : L$, $n_2 : M$ for which L and M are disjoint, then all nets built with [S] and $\|$ will have exactly one event for each label in their sort].

To illustrate with cyclers, we have, for $c_i = c[\alpha_i/\alpha, \beta_i/\beta, \gamma_i/\gamma, \bar{\gamma}_{i+1}/\delta]$:

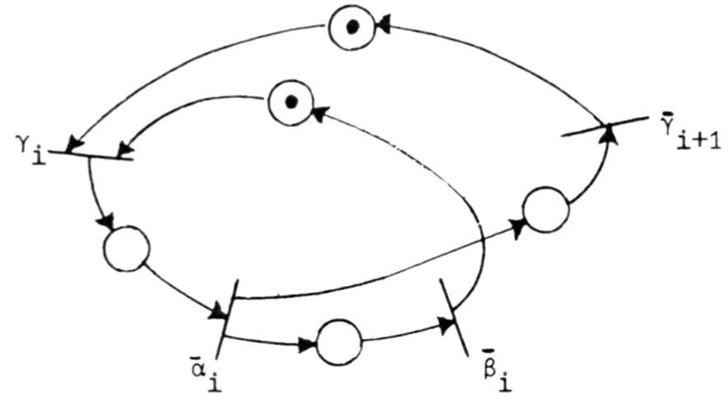

and for $c_1 \| c_2$:

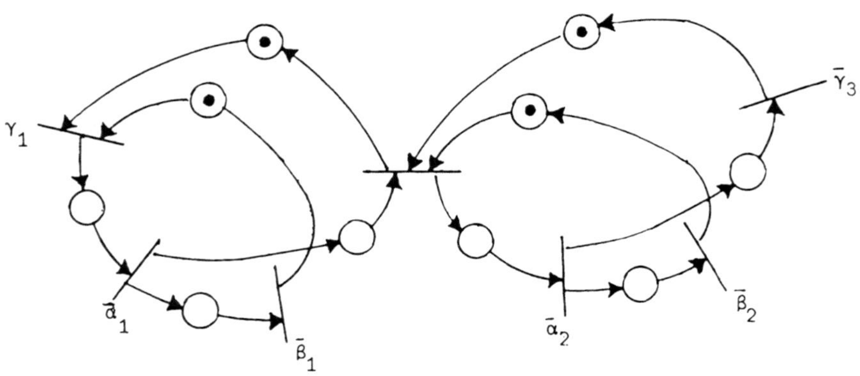

Finally we give the diagram for a scheduler of size 5 on which you can play the token game:

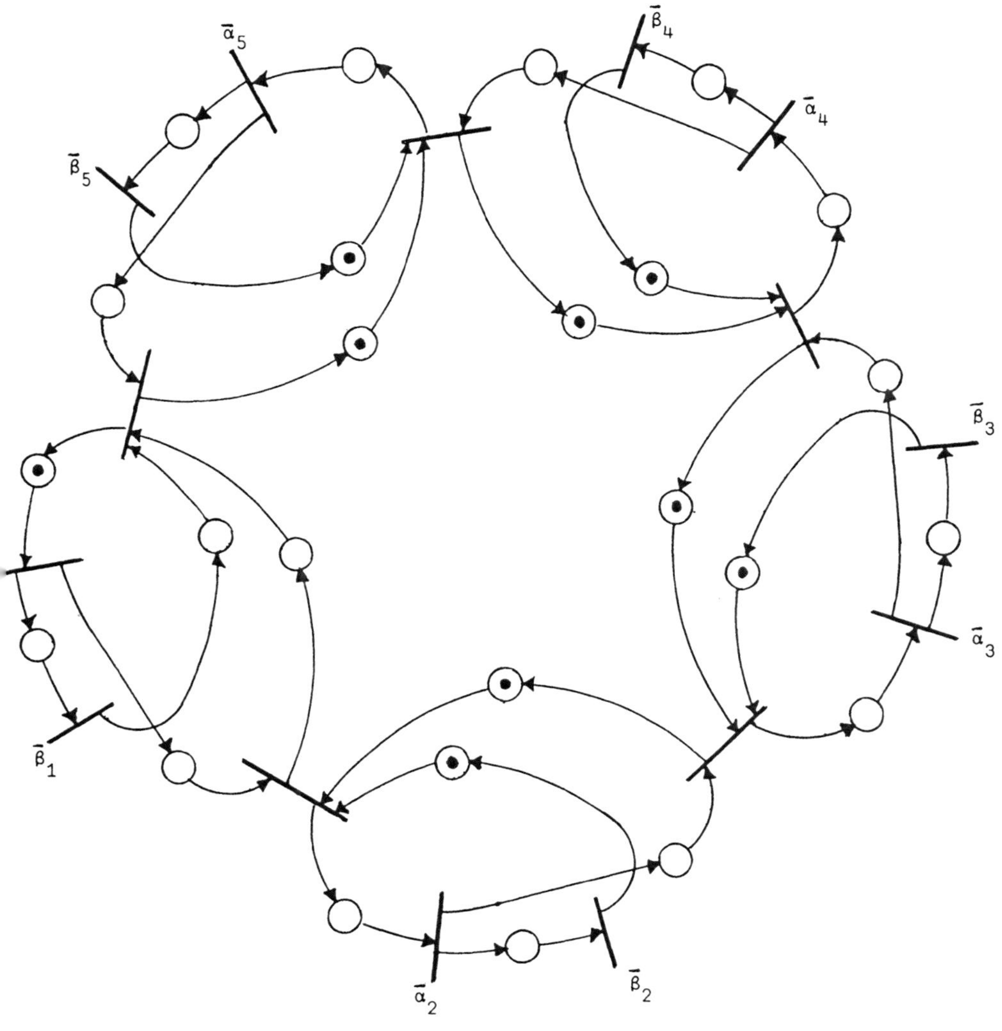

The Petri Net for the scheduler

Notice the slight cheat: c_1 has been given a different initial marking. This would not have been needed if we had included a part of the net for our start button, and in building the net we would then find the need for more than one event labelled γ_1 - which corresponds to the shared port of c in the picture of Sch, §3.1.

There is a growing body of techniques for analysis of Petri Nets. For example, the behaviour of Marked Graphs is well understood [CoH]; a marked graph is a Petri net in which each place has indegree and outdegree equal to 1, and our scheduler is indeed a marked graph. Further, much can be discovered of the behaviour of arbitrary nets using techniques from Linear Algebra due to Kurt Lautenbach (GMD, Bonn) to discover Invariants (properties which holds for all accessible markings, or token distributions) Kurt Jensen has pointed out that these techniques are strong enough to tell us that our scheduler net indeed satisfies the two constraints specified.

Nevertheless we shall tackle the proof of correctness of the scheduler by our own methods, since we shall see later that they apply also to systems which are not so readily represented as Petri Nets (e.g. Systems whose communication structure does not remain fixed).

3.3 Observation equivalence

It is now time to be completely precise about the form of equivalence of agents that we wish to adopt. The discussion in Chapter 1 was imprecise, deliberately so; but now that we have a case study in hand where correctness of an agent has been expressed as equivalence between the agent and its specification, we have enough motivation to study equivalence seriously.

We may forget our algebra temporarily, and imagine simply that we have a set P of agents (or behaviours) together with a family $\{ \xrightarrow{\mu} ;\ \mu \in \Lambda \cup \{\tau\} \}$ of binary relations over P . Λ is our label set, but we can also forget temporarily that $\Lambda = \Delta \cup \bar{\Delta}$. We shall consistently use λ

to range over Λ, and μ,ν to range over $\Lambda \cup \{\tau\}$.

$p \xrightarrow{\lambda} p'$ means "p admits a λ-experiment, and can transform into p' as a result"

$p \xrightarrow{\tau} p'$ means "p can transform to p' unobserved"

We shall write $p \xrightarrow{s} p'$, for $s = \mu_1 \cdots \mu_n \in (\Lambda \cup \{\tau\})^*$, to mean that for some $p_0, \ldots, p_n$ $(n \geq 0)$

$$p = p_0 \xrightarrow{\mu_1} p_1 \xrightarrow{\mu_2} p_2 \cdots \xrightarrow{\mu_n} p_n = p' .$$

Now consider the result(s) of performing a sequence $\lambda_1, \ldots, \lambda_n$ of atomic experiments on p $(n \geq 0)$. The result may be any p' for which

$$p \xrightarrow{\tau^{k_0}\lambda_1\tau^{k_1}\lambda_2 \cdots \lambda_n\tau^{k_n}} p' \qquad (k_i \geq 0) \qquad ;$$

that is, an arbitrary number of silent moves may occur before, among and after the λ_i.

<u>Definition</u> for $s \in \Lambda^*$, define the relation $\overset{s}{\Rightarrow}$ by: if $s = \lambda_1 \ldots \lambda_n$, then

$p \overset{s}{\Rightarrow} p'$ iff for some $k_0, \ldots, k_n \geq 0$

$$p \xrightarrow{\tau^{k_0}\lambda_1\tau^{k_1}\lambda_2 \cdots \lambda_n\tau^{k_n}} p'$$

We may talk of an <u>s-experiment</u> $(s \in \Lambda^*)$, and then $p \overset{s}{\Rightarrow} p'$ means " p admits an s-experiment and can transform to p' as a result" ; we may also say more briefly " p can produce p' under s ".

Note that for the empty sequence $\varepsilon \in \Lambda^*$, an ε-experiment consists of letting the agent proceed silently as it wishes, while observing nothing; for we have

$$p \overset{\varepsilon}{\Rightarrow} p' \text{ iff for some } k \geq 0 \quad p \xrightarrow{\tau^k} p' .$$

Note also the special case $p \overset{\varepsilon}{\Rightarrow} p$ when $k = 0$.

Now we can state in words what we shall mean by equivalent agents.

p and q are equivalent iff for every $s \in \Lambda^*$

(i) For every result p' of an s-experiment on p, there is an equivalent result q' of a s-experiment on q.

(ii) For every result q' of an s-experiment on q, there is an equivalent result p' of a s-experiment on p.

This appears to be a circular definition (the formal definition will take care of this point) but note first that it implies that, for each s ,

$$p \text{ admits an } s\text{-experiment iff } q \text{ does.}$$

But it implies much more; for example, the two ST's

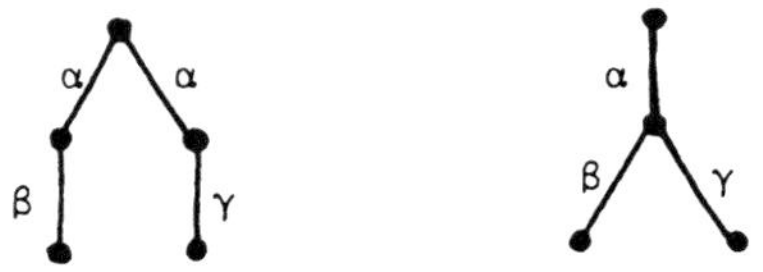

admit exactly the same s-experiments, but neither of the two possible results of an α-experiment on the first tree is equivalent to the result of an α-experiment on the second.

The motivation for our definition is this: we imagine switching p on, performing an experiment, and switching it off again. For q to be equivalent, it must be possible to switch q on, do the same experiment, and switch it off in a state equivalent to the state in which p was switched off (and the same, interchanging p and q).

Our formal definition is in terms of a decreasing sequence $\approx_0, \approx_1, \ldots, \approx_k, \ldots$ of (finer and finer) equivalence relations:

<u>Definition</u> (Observation equivalence) $p \approx_0 q$ is always true;

$p \approx_{k+1} q$ iff $\forall s \in \Lambda^*$

(i) if $p \overset{s}{\Rightarrow} p'$ then for some q', $q \overset{s}{\Rightarrow} q'$ and $p' \approx_k q'$;

(ii) if $q \overset{s}{\Rightarrow} q'$ then for some p', $p \overset{s}{\Rightarrow} p'$ and $p' \approx_k q'$;

$p \approx q$ iff $\forall k \geq 0.\ p \approx_k q$ (i.e. $\approx = \bigcap_k \approx_k$) .

<u>Exercise 3.3</u> (a) Prove that each $\approx_k$ is an equivalence relation, by induction on k . (b) Prove by induction that $\approx_{k+1} \subseteq \approx_k$, i.e. that $p \approx_{k+1} q$ implies $p \approx_k q$.

This equivalence relation has many interesting properties, which we need not examine until Chapter 7 - except one or two.

First, it is not <u>necessarily</u> true that $\approx$ itself satisfies the recurrence relation defining $\approx_{k+1}$ in terms of $\approx_k$, that is, the property

$$p \approx q \text{ iff } \forall s \in \Lambda^* \qquad (*)$$
$$\text{(i) if } p \overset{s}{\Rightarrow} p' \text{ then } \exists q'.q \overset{s}{\Rightarrow} q' \ \& \ p' \approx q'$$
$$\text{(ii) if } q \overset{s}{\Rightarrow} q' \text{ then } \exists p'.p \overset{s}{\Rightarrow} p' \ \& \ p' \approx q'$$

(which is a formal version of our verbal recursive definition of equivalence given earlier in this section). It <u>is</u> true if p and q are finite STs, but not in general. However, our definition has nicer properties than one which satisfies (*).

For STs, our binary relations $\xrightarrow{\lambda}$ and $\xrightarrow{\tau}$ are obvious; $t \xrightarrow{\lambda} t'$ (resp. $t \xrightarrow{\tau} t'$) iff t has a branch $\lambda t'$ (resp. $\tau t'$). In this case we shall call t' a <u>λ-son</u> (resp. <u>τ-son</u>) of t.

<u>Exercise 3.4</u> Prove that $t \approx \tau t$ for STs. (You need a very simple inductive proof that $t \approx_k \tau t$).

Let us consider one example of equivalent STs:

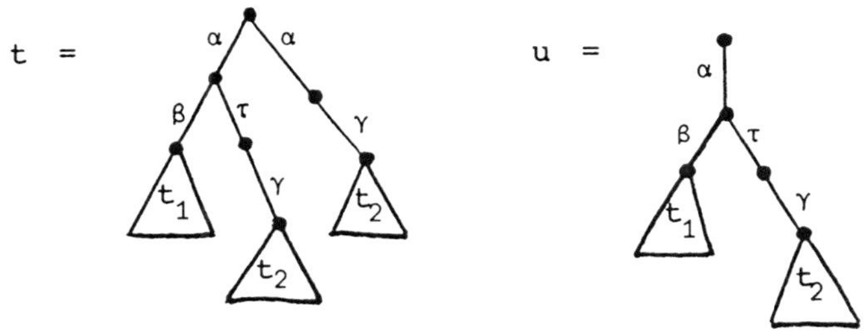

To check equivalence, i.e. $t \approx_k u$ for all k, we must prove the inductive step: $t \approx_k u$ implies $t \approx_{k+1} u$. Now for every $s \neq \varepsilon$, t and u produce identical trees under s; under ε, t produces only t and u only u, and $t \approx_k u$ by induction.

<u>Definition</u> If $p \overset{s}{\Longrightarrow} p'$ $(\sigma \in \Lambda^*)$ then p' is an <u>s-derivative</u> of p.

(Note that p is always an ε-derivative of itself). We can thus rephrase the definition of $\approx_{k+1}$ in terms of $\approx_k$:

" $p \approx_{k+1} q$ iff, for all $s \in \Lambda^*$,
p and q have the same s-derivatives
up to $\approx_k$ equivalence. "

<u>Exercise 3.5</u> Re-examine Exercise 1.4, and verify precisely which pairs ar observation equivalent. You should find exactly four pairs.

<u>Exercise 3.6</u> (<u>Deadlock</u>) Prove that if $p \approx q$ then the following statement is true of <u>both</u> or of <u>neither</u>, for given $\lambda_1, \ldots, \lambda_n, \lambda_{n+1}$:

"It is possible to do a $\lambda_1 \ldots \lambda_n$ experiment and reach a state where a λ_{n+1}-experiment is impossible"

One property of agents is not respected by our equivalence. It is possible for p and q to be equivalent even though p possesses an infinite silent computation

$$p \xrightarrow{\tau} p_1 \xrightarrow{\tau} p_2 \xrightarrow{\tau} \ldots\ldots p_k \xrightarrow{\tau} p_{k+1} \xrightarrow{\tau} \ldots$$

(<u>divergence</u>) while q cannot diverge in this way. The equivalence can be refined to exclude this possibility. See the remarks in §7.3.

3.4 Proving the scheduler

It is cumbersome to use the direct definition of $\approx$; we shall instead use a few of its key properties, which are derived formally in Chapter 7. We begin by listing them, so that Chapter 7 need not be read first.

($\approx$ 1) $t \approx \tau t$ (see Exercise 3.4)

Now we can see that $\approx$ is not a congruence relation; that is, replacing t by t' (when $t \approx t'$) in u to get u' does not ensure $u \approx u'$. For example, $NIL \approx \tau NIL$, but $\alpha NIL + NIL \not\approx \alpha NIL + \tau NIL$.

Exercise 3.7 Verify this fact.

So in general $t \approx t'$ does not imply $t + u \approx t' + u$. But all our other operations do preserve $\approx$.

($\approx$ 2) $t \approx t'$ implies $\begin{cases} \mu t \overset{c}{\approx} \mu t' & \text{(see below for } \overset{c}{\approx}\text{)} \\ t|u \approx t'|u \text{ and } u|t \approx u'|t \\ t\backslash\alpha \approx t'\backslash\alpha \\ t[S] \approx t'[S] \end{cases}$

Fortunately, too, when we apply a guard μ to equivalent STs t,t' we get not only $\mu t \approx \mu t'$, but $\mu t \overset{c}{\approx} \mu t'$, where $\overset{c}{\approx}$ is a stronger relation than $\approx$ which is preserved by all our operations.

($\approx$ 3) $\overset{c}{\approx}$ is a congruence relation, and
$t \overset{c}{\approx} t'$ implies $t \approx t'$.

Beyond these, we need one more property which may look a little surprising; we leave its discussion to Chapter 7 .

($\approx$ 4) $t + \tau t \overset{c}{\approx} \tau t$

Apart from this, the proof below will use only rather natural properties of our operations, including the Expansion Theorem, all justified by Chapter 5.

We treat only the first constraint, namely

$$Sch \parallel (\beta_1^{\omega} | \ldots | \beta_n^{\omega}) \approx (\bar{\alpha}_1 \ldots \bar{\alpha}_n)^{\omega} \tag{1}$$

Define the left hand side to be Sch' . We shall actually show that Sch' satisfies the defining equation of $(\bar{\alpha}_1 \ldots \bar{\alpha}_n)^{\omega}$, namely

$$Sch' \approx \bar{\alpha}_1 \ldots \bar{\alpha}_n \, Sch' . \tag{2}$$

from which (1) follows, by general principles which we shall not treat here (but see Exercise 7.7).

We may write Sch' as

$$Sch' = (s \mid c_1' \mid \ldots \mid c_n')\backslash\gamma_1 \ldots \backslash\gamma_n \tag{3}$$

(using general properties of $|$ and $\backslash\alpha$), where

$$c_i' = (c_i \mid \beta_i^{\omega})\backslash\beta_i \tag{4}$$

represents the ith cycler with $\bar{\beta}_i$ permitted. Now we shall discover below that

$$c_i' \overset{c}{\approx} \gamma_i \bar{\alpha}_i \bar{\gamma}_{i+1} c_i' \qquad (5)$$

so we can use these expressions interchangably, by ($\approx$ 3), to assist our expansion of Sch', which runs as follows:

$$\begin{aligned}
\text{Sch}' &\overset{c}{\approx} (\bar{\gamma}_1 \text{NIL} | \gamma_1 \bar{\alpha}_1 \bar{\gamma}_2 c_1' | \dots | \gamma_n \bar{\alpha}_n \bar{\gamma}_1 c_n') \backslash \gamma_1 \dots \backslash \gamma_n \\
&\overset{c}{\approx} \tau(\text{NIL} | \bar{\alpha}_1 \bar{\gamma}_2 c_1' | \gamma_2 \bar{\alpha}_2 \bar{\gamma}_3 c_2' | \dots | \gamma_n \bar{\alpha}_n \bar{\gamma}_1 c_n') \backslash \gamma_1 \dots \backslash \gamma_n \\
&\qquad \text{(the start button has worked)} \\
&\overset{c}{\approx} \tau\bar{\alpha}_1 \tau\bar{\alpha}_2 \dots \tau\bar{\alpha}_n (\text{NIL} | c_1' | c_2' | \dots | \bar{\gamma}_1 c_n') \backslash \gamma_1 \dots \backslash \gamma_n \\
&\qquad \text{(leaving } c_1' \text{ to be reenabled)} \\
&\overset{c}{\approx} \tau\bar{\alpha}_1 \tau\bar{\alpha}_2 \dots \tau\bar{\alpha}_n \tau(\text{NIL} | \bar{\alpha}_1 \bar{\gamma}_2 c_1' | c_2' | \dots | c_n') \backslash \gamma_1 \dots \backslash \gamma_n \\
&\approx \bar{\alpha}_1 \bar{\alpha}_2 \dots \bar{\alpha}_n \, \text{Sch}' \quad \text{as required, by } (\approx 1) \text{ and } (\approx 2).
\end{aligned}$$

Let us now show (5) , for $i = 1$ say.

$$\begin{aligned}
c_1' &= (\gamma_1 \bar{\alpha}_1 (\bar{\beta}_1 \bar{\gamma}_2 c_1 + \bar{\gamma}_2 \bar{\beta}_1 c_1) | \beta_1^{\omega}) \backslash \beta_1 \\
&= \gamma_1 \bar{\alpha}_1 (\tau \bar{\gamma}_2 c_1' + \bar{\gamma}_2 \tau c_1') \quad \text{by expansion.}
\end{aligned}$$

But $\bar{\gamma}_2 \tau c_1' \overset{c}{\approx} \bar{\gamma}_2 c_1'$ by ($\approx$ 1) and ($\approx$ 2), so

$$\begin{aligned}
\tau \bar{\gamma}_2 c' + \bar{\gamma}_2 \tau c_1' &\overset{c}{\approx} \tau \bar{\gamma}_2 c_1' + \bar{\gamma}_2 c_1' \quad \text{by } (\approx 3) \\
&\overset{c}{\approx} \tau \bar{\gamma}_2 c_1' \quad \text{by } (\approx 4),
\end{aligned}$$

and by substituting in the expansion of c_1' we get by ($\approx$ 1),($\approx$ 2)

$$c_1' \overset{c}{\approx} \gamma_1 \bar{\alpha}_1 \bar{\gamma}_2 c_1' \quad \text{as required.}$$

We leave the verification of the second constraint on the scheduler as an exercise in Chapter 8. It is not hard, but uses a slightly more general property than ($\approx$ 4).

CHAPTER 4

Case studies in value-communication

4.1 Review

So far, we have seen how behaviours (STs) may be built using six kinds of operation, together with the all-important use of recursion. The operations fall into two classes:

(1) Dynamic operations (Chapter 1)

Inaction	NIL
Summation	+
Action	$\mu \in \Lambda \cup \{\tau\}$

The dynamic operations build nondeterministic sequential behaviours.

(2) Static operations (Chapter 2)

Composition	$\mid$	
Restriction	$\backslash\alpha$	$(\alpha \in \Delta)$
Relabelling	$[S]$	

The static operations establish a fixed linkage structure among concurrently active behaviours.

The examples given were static combinations of sequential behaviours, yielding systems with fixed linkage structure. But dynamically-evolving structures can be gained by defining recursive behaviours involving composition. The possibilities are quite rich; we give an example, not for its usefulness (which is doubtful) but to illustrate the power of CCS.

First, let us define an operation which has wide application. If $x : L$, $y : M$ and $L \cap \bar{M} = \emptyset$, with $\bar{\beta} \in L$ and $\alpha \in M$, the chaining operation $\frown$ is given by

$$x \frown y = (x[\delta/\beta] \mid y[\delta/\alpha])\backslash\delta$$

where $\delta \notin \text{names}(L \cup M)$. In pictures:

(See §8.3 for a proof that $\frown$ is associative; this even holds if $L \cap \bar{M} \neq \emptyset$.)

Now consider in particular $p:\{\alpha,\bar{\beta},\gamma\}$ and $q:\{\alpha\}$ given by

$$p = \alpha\bar{\beta}\gamma(p^\frown p) \quad , \quad q = \alpha q$$

and consider the following derivation:

$$p^\frown q$$

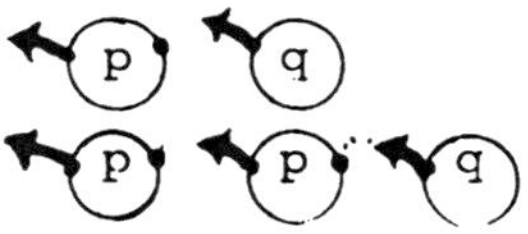

$$\overset{\alpha\gamma}{\Longrightarrow} p^\frown p^\frown q$$

$$\overset{\alpha\gamma^2}{\Longrightarrow} p^\frown p^\frown p^\frown p^\frown q$$

$$\overset{\alpha\gamma^4}{\Longrightarrow} p^\frown p^\frown p^\frown p^\frown p^\frown p^\frown p^\frown p^\frown q$$

..etc.....

After n α's, $2^n - 1$ γ's (and no more) can have occurred.

Exercise 4.1 (For fun). Describe the behaviour of $p^\frown q$ a bit more precisely - e.g. how many γ's must have occurred after n α's?

Exercise 4.2 Build a counter of sort $\{\iota,\delta,\zeta\}$
which (i) Can always be incremented by an ι-experiment;
(ii) Can be decremented by a δ-experiment if non-zero;
(iii) Can admit a ζ-experiment only when it is zero.

Hint: in state n, it will be something like a chain of about n cells. Incrementing must increase the cell-count by one; decrementing must decrease the cell-count by one by causing one cell to die - i.e. become NIL. You may need a doubly linked chain, built by a suitably generalised chaining operator, and looking like

But our calculus so far has an important restriction which makes it inadequate for programming; all communication is pure synchronization, and no data-values are passed from one agent to another. True, we could in principle 'read' the contents of the counter of Exercise 4.2 by seeing how many decrements (δ) are needed before a ζ (test for zero) is offerred. This would be cumbersome, to say the least, and for the counter as specified it would destroy the count stored in it!

So we now proceed to a generalisation of the algebra. In doing so we are forced to abandon our ST interpretation. What takes its place must wait till Chapters 5 and 6; meanwhile the reader must realise that - for example - the equality symbol between our more general behaviour expressions is not explained in this chapter.

4.2 Passing values

Consider the simple behaviour

$$p = \alpha\ \beta\ \bar{\gamma}\ p$$

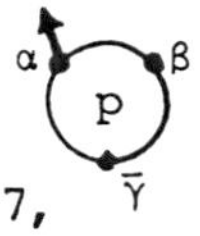

It's no more than the cycler of Exercise 2.7, but if we think of positive labels (α,β) as accepting input pulses, and negative labels $(\bar{\gamma})$ as giving output pulses, then p becomes a behaviour which "gives an output whenever it has received two inputs" (the inputs being demanded in a particular order).

Suppose that an input at α consists of more than a pulse; it is a value (an integer, say). That is, attempting an α-experiment on p consists of <u>offerring a value to p at α</u>. We may then wish to represent p's behaviour as

$$p = \alpha x.---$$

where x is a variable (supposed to become bound to the value received in an α-experiment), and --- is some behaviour expression dependent upon x, i.e. containing x as a free variable. We say that the variable x is <u>bound by α</u>, and its <u>scope</u> is --- .

(This is very familiar to anyone who knows the λ-calculus; the difference here is that any positive label α may bind a variable, while in the λ-calculus there is only one binder - the symbol "λ".)

We can go further, in our aim to transform p into a behaviour whose output values depend on its input values, and write

$$p = \alpha x.\beta y.\ ---$$

where β binds the variable y. Note that the scope of x is $\beta y.---$, while the scope of y is just ---. (It would be stupid to write $\alpha x.\beta x.---$ since then any occurence of x in --- would refer to the value bound by β to x; the value bound by α to x is inaccessible.)

Suppose we want the sum of x and y to be output at $\bar{\gamma}$. That is, in general for negative labels, attempting a $\bar{\gamma}$-experiment on p consists of demanding a value from p at $\bar{\gamma}$. Thus negative labels do not bind variables - instead they qualify value expressions (which may contain variables). So we write

$$p = \alpha x.\beta y.\bar{\gamma}(x+y).p$$

It is now proper to talk of an "α v-experiment" rather than an "α-experiment", where v is the value submitted by the observer, and similarly of a "$\bar{\gamma}$ v-experiment" where v is the value received by the observer. So, generalising the relation $\xrightarrow{\lambda}$ of §3.3, we say

$p \xrightarrow{\lambda v} p'$ means "p admits a λv-experiment, and can transform to p' as result".

(Note the different sense, according to the sign of λ.)
As a general rule then, we can state

$$\alpha x.B \xrightarrow{\alpha v} B\{v/x\}$$

where v is any value, B is a behaviour expression, and B{v/x} means the result of replacing all unbound occurrences of x in B by v. And similarly (more simply)

$$\bar{\gamma}v.B \xrightarrow{\bar{\gamma}v} B$$

for the particular value v. So the following derivation is possible on p :

$$\begin{array}{lr} p = \alpha x.\beta y.\bar{\gamma}(x+y).p & \\ \xrightarrow{\alpha 3} \quad \beta y.\bar{\gamma}(3+y).p & \\ \xrightarrow{\beta 4} \quad \bar{\gamma}(3+4).p & \\ \xrightarrow{\bar{\gamma}7} \quad p & \end{array}$$

(See §4.4 for more about derivations.)

Now we have hardly anything more to add to our language before finding that it can be used conveniently for programming. As for its interpretation, we can introduce a generalised form of ST which we call Communication Trees (CT), but for the present we wish to rely on intuitive understanding.

We shall usually be handing expressions of the form

$$\sum_i \alpha_i x_i . B_i \quad + \quad \sum_j \bar{\beta}_j E_j . B'_j \quad + \quad \sum_k \tau . B''_k$$

where B_i, B'_j, B''_k are behaviour expressions, the x_i are variables, and the E_j are value expressions. As for expressions involving composition ($|$) and the other operations, it will be enough to look at a simple example and then give a generalised Expansion Theorem (§2.5).

Consider

$$B = (\alpha x.B_1 + \beta y.B_2) \mid \bar{\alpha} v.B_3$$

We expect a sum of 4 terms, one involving τ :

$$B = \alpha x.(B_1 | \bar{\alpha} v.B_3) + \beta y.(B_2 | \bar{\alpha} v.B_3)$$
$$+ \bar{\alpha} v.((\alpha x.B_1 + \beta y.B_2) \mid B_3) + \tau.(B_1\{v/x\} | B_3)$$

Note that the "label" τ does not bind a variable or qualify a value expression. We shall also reserve the right to use other labels in this simple way when they only represent synchronization. In fact we shall allow a positive label to bind a tuple $\tilde{x} = x_1,\ldots,x_n$ of (distinct) variables, and a negative label, to qualify a tuple $\tilde{E} = E_1,\ldots,E_n$ of value expressions; then for pure synchronization we just use 0-tuples.

We shall use the term <u>guard</u> to comprise the prefixes $\alpha\tilde{x}, \overline{\beta}\tilde{E}$ and τ, and use g to stand for a guard. Dijkstra [Dij] invented the notion of guard, to stand for some condition to be met before the execution of a program part. It is natural to adapt it to the case where the condition is the acceptance of an offerred communication, as Hoare [Hoa 3] has also done in his CSP. We then find that the analogue of Dijkstra's guarded commands is provided by summation; we refer to an expression $\Sigma g_k . B_k$ as a <u>sum of guards</u>, and call each $g_k . B_k$ a <u>summand</u> of the expression. We denote the name of g's label by name(g).

<u>Expansion Theorem</u> (stated and proved as Theorem 5.8).

Let $B = (B_1 | \ldots | B_m) \backslash A$, where each B_i is a sum of guards. Then

$$B = \sum\{g.((B_1|\ldots|B'_i|\ldots|B_m)\backslash A) \;;\; g.B'_i \text{ a summand of } B_i,\ \text{name}(g) \notin A\}$$
$$+ \sum\{\tau.((B_1|\ldots|B'_i\{\tilde{E}/\tilde{x}\}|\ldots|B'_j|\ldots|B_m)\backslash A);\ \alpha\tilde{x}.B'_i \text{ a summand of } B_i,\ \overline{\alpha\tilde{E}}.B'_j \text{ a summand of } B_j\ ,\ i \neq j\}$$

provided that, in the first term, no free variable in $B_k (k \neq i)$ is bound by g . ☒

The meaning of the Theorem is that all unrestricted actions and all internal communications in B may occur.

Note that our language contains two distinct kinds of expression - value expressions and behaviour expressions. Consider $\bar{\alpha}$ E.B ; E is the first kind, B the second. We allow the following simple but important constructs in our language:

(i) Conditional behaviour expressions.

<u>if</u> E <u>then</u> B_1 <u>else</u> B_2

where E is boolean-valued. Consider for example

$\alpha x.$(<u>if</u> $x \geq 0$ <u>then</u> $\bar{\beta}x.B$ <u>else</u> $\bar{\gamma}x.B$)

(ii) Parameterised behaviour definitions. For example:

$a(y) = \alpha x.$(<u>if</u> $x \geq y$ <u>then</u> $\bar{\beta}x.a(y)$<u>else</u> $\bar{\gamma}x\ a(y)$)

(iii) Local variable declarations. We shall allow constructs like

<u>let</u> $x = 6$ <u>and</u> $y = 10$ <u>in</u> B

and

B <u>where</u> $x = 6$ <u>and</u> $y = 10$.

They mean exactly the same - namely, the same as substituting 6 for x and 10 for y throughout B.

We hope that the language is simple enough to be understood intuitively, without formal syntax. Exact formulation comes later!

4.3 An example - Data Flow

We will now show how to build and verify a simple system which bears a strong relation to the Data Flow Schemata of Dennis et al [DFL].
The task is to build a net which will compute 2^x for arbitrary non-negative integer x , given components for computing more primitive functions and predicates, and some standard gating and switching components. That is, we want a net whose behaviour is observation equivalent to

$$a = \iota x.\bar{o}2^x.\ a \tag{1}$$

(We shall often use ι for input, $\bar{o}$ for output). First, we define some standard components.

(i) Unary function agent

For arbitrary unary function f , we define the agent

$$\mathrm{DO}\ f \;=\; \iota x.\bar{o}(f(x)).(\mathrm{DO}\ f) \qquad (2)$$

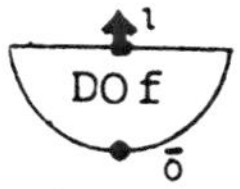

we shall only use simple f's ; we are actually trying to build the behaviour

DO bexp

where $\mathrm{bexp}(x) = 2^x$, as you can see by comparing (1) and (2).

(ii) Unary predicate agent

For arbitrary unary predicate p , we define

$$\mathrm{ASK}\ p = \iota x.\ \underline{\text{if}}\ p(x)\ \underline{\text{then}}\ \bar{o}_1 x.(\mathrm{ASK}\ p)\ \underline{\text{else}}\ \bar{o}_2 x.(\mathrm{ASK}\ p)$$

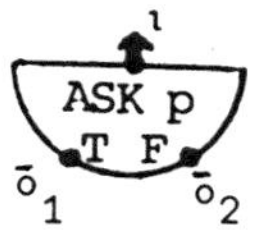

Note that the value x is passed unchanged out of one of the output ports.

(iii) A gate

$$\mathrm{GATE} \;=\; \iota x.\bar{o}x.\gamma.\mathrm{GATE}$$

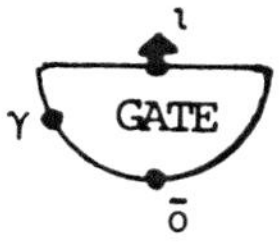

The gate transmits a value unchanged, but must be re-opened at γ to repeat.

(iv) A trigger

$$\mathrm{TRIG} \;=\; \iota x.\gamma.\bar{o}x.\mathrm{TRIG}$$

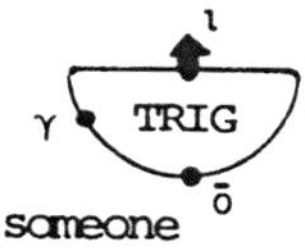

Like a gate, but must be triggered (or trigger someone else!) after receipt and before transmission.

(v) A source

For arbitrary constant value v , a permanent source of v's is given by

$$\mathrm{DO}v \;=\; \iota.\bar{o}v.(\mathrm{DO}v)$$

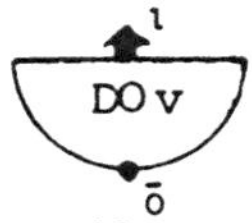

We use DO , because the unary function agent is easily generalised to n-ary function agents, and constants are just o-ary functions.

(vi) A sink

$$\text{SINK} = \iota x.\text{SINK}$$

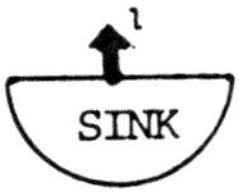

For discarding unwanted values.

(vii) A switch

$$\text{SWITCH} = \iota x.(\gamma_1.\bar{o}_1 x.\text{SWITCH} + \gamma_2.\bar{o}_2 x.\text{SWITCH})$$

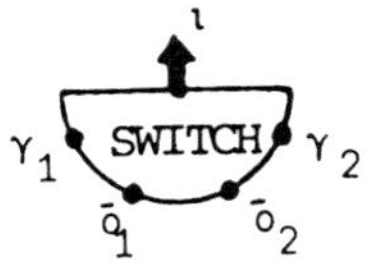

A generalisation of a trigger;
triggering γ_i selects output port $\bar{o}_i$.

This is all we need for our example; it is not a complete (or necessarily best) set, and it would be interesting to design a good set of components which could be shown adequate for a wide class of data-flow computations.

We would like to factor our design into a control part and a controlled part. For the control part, it will be convenient to build an agent observation-equivalent to

$$\text{CONTROL} = \iota x.\overbrace{\gamma.\cdots\cdot\gamma.}^{x \text{ times}}\delta.\text{CONTROL} \tag{3}$$

i.e. for input x it will admit x γ-experiments followed by a δ-experiment and return to its original 'state'. We show the net for realising CONTROL; it can be shown by Expansion to satisfy an equation like (3) with many intervening τ's, and this is observation equivalent to CONTROL, as we shall see in Chapter 7.

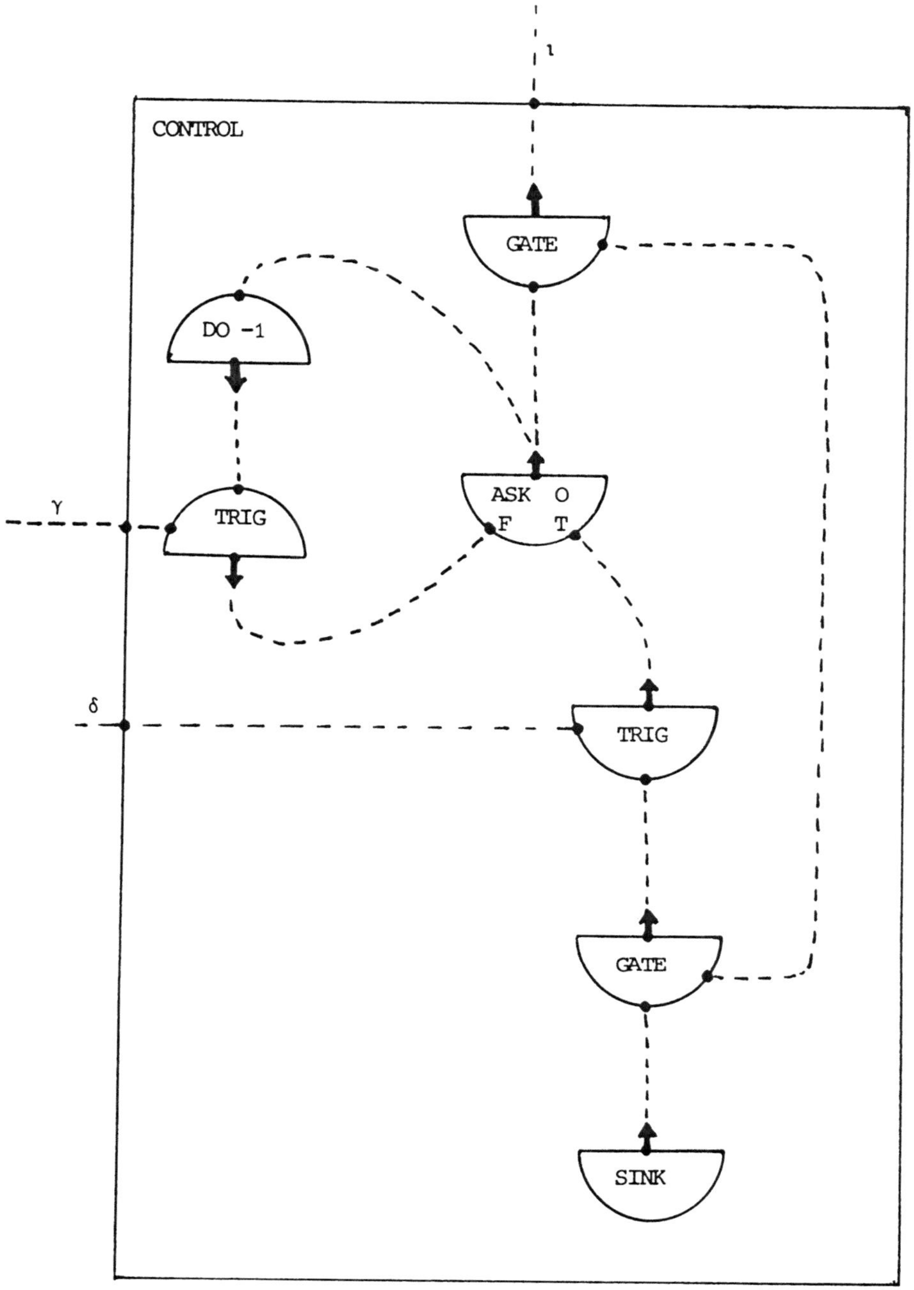

One can check for the right behaviour informally, by "arrow-swinging". Note that the initial state is restored, and that if either trigger is replaced by a gate then 'overtaking' can occur, yielding the wrong behaviour.

The controlled part, or body, is to admit a value v at ι', then after n $\bar{\gamma}$-experiments followed by a $\bar{\delta}$-experiment it will emit $2^n \times v$ at $\bar{o}$ and restore itself. That is, we want to realise

$$\begin{aligned} \text{BODY} &= \iota'y.\ b(y) \quad \text{where} \\ b(y) &= \bar{\gamma}.b(2y) + \bar{\delta}.\bar{o}y.\text{BODY} \end{aligned} \tag{4}$$

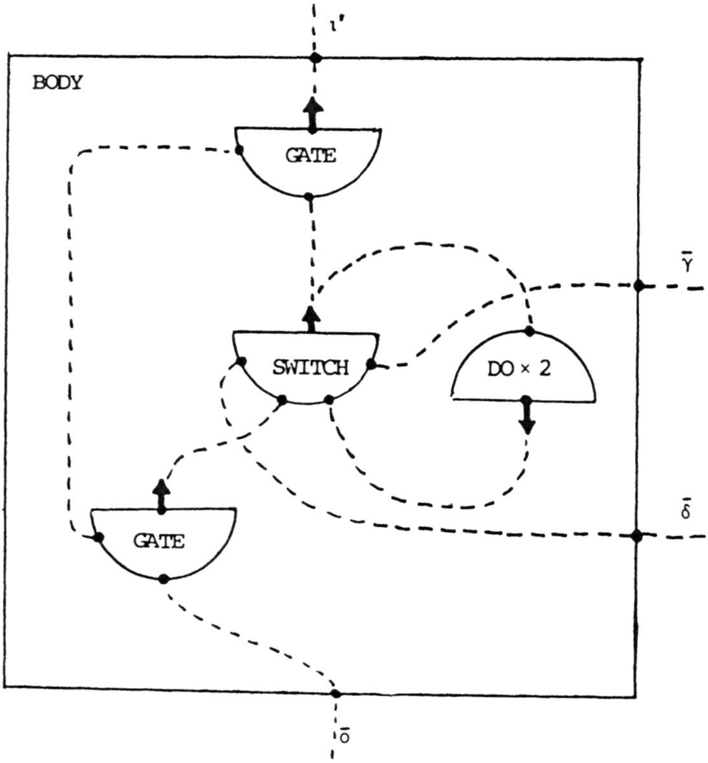

Exercise 4.3 Put this net together, as a restricted composition of relabelled standard components, and show that it satisfies an equation like (4) (but with intervening τ's), using the Expansion Theorem.

Having established the behaviour of BODY and CONTROL, it is a simple matter to put them together in such a way that an input x to the whole system first gates a 1 into BODY, then enters CONTROL itself. The outer pair of gates (present also in BODY and CONTROL) is to prevent overlapping of successive computations.

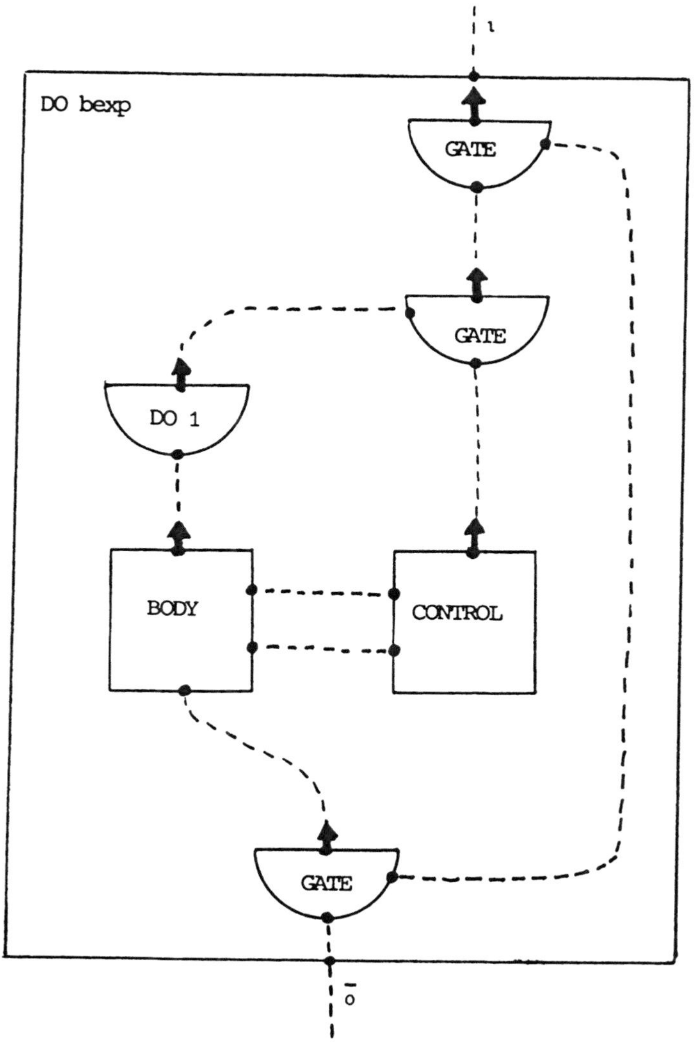

<u>Exercise 4.4</u> Treating BODY and CONTROL as given by (3) and (4), put the net together as in the last exercise, and show that it behaves like DO bexp, but with intervening τ's. See (1) and (2).

The example shows how nets may be built in modules which are verified separately. There are two remarks:

(i) The use of the Expansion Theorem is tedious, but as we mentioned earlier it can be mechanised.

(ii) We have implicitly assumed that if two behaviours are observation equivalent, then replacing one by another in any system context will yield an observation equivalent system. (This is what justified our treatment of BODY and CONTROL - replacing them by their <u>specified</u> behaviours). This assumption is justified for the contexts we have considered, but it is not trivial to prove that this is so.

<u>Exercise 4.5</u> Construct data flow nets to compute the value of y from input values x and y , for each of the following programs:

(i) <u>while</u> p(x) <u>do</u> (y:= f(x,y) ; x:= g(x))

(ii) <u>while</u> p(y) <u>do</u> (y:= <u>if</u> q(x,y) <u>then</u> f(x,y) <u>else</u> f(y,x) ;
x:= g(x))

You will almost certainly need some other 'standard' agents, and a different way of handling predicates - since the construct 'ASK q' doesn't generalise very well for non-unary predicates.

4.4 <u>Derivations</u>

In §4.2 we gave an example of a derivation of $p = \alpha x.\beta y.\bar{\gamma}(x+y).p$:

$$p \xrightarrow{\alpha 3} \beta y.\bar{\gamma}(3+y).p \xrightarrow{\beta 4} \bar{\gamma}(3+4).\ p \xrightarrow{\bar{\gamma} 7} p\ .$$

Similarly, $B = ((\alpha x.B_1 + \beta y.B_2) \mid \bar{\beta}v.\gamma z.B_3)\backslash\beta$ has derivations

$$B \xrightarrow{\alpha 5} (B_1\{5/x\} \mid \bar{\beta}v.\gamma z.B_3)\backslash\beta\ ;$$

$$B \xrightarrow{\tau} (B_2\{v/y\} \mid \gamma z.B_3)\backslash\beta \xrightarrow{\gamma 7} (B_2\{v/y\} \mid B_3\{7/z\})\backslash\beta\ .$$

A general derivation takes the form

$$B \xrightarrow{\mu_1 v_1} B_1 \xrightarrow{\mu_2 v_2} B_2 \longrightarrow \cdots \xrightarrow{\mu_n v_n} B_n$$

(which has length n) or may be infinite. We shall often write a derivation of length n as

$$B \xrightarrow{\mu_1 v_1} \cdot \xrightarrow{\mu_2 v_2} \cdot \;\ldots\; \cdot \xrightarrow{\mu_n v_n} B_n \quad , \text{ or } \quad B \xrightarrow{\mu_1 v_1 \cdot \mu_2 v_2 \cdot \;\ldots\; \cdot \mu_n v_n} B_n$$

we can abbreviate $B \xrightarrow{\tau^n} B'$ by $B \overset{\varepsilon}{\Longrightarrow} B'$ $(n \geq 0)$

and abbreviate $B \xrightarrow{\tau^m . \mu v . \tau^n} B'$ by $B \overset{\mu v}{\Longrightarrow} B'$ $(m,n \geq 0)$.

(see also §3.3).

A complete derivation is either an infinite derivation, or a finite derivation which cannot be extended (this means B_n = NIL).

Exercise 4.6 Using equations (3) and (4) in 4.3, write some of the derivations of BODY, CONTROL and $(\text{BODY} \mid \text{CONTROL})\backslash\gamma\backslash\delta$. What complete derivations are there?

A complete finite derivation of B represents a possibility that B can reach a point where no further action is possible; it may deadlock.

4.5 An example - Zero searching

We want to set two agents p and q to work together in finding a root for the equation $f(X) = 0$ in the range $[A,B]$, for a continuous function f , knowing that such a root exists - i.e. $f(A) \times f(B) \leq 0$. It is natural to make p and q calculate $f(A')$ and $f(B')$ respectively, and concurrently, for two internal points A' and B'.

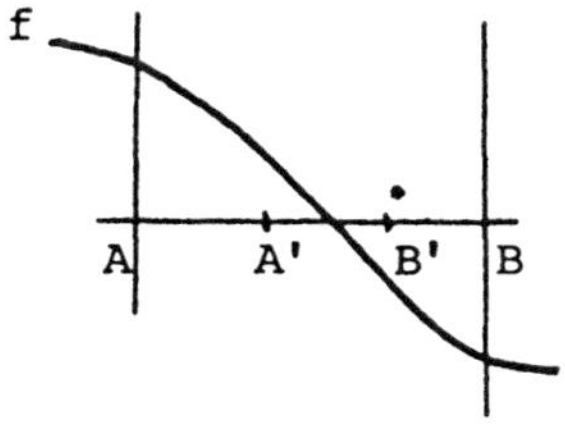

If p finishes first, and finds that $f(A')$ differs in sign from $f(A)$, he can leave a message for q to come and help him in the new interval $[A,A']$, and begin to work within this interval himself.

If he finds f(A') to have the same sign as f(A), then he should go to help q in the interval [A',B].

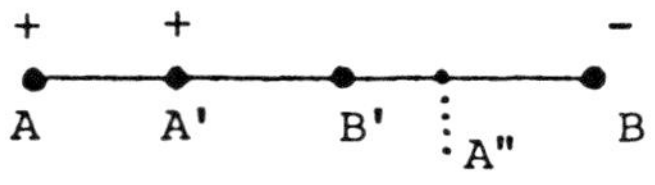

He could choose a point A" in [A',B'] or in [B',B]. Kung [Kun, Section 3] made the elegant suggestion that the points A',B' should not trisect [A,B], but rather divide it so that the ratios AA':AB, B'B:AB and A'B':A'B are equal; then in the case above A may pick the new point A" so that the new interval [A',B] is subdivided by the working points in the same ratio as [A,B] was subdivided.

This determines A',B' as the golden sections of A,B;

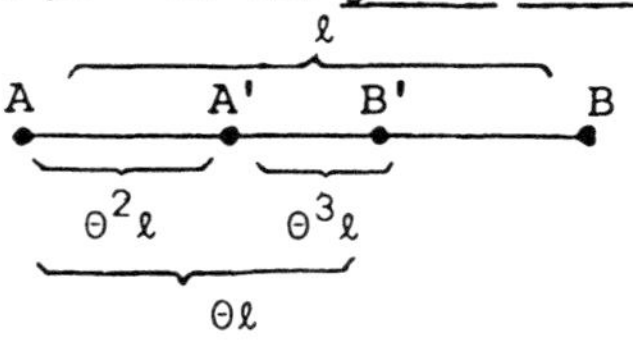

$\theta^2 + \theta = 1$;

$\theta = \frac{\sqrt{5}-1}{2} \approx .618$

At any moment then, there are two possibilities:

(i) p and q are both working on golden sections of [A,B];

(ii) One of them is working on a golden section point, and the other on a point outside the interval (because the other agent has shrunk the interval).

The computation stops when the interval has been reduced to less than some predetermined value 'eps'.

As Kung observed, the algorithm can be implemented by giving p a local variable X (his working point), q a local variable Y similarly, and representing the interval by a few global variables which either p or q may inspect and update, using a critical section for the purpose. Thus an outline program for P , using conventional and obvious notation, is:

p = <u>while</u> interval ≥ eps <u>do</u> <u>begin</u> compute f(X) ; update globals (CRITICAL SECTION) <u>end</u> ;

similarly for q , and the whole program is

<u>cobegin</u> p || q <u>coend</u> .

. Müldner has given the complete algorithm [Mül]. I am grateful to
. Salwicki for drawing my attention to this example, which is a good
ne to illustrate different concurrent programming disciplines.

Now in a sense p and q are <u>sharing a resource</u>, i.e. the nterval, represented by global variables. Hoare and others have ade the point that code and data associated with shared resources are etter located at one site, rather than distributed over the sharing gents; Hoare proposed <u>Monitors</u> as a device to achieve this modularity Hoa 2].

Here we propose to represent the interval as a separate agent, ithout the need for any extra programming construct for the purpose.

The idea is that p or q submits the result of his evaluation o the interval agent, which then hands him a new evaluation point. , working on X , is represented by

$$p(X) = \bar{\alpha}_1(X,f(X)).\alpha_2 X'.p(X')$$

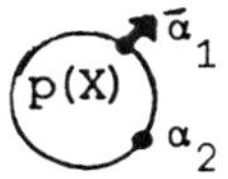

nd q , working on Y, by

$$q(Y) = \bar{\beta}_1(Y,f(Y)).\beta_2 Y'.q(Y')$$

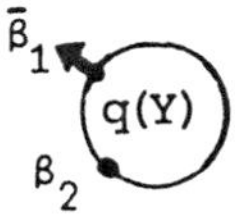

otice that each submits a <u>pair</u>, argument and function-value, to the nterval.

The interval Int is parameterised on A,B,a,b where initially and always later) $a = f(A)$, $b = f(B)$ and $a \times b \leq 0$.

By carefully reversing the direction of the interval when necessary, nt ensures that at any time

p is working either at ℓ[A,B] (left section) or outside the interval;
q " " " " r[A,B] (right section) " " " " .

he interval agent has sort $\{\alpha_1,\bar{\alpha}_2,\beta_1,\bar{\beta}_2,\bar{\rho}\}$, and delivers the root inally at $\bar{\rho}$. It is defined as follows:

```
Int(A,B,a,b) =
if  |A - B| < eps then  ρ̄A.NIL else
(α1(X,x).  if X =  A'  then

                    if  x × a ≤ 0
                    then  ᾱ2ℓ[A,A'].Int(A,A',a,x)
                    else  ᾱ2ℓ[B,A'].Int(B,A',b,x)
               else  ᾱ2A'.Int(A,B,a,b)

+ β1(Y,y). if  Y = B'  then
                    if  y × b ≤ 0
                    then  β̄2r[B',B].Int(B',B,y,b)
                    else  β̄2r[B',A].Int(B',A,y,a)
               else  β̄2B'.Int(A,B,a,b)
 ) where  A',B' = ℓ[A,B],r[A,B]
```

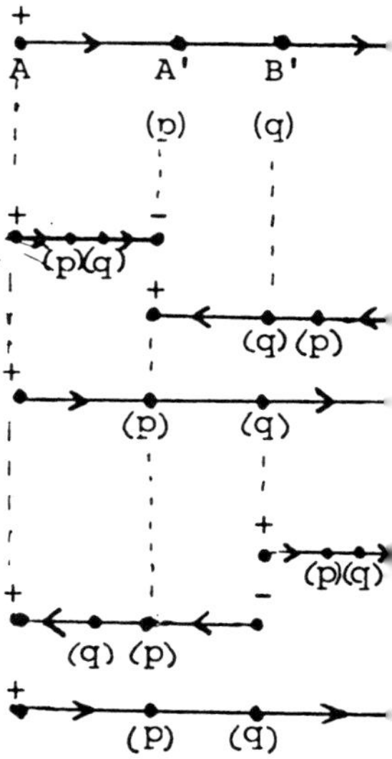

The complete system is $\text{Sys}(A,B,a,b,X,Y) =$

$$(p(X) \mid \text{Int}(A,B,a,b) \mid q(Y))\backslash\alpha_1\backslash\alpha_2\backslash\beta_1\backslash\beta_2$$

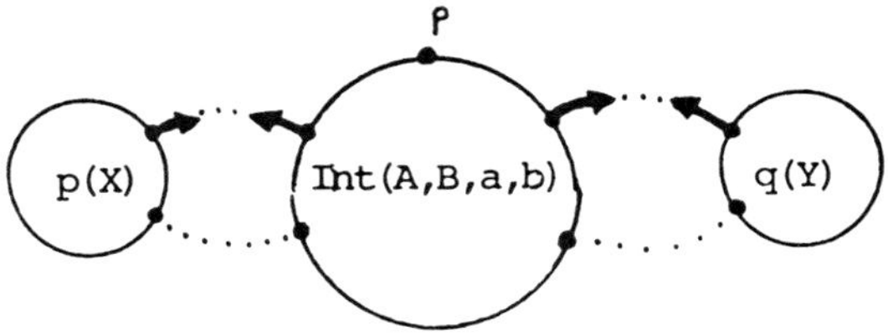

(The arrows are marked assuming the case $|A-B| \geq$ eps.)

What do we want to prove about Sys? Simply that every possible derivation computes a near-root of f in [A,B]. (By a near-root Z of f, we mean a Z such that [Z - eps, Z + eps] contains a root.) More precisely, we require

<u>if</u> (i) $a = f(A)$, $b = f(B)$, $a \times b \leq 0$,
<u>and</u> (ii) $X = \ell[A,B]$ or $Y = r[A,B]$,
<u>then</u> every complete derivation of
Sys(A,B,a,b,X,Y) takes the form

$$\text{Sys}(A,B,a,b,X,Y) \xrightarrow{\bar{\rho} Z} \text{NIL}$$

where $Z \in [A,B]$ is a near-root of f.

It's convenient to prove this by induction on the size of [A,B], defined as the least n such that $\theta^n \times |A-B| < \text{eps}$. For size = 0 we have

$$\text{Sys}(A,B,a,b,X,Y) \xrightarrow{\bar{\rho} A} \text{NIL}$$

as the only complete derivation, and we are done. For size > 0, we can use the Expansion Theorem to show the following, which is enough to complete the proof:

Under conditions (i) and (ii), every complete derivation of Sys(A,B,a,b,X,Y) extends a derivation

$$\xrightarrow{\tau.\tau} \text{Sys}(A',B',a',b',X',Y')$$

where the parameters again satisfy (i) and (ii), and
(a) if $X = \ell[A,B]$ and $Y = r[A,B]$ then $[A',B']$ has smaller size;
(b) otherwise <u>either</u> $[A',B']$ has smaller size <u>or</u> $[A',B'] = [A,B]$, $X' = \ell[A,B]$ and $Y' = r[A,B]$.

<u>Exercise 4.7</u> Verify the above statement by expanding Sys(A,B,a,b,X,Y). Note that the interval decreases in size after two computations, though not always after one.

<u>Exercise 4.8</u> It isn't necessary for p and q to access Int through distinct ports. Redesign Int so that ports $\bar{\alpha}_1$, $\bar{\beta}_1$ are identified, and similarly α_2, β_2; it's easy but not completely trivial.

<u>Exercise 4.9</u> Kung remarks that a root-searching algorithm for <u>three</u> cooperating agents can be designed so that the interval subdivision adopts one of the two patterns

Program this algorithm.

<u>Exercise 4.10</u> Suppose that p (q similarly) can pause during its evaluation of f(X) at certain times, to ask the interval "should I continue or start on a new point?" Adjust the interval agent to respond to these interrupts.

CHAPTER 5

Syntax and Semantics of CCS

5.1 Introduction

We have seen some examples of expressions of CCS, representing both programs and their specifications. We saw that, with the introduction of value-passing, we had to abandon the simple interpretation of behaviour expressions as synchronization trees, but in §4.2 we talked of atomic experiments on behaviour expressions (or on the behaviours for which they stand), and this was developed further in §4.4 on derivations.

We are now ready to present CCS precisely, and to define precisely the atomic actions (and hence the derivations) of every CCS program. On this basis, we proceed in this chapter and in Chapter 7 to develop our central notion, observation equivalence of programs. From this it is a short step to a congruence relation; two programs are observation congruent iff they are observation equivalent (i.e. indistinguishable by observation) in every context. Our proposal is that an observation congruence class is a behaviour, so that CCS is indeed an algebra of behaviours, in which each program stands for its congruence class.

This main development is independent of the notion of ST. STs may now be regarded as a first approximation (not sufficiently abstract) to a model of CCS without value-passing, and in Chapter 6 we show how they may be generalised to CTs (communication trees) to give a first approximation to a model of CCS with value-passing; again, the main development is independent of CTs, which are only discussed to aid understanding. When we eventually define observation equivalence over programs in Chapter 7, it will look just like the corresponding definition in §3.3 over STs, which generalises to CTs in an obvious way. Indeed, we expect to find that two programs are equivalent iff the corresponding CTs are so; in that case CTs, though not technically essential, fit naturally into our picture.

This chapter is devoted to a congruence over programs which we call strong congruence, since it is stronger than the observation congruence studied in Chapter 7. By approaching our proposal in two stages we introduce the properties of behaviour gradually, and with greater insight than if we tackled observation congruence immediately. In fact we even subdivide the first stage in this chapter, approaching strong congruence via an even stronger relation called <u>direct equivalence</u>.

The CCS language was introduced in the author's "Synthesis of Communicating Behaviour" [Mil 3]. However, the semantic specification by derivations was not given there in detail.

5.2 Syntax

Value expressions E

Value expressions are built from

(i) Variables $x, y, \ldots$
(ii) Constant symbols, and function symbols standing for known total functions over values

using conventional notation. We also allow tuples $(E_1, \ldots, E_n)$ of value expressions. Thus each value expression without variables stands for a uniquely defined value; we shall not worry about the distinction between such expressions and their values.

We shall also avoid details about the types of values and value expressions, though we shall have to mention some syntactic constraints depending on such details (which are standard).

Labels, sorts and relabelling

As in Chapter 2, our labels are $\Lambda = \Delta \cup \bar{\Delta}$, together with τ. We use $\alpha, \beta, ..$ to range over Δ, λ over Λ, and $\mu, \nu, \ldots$ to range over $\Lambda \cup \{\tau\}$. A sort L is a subset of Λ; to each behaviour expression B will be assigned a sort L(B). †

A relabelling $S : L \to M$ between sorts L and M is as in §2.2. However, some positive labels α will be used to bind (tuples of) variables and then $\bar{\alpha}$ will qualify (tuples of) value expressions; we must ensure that S preserves the sign of such labels (i.e. $S(\alpha) \in \Delta$). Moreover, in a complete treatment we should have to assign types to value variables and value expressions, hence also to labels, and to ensure that relabellings respect the types of labels. We will avoid these details; they need care, but would only obscure the more important aspects of semantics which we want to discuss here.

† We shall only meet <u>finite</u> sorts in examples. However, all we need to assume - for technical reasons - is that Λ is never exhausted. Infinite sorts may be of use; see the end of Chapter 6.

Behaviour identifiers b

We presuppose a collection of such identifiers, each having preassigned

(i) an arity n(b) - the number of value parameters.
(ii) a sort L(b).

We assume that the meaning of such identifiers is given, often recursively, by a behaviour expression. For example, in §4.5 we gave meaning to the behaviour identifier p by

$$p(x) = \bar{\alpha}_1(x,f(x)).\alpha_2 x'.\ p(x')$$

where $n(p) = 1$, $L(p) = \{\bar{\alpha}_1, \alpha_2\}$.

Again, a complete treatment would specify not just an arity but a type (i.e. list of parameter types) for each b .

Behaviour expressions B

Behaviour expressions are formed by our six kinds of behaviour operator (§4.1), by parameterising behaviour identifiers, and by conditionals. It's convenient to present the formation rules as a table (see below), giving for each expression B its sort L(B) and its free variable set FV(B).

We should regard the language given by the table as a core language, which we are free to extend by defining derived behaviour operators (the chaining combinator $\frown$ of §4.1 for example) and by alternative syntax for commonly occurring patterns.

In what follows, we shall use

$$B\{E_1/x_1,\ldots,E_n/x_n\}$$

to denote the result of substituting expression E_i for variable x_i $(1 \leq i \leq n)$ at all its free occurrences within B . Sometimes we shall abbreviate vectors (tuples) of variables and expressions as $\tilde{x}$ and $\tilde{E}$, and write a substitution as

$$B\{\tilde{E}/\tilde{x}\} .$$

(As usual, such substitutions may require change of bound variables, to avoid clashes.)

SYNTAX TABLE FOR BEHAVIOUR EXPRESSIONS

Form	B"	L(B")	FV(B")
Inaction	NIL	$\emptyset$	$\emptyset$
Summation	$B + B'$	$L(B) \cup L(B')$	$FV(B) \cup FV(B')$
Action	$\alpha x_1,\ldots,x_n \,.\, B$	$L(B) \cup \{\alpha\}$	$FV(B) - \{x_1,\ldots,x_n\}$
	$\bar{\alpha} E_1,\ldots,E_n \,.\, B$	$L(B) \cup \{\bar{\alpha}\}$	$FV(B) \cup \bigcup_i FV(E_i)$
	$\tau.B$	$L(B)$	$FV(B)$
Composition	$B \mid B'$	$L(B) \cup L(B')$	$FV(B) \cup FV(B')$
Restriction	$B \backslash \alpha$	$L(B) - \{\alpha,\bar{\alpha}\}$	$FV(B)$
Relabelling	$B[S]$	$S(L(B))$	$FV(B)$
Identifier	$b(E_1,\ldots,E_{n(b)})$	$L(b)$	$\bigcup_i FV(E_i)$
Conditional	<u>if</u> E <u>then</u> B <u>else</u> B'	$L(B) \cup L(B')$	$FV(E) \cup FV(B) \cup FV(B')$

The table shows how B" of sort L(B") may be built from B,B' of sorts L(B),L(B'). Parentheses are to be used to make parsing unambiguous, or to emphasize structure; to avoid excessive use of parentheses we assume the operator precedences

$$\left\{\begin{matrix}\text{Restriction}\\ \text{Relabelling}\end{matrix}\right\} > \text{Action} > \text{Composition} > \text{Summation} .$$

Thus for example

$$B \mid \tau.B'\backslash\alpha + B''[S] \quad \text{means} \quad (B \mid (\tau.(B'\backslash\alpha))) + (B''[S]) .$$

5.3 Semantics by derivations

We proceed to define a binary relation $\xrightarrow{\mu v}$ over behaviour expressions, for each $\mu \in \Lambda \cup \{\tau\}$ and value v (of type appropriate to μ). $B \xrightarrow{\mu v} B'$ may be read "B produces (or can produce) B' under μv"; thus if B, B' are in the relation $\xrightarrow{\mu v}$, a particular atomic action of B - resulting in B' - is indicated.

Referring back to §3.3, we are taking behaviour expressions to be our agents; towards the end of §3.3 we chose STs as agents, and we shall see in the next chapter how to regard CTs as agents.

Note that $\xrightarrow{\tau}$ is a particular case of our relations, since the only value of type appropriate to τ is the 0-tuple.

The relations $\xrightarrow{\mu v}$ are defined by induction on the structure of behaviour expressions. This means that all the atomic actions of a compound expression can be inferred from the atomic actions of its component(s).

Such a relation, though not indexed as here by μv, probably first appeared in connection with the λ-calculus. It was called a reduction relation, and the clauses of its definition were called reduction rules. Gordon Plotkin first made me aware of the power and flexibility of such relations in giving meaning-by-evaluation to programming languages. (In passing we may note that the original definition of ALGOL 68, though strongly verbal, is in essence a set of reduction rules.)

Inaction

NIL has no atomic actions.

Summation

From $B_1 \xrightarrow{\mu v} B_1'$ infer $B_1 + B_2 \xrightarrow{\mu v} B_1'$

From $B_2 \xrightarrow{\mu v} B_2'$ infer $B_1 + B_2 \xrightarrow{\mu v} B_2'$

Thus the atomic actions of a sum are exactly those of its summands. We adopt the following presentation of such inference rules:

Sum → (1) $\dfrac{B_1 \xrightarrow{\mu v} B_1'}{B_1 + B_2 \xrightarrow{\mu v} B_1'}$ (2) $\dfrac{B_2 \xrightarrow{\mu v} B_2'}{B_1 + B_2 \xrightarrow{\mu v} B_2'}$

Action

$$\underline{\text{Act}\rightarrow}\quad \begin{array}{ll} (1) & \alpha x_1,\ldots,x_n.B \xrightarrow{\alpha(v_1,\ldots,v_n)} B\{v_1/x_1,\ldots,v_n/x_n\} \\ (2) & \bar{\alpha}v_1,\ldots,v_n.B \xrightarrow{\bar{\alpha}(v_1,\ldots,v_n)} B \\ (3) & \tau.B \xrightarrow{\tau} B \end{array}$$

Notes: (i) These are not inference rules, but axioms.

(ii) Act → (1) holds for all tuples $(v_1,\ldots,v_n)$ (of appropriate type for α), while Act → (2) holds just for the tuple qualified by $\bar{\alpha}$.

(iii) See §5.5 below for why we consider only values $v_1,\ldots,v_n$ (not expressions $E_1,\ldots,E_n$) in Act → (2) .

Composition

$$\underline{\text{Com}\rightarrow}\quad (1)\ \frac{B_1 \xrightarrow{\mu v} B_1'}{B_1|B_2 \xrightarrow{\mu v} B_1'|B_2} \qquad (2)\ \frac{B_2 \xrightarrow{\mu v} B_2'}{B_1|B_2 \xrightarrow{\mu v} B_1|B_2'}$$

$$(3)\ \frac{B_1 \xrightarrow{\lambda v} B_1' \qquad B_2 \xrightarrow{\bar{\lambda} v} B_2'}{B_1|B_2 \xrightarrow{\tau} B_1'|B_2'}$$

Notes: (i) Com → (1) and (2) express the idea that an action of B_1 or of B_2 in the composition $B_1|B_2$ yields an action of the composite in which the other component is unaffected.

(ii) Com → (3) expresses that communication of components yields a τ-action of the composite.

striction

s → $$\frac{B \xrightarrow{\mu v} B'}{B\backslash\alpha \xrightarrow{\mu v} B'\backslash\alpha}\;,\quad \mu\notin\{\alpha,\bar{\alpha}\}$$

Note: the side condition ensures that $B\backslash\alpha$ has no αv or $\bar{\alpha}v$ actions.

labelling

l → $$\frac{B \xrightarrow{\mu v} B'}{B[S] \xrightarrow{(S\mu)v} B'[S]}$$

Note: recall our convention that $S\tau = \tau$.

entifier. Suppose that identifier b is defined by the (possibly cursive) clause

$$b(x_1,\ldots,x_{n(b)}) \Leftarrow B_b \qquad (FV(B_b) \subseteq \{x_1,\ldots,x_{n(b)}\})$$

shall discuss such definitions shortly. Our rule is

e → $$\frac{B_b\{v_1/x_1,\ldots,v_{n(b)}/x_{n(b)}\} \xrightarrow{\mu v} B'}{b(v_1,\ldots,v_{n(b)}) \xrightarrow{\mu v} B'}$$

Note: the rule says, in effect, that each parameterized identifier has exactly the same actions as the appropriate instance of the right-hand side of its definition.

nditional

n → (1) $$\frac{B_1 \xrightarrow{\mu v} B_1'}{\underline{\text{if}}\ \text{true}\ \underline{\text{then}}\ B_1\ \underline{\text{else}}\ B_2 \xrightarrow{\mu v} B_1'}$$ (2) $$\frac{B_2 \xrightarrow{\mu v} B_2'}{\underline{\text{if}}\ \text{false}\ \underline{\text{then}}\ B_1\ \underline{\text{else}}\ B_2 \xrightarrow{\mu v} B_2'}$$

Note: As with all value expressions without variables, we assume that boolean-valued expressions evaluate 'automatically' to their boolean values. See §5.5 below for why we need not consider value-expressions containing variables in these rules.

5.4 Defining behaviour identifiers

We shall now assume that every behaviour identifier b is defined by a clause

$$b(x_1,\ldots,x_{n(b)}) \Leftarrow B_b$$

where $x_1,\ldots,x_{n(b)}$ are distinct variables, and where $FV(B_b) \subseteq \{x_1,\ldots,x_{n(b)}$
The symbol '$\Leftarrow$' is preferred to ' = ' since we are not yet talking of the behaviours denoted by behaviour expressions (so ' = ', in the sense of equality of meaning, would be out of place), and also because we will later in this chapter use ' =' to mean <u>identity</u> between expressions.

We thus have a collection of clauses defining our b's, and they may be mutually recursive. Although not actually essential, we shall impose a slight constraint on the collection, which will forbid such definitions as

$$b(x) \Leftarrow \bar{\alpha}x.NIL + b(x+1)$$

or

$$\begin{cases} b_1 \Leftarrow b_2 + \alpha.b_3 \\ b_2 \Leftarrow b_1 \mid \beta.b_4 \end{cases}$$

in which a behaviour may 'call itself recursively without passing a guard'. Thus the following are permitted:

$$b(x) \Leftarrow \bar{\alpha}x.NIL + \tau.b(x+1)$$

and

$$\begin{cases} b_1 \Leftarrow b_2 + \alpha.b_3 \\ b_2 \Leftarrow \tau.b_1 \mid \beta.b_4 \end{cases}$$

More precisely, we say that <u>b is unguarded in B</u> if it occurs in B without an enclosing guard. The restriction on our defining clauses for the b's is that there must be no infinite sequence $b_{i(1)}, b_{i(2)}, \ldots$ such that, for each j , $b_{i(j+1)}$ is unguarded in $b_{i(j)}$. (In the forbidden examples above there are such sequences: b,b,b,.... and $b_1,b_2,b_1,b_2,\ldots$ respectively.) Further, for correctness of sorts, we require

$$L(B_b) \subseteq L(b)$$

When the above constraints are met, we shall say that the behaviour identifiers are <u>guardedly well-defined</u>.

5.5 Sorts and programs

Our formation rules ascribe a unique sort L(B) each behaviour expression B ; we write

$$B : L(B)$$

to mean 'B possesses sort L(B)' . For many reasons, it is convenient to allow B to possess all larger sorts as well; so we declare

$$B : L \ \& \ L \subseteq M \ \text{ implies } \ B : M$$

For example, this allows us to make sense of an expression like

$$NIL[\beta/\alpha]$$

since $\beta/\alpha : \{\alpha\} \to \{\beta\}$ is a relabelling, and NIL : $\{\alpha\}$ since NIL : $\emptyset$.

An important property of atomic actions as defined in §5.3 is the following:

Proposition 5.1 If $B \xrightarrow{\mu v} B'$, and B : L , then

$$\mu \in L \cup \{\tau\} \ \text{ and } \ B' : L$$

Proof By induction on the length of the inference which ensures $B \xrightarrow{\mu v} B'$, using the ascription of sorts by the formation rules. ☒

Although our rules for atomic actions apply to arbitrary behaviour expressions, they fail to describe fully the meaning of expressions with free variables. For example, the rule Act→ gives no action for

$$\bar{\alpha}(x+1).\,NIL$$

and Con→ says nothing for

$$\underline{\text{if}} \ \ x \ge 0 \ \ \underline{\text{then}} \ \ \bar{\alpha}x.NIL \ \underline{\text{else}} \ \bar{\beta}(-x).NIL$$

Clearly they could not determine the actions of these expressions, since actions involve values, not variables, and in the second example even the label of the possible action depends upon the 'value' of x .

We choose to regard the meaning of a behaviour expression B with free variables $\tilde{x}$ as determined by the meanings of $B\{\tilde{v}/\tilde{x}\}$ for all value-vectors $\tilde{v}$.

Definition We define a program to be a closed behaviour expression, i.e. one with no free variables.

Now the fact that our rules describe the meanings of programs satisfactorily is due to the following:

<u>Proposition 5.2</u> If B is a program and $B \xrightarrow{\mu v} B'$, then B' is also a program.

<u>Proof</u> By induction on the length of the inference which ensures $B \xrightarrow{\mu v} B'$. The condition on the free variables of each B_b, and the substitution involved in <u>Act→(1)</u>, are critical. ⊠

5.6 Direct equivalence of behaviour programs

(In §5.6 and §5.7 we are concerned only with programs).

We now take up the question, posed in §5.1, of which behaviour programs possess the same derivations; this will yield an equivalence relation, which will also be a <u>congruence</u> - that is, any program may be replaced by an equivalent one in any context, without affecting the behaviour (derivations) of the whole. For example,

$$B + B' \qquad \text{and} \qquad B' + B$$

are different programs, but we clearly expect them to be interchangeable in this sense.

A first approximation to what we want may be called <u>direct equivalence</u> we denote it by $\equiv$, and define it as follows:

<u>Definition</u> $B_1 \equiv B_2$ (B_1 and B_2 are directly equivalent) iff for every μ, v and B

$$B_1 \xrightarrow{\mu v} B \Leftrightarrow B_2 \xrightarrow{\mu v} B .$$

(<u>Warning</u>: $\equiv$ is not a congruence relation. For example, we may have $B_1 \equiv B_2$, but in general

$B | B_1 \not\equiv B | B_2$. For example,

$$\left.\begin{array}{l} \alpha.\mathrm{NIL} \,|\, B_1 \xrightarrow{\alpha} \mathrm{NIL} \,|\, B_1 \\ \alpha.\mathrm{NIL} \,|\, B_2 \xrightarrow{\alpha} \mathrm{NIL} \,|\, B_2 \end{array}\right\} \text{not identical!}$$

But the congruence relation we want will be <u>implied</u> by $\equiv$, and so the following laws for $\equiv$ will hold for the congruence also.)

In what follows it is often convenient to let g stand for an arbitrary guard $\alpha\tilde{x}$, $\bar{\alpha}\tilde{E}$ or τ. The result Sg of relabelling a guard is given by $S(\alpha\tilde{x}) = (S\alpha)\tilde{x}$, $S(\bar{\alpha}\tilde{E}) = (S\bar{\alpha})\tilde{E}$ and $S\tau = \tau$. The name of the label in g is denoted by $\mathrm{name}(g)$.

Theorem 5.3 (Direct Equivalences). The following direct equivalences hold (classified by the leading operator on the left side):

Sum ≡	(1) $B_1 + B_2 \equiv B_2 + B_1$	(2) $B_1 + (B_2 + B_3) \equiv (B_1 + B_2) + B_3$
	(3) $B + \mathrm{NIL} \equiv B$	(4) $B + B \equiv B$

Act ≡	$\alpha\tilde{x}.B \equiv \alpha\tilde{y}.B\{\tilde{y}/\tilde{x}\}$ (change of bound variables) where $\tilde{y}$ are distinct variables not in B

Res ≡	(1) $\mathrm{NIL}\backslash\beta \equiv \mathrm{NIL}$	(2) $(B_1 + B_2)\backslash\beta \equiv B_1\backslash\beta + B_2\backslash\beta$
	(3) $(g.B)\backslash\beta \equiv \begin{cases} \mathrm{NIL} & \text{if } \beta = \mathrm{name}(g) \\ g.B\backslash\beta & \text{otherwise} \end{cases}$	

Rel ≡	(1) $\mathrm{NIL}[S] \equiv \mathrm{NIL}$	(2) $(B_1 + B_2)[S] \equiv B_1[S] + B_2[S]$
	(3) $(g.B)[S] \equiv Sg.B[S]$	

Now in view of Sum ≡ the following notations are unambiguous:

$\sum_{1\le i\le n} B_i$ meaning $B_1 + \ldots + B_n$ (NIL, if $n = 0$)

$\sum\{B_i \, ; i \in I\}$ more generally, where I is finite.

If each B_i is of form $g_i.B_i'$, we call such a sum a sum of guards, and each B_i a summand.

Com ≡ Let B and C be sums of guards. Then

$$\begin{aligned} B|C \equiv\ & \textstyle\sum\{g.(B'|C) \;;\; g.B' \text{ a summand of } B\} \\ &+ \textstyle\sum\{g.(B|C') \;;\; g.C' \text{ a summand of } C\} \\ &+ \textstyle\sum\{\tau.(B'\{\tilde{v}/\tilde{x}\}|C') \;;\; \alpha\tilde{x}.B' \text{ a summand of } B \text{ and } \bar{\alpha}\tilde{v}.C' \text{ a summand of } C\} \\ &+ \textstyle\sum\{\tau.(B'|C'\{\tilde{v}/\tilde{x}\}) \;;\; \bar{\alpha}\tilde{v}.B' \text{ a summand of } B \text{ and } \alpha\tilde{x}.C' \text{ a summand of } C\} \end{aligned}$$

Ide ≡	Let identifier b be defined by $b(\tilde{x}) \Leftarrow B_b$; then $b(\tilde{v}) \equiv B_b\{\tilde{v}/\tilde{x}\}$

Con ≡	(1) **if** true **then** B_1 **else** $B_2 \equiv B_1$ (2) **if** false **then** B_1 **else** $B_2 \equiv B_2$

Proof To prove each law is a routine application of the definition of the relations $\xrightarrow{\mu v}$. We consider three laws:

(i) Sum ≡ (2): $B_1+(B_2+B_3) \equiv (B_1+B_2)+B_3$
Let $B_1+(B_2+B_3) \xrightarrow{\mu v} B$. This can only be due to
either rule Sum → (1), because $B_1 \xrightarrow{\mu v} B$
or rule Sum → (2), because $B_2+B_3 \xrightarrow{\mu v} B$,
and in the latter case, similarly, either $B_2 \xrightarrow{\mu v} B$ or $B_3 \xrightarrow{\mu v} B$.
In each of the three cases, rules Sum → (1) and Sum → (2) yield

$$(B_1+B_2)+B_3 \xrightarrow{\mu v} B \ .$$

The reverse implication is similar.

(ii) Res ≡ (3) : $(\alpha\tilde{x}.B)\backslash\beta \equiv \begin{cases} \text{NIL} & (\beta=\alpha) \\ \alpha\tilde{x}.(B\backslash\beta) & (\beta\neq\alpha) \end{cases}$

By Act → (1) , the only actions of $\alpha\tilde{x}.B$ are of form

$$\alpha\tilde{x}.B \xrightarrow{\alpha\tilde{v}} B\{\tilde{v}/\tilde{x}\} \quad \text{(for arbitrary } \tilde{v}\text{)}.$$

Thus $(\alpha\tilde{x}.B)\backslash\alpha$ has no actions (since Res → yields none) ; neither has NIL, which settles the case $\beta=\alpha$.
For $(\beta\neq\alpha)$, by Res → the only actions of $(\alpha\tilde{x}.B)\backslash\beta$ are

$$(\alpha\tilde{x}.B)\backslash\beta \xrightarrow{\alpha\tilde{v}} B\{\tilde{v}/\tilde{x}\}\backslash\beta \ = \ (B\backslash\beta)\{\tilde{v}/\tilde{x}\}$$

and these are exactly the actions of $\alpha\tilde{x}.(B\backslash\beta)$.
The proof for guards $\bar{\alpha}\tilde{v}$ and τ is similar.

(iii) Com ≡ : $B|C \equiv \sum\cdots+\sum\cdots+\sum\cdots+\sum\cdots$.
(We use X to abbreviate the right-hand side.)
Let $B|C \xrightarrow{\mu v} D$. There are several cases.
(a) $B \xrightarrow{\mu v} B''$, and $D = B''|C$ (by Com → (1)).
Then B has a summand $g.B'$ for which $g.B' \xrightarrow{\mu v} B''$ (by Sum →). This action must be an instance of Act →

from which we can also find that $g.(B'|C) \xrightarrow{\mu v} B''|C$ (considering the three types of guard).
Hence also $X \xrightarrow{\mu v} B''|C = D$.

(b) $C \xrightarrow{\mu v} C''$, and $D = B|C''$ (by Com→(2))
The argument that $X \xrightarrow{\mu v} D$ is similar.

(c) $B \xrightarrow{\alpha\tilde{u}} B''$, $C \xrightarrow{\bar{\alpha}\tilde{u}} C'$ and $\mu v = \tau$, $D = B''|C'$
(by Com→(3) ; there is a similar case with $\alpha, \bar{\alpha}$ exchanged)
Then by Sum→ and Act→ , B has a summand $\alpha\tilde{x}.B'$ and $B'' = B'\{\tilde{u}/\tilde{x}\}$, while C has a summand $\bar{\alpha}\tilde{u}.C'$.
Hence, since X has a summand $\tau.(B'\{\tilde{u}/\tilde{x}\}|C')$, we have

$$X \xrightarrow{\tau} B''|C' = D \text{ , as required .}$$

We have now shown by (a), (b) & (c) that for all μ, v and D

$$B|C \xrightarrow{\mu v} D \Rightarrow X \xrightarrow{\mu v} D$$

and the reverse implication can be argued similarly.

⊠

Exercise 5.1 Prove some more of the equivalences claimed; e.g. Sum ≡ (1), Res ≡ (2), Rel ≡ (2) and Con ≡ (1) . They are all as easy as Sum ≡ (2) .

5.7 Congruence of behaviour programs

We now propose to extend or widen our direct equivalence relation to a congruence relation. Apart from the wish to get a congruence relation (so that equivalence is preserved by substitution of equivalent programs) there is another motivation; '≡' requires that the results of actions of equivalent programs should be identical, and it is reasonable to ask only that the results should be equivalent again.

We therefore define the relation '~' over programs, which we call strong equivalence (we define it analogously to the observation equivalence of §3.3, but it is stronger because we do not allow arbitrary τ-actions to interleave the observable actions). We define it in terms of a decreasing sequence $\sim_0, \sim_1, \ldots, \sim_k, \ldots$ of equivalence relations:

Definition $B \sim_0 C$ is always true;

$B \sim_{k+1} C$ iff for all μ, v

(i) if $B \xrightarrow{\mu v} B'$ then for some C', $C \xrightarrow{\mu v} C'$ and $B' \sim_k C'$,

(ii) if $C \xrightarrow{\mu v} C'$ then for some B', $B \xrightarrow{\mu v} B'$ and $B' \sim_k C'$;

$B \sim C$ iff $\forall k \geq 0.\ B \sim_k C$ (i.e. $\sim = \bigcap_k \sim_k$) .

We leave out the simple proofs that each $\sim_k$ is an equivalence relation, and that $B \sim_{k+1} C$ implies $B \sim_k C$ (i.e. the sequence of equivalences is decreasing).

Exercise 5.2 Show that $B \equiv C$ implies $B \sim_k C$ for each k, and hence implies $B \sim C$.

Theorem 5.4 $\sim$ is a congruence relation.

More precisely, $B_1 \sim B_2$ implies

$$B_1 + C \sim B_2 + C, \quad C + B_1 \sim C + B_2$$
$$\bar{\alpha}\,\tilde{v}.B_1 \sim \bar{\alpha} v.B_2\ , \quad \tau.B_1 \sim \tau.B_2$$
$$B_1|C \sim B_2|C\ , \quad C|B_1 \sim C|B_2$$
$$B_1\backslash\alpha \sim B_2\backslash\alpha\ , \quad B_1[S] \sim B_2[S]$$

and $B_1\{\tilde{v}/\tilde{x}\} \sim B_2\{\tilde{v}/\tilde{x}\}$ (for all $\tilde{v}$) implies

$$\alpha\tilde{x}.B_1 \sim \alpha\tilde{x}.B_2$$

Proof We give the proof only for composition. We prove by induction on k that

$$B_1 \sim_k B_2 \ \text{ implies } \ B_1|C \sim_k B_2|C$$

For $k = 0$ it is trivial. Now assume $B_1 \sim_{k+1} B_2$.

Let $B_1|C \xrightarrow{\mu v} D_1$. We want D_2 such that

$$B_2|C \xrightarrow{\mu v} D_2 \sim_k D_1$$

There are three cases:

(a) $B_1 \xrightarrow{\mu v} B_1'$, and $D_1 = B_1'|C$ (by <u>Com→(1)</u>)

Then $B_2 \xrightarrow{\mu v} B_2' \sim_k B_1'$. for some B_2',

whence $B_2|C \xrightarrow{\mu v} B_2'|C$ by <u>Com→(1)</u>

$\sim_k D_1 (= B_1'|C)$ by inductive hypothesis.

(b) $C \xrightarrow{\mu v} C'$ and $D_1 = B_1|C'$ (by <u>Com→(2)</u>)

Then $B_2|C \xrightarrow{\mu v} B_2|C'$ by <u>Com→(2)</u>

But $B_1 \sim_k B_2$ (since $B_1 \sim_{k+1} B_2$), hence $B_1|C' \sim_k B_2|C'$ by inductive hypothesis.

(c) $B_1 \xrightarrow{\lambda\tilde{u}} B_1'$, $C \xrightarrow{\bar{\lambda}\tilde{u}} C'$ and $\mu v = \tau$, $D_1 = B_1'|C'$ (by Com →(3))
Then $B_2 \xrightarrow{\lambda\tilde{u}} B_2' \sim_k B_1'$, for some B_2' ,
whence $B_2|C \xrightarrow{\tau} B_2'|C'$ by Com →(3)

$\sim_k D_1$ by inductive hypothesis .

By symmetry, of course, if $B_2|C \xrightarrow{\mu v} D_2$ then we find D_1 such that $B_1|C \xrightarrow{\mu v} D_1 \sim_k D_2$.

∎

Exercise 5.3 (i) Prove that $B_1 \sim_k B_2$ implies $\bar{\alpha}\tilde{v}.B_1 \sim_{k+1} \bar{\alpha}\tilde{v}.B_2$; this shows that $B_1 \sim B_2$ implies $\bar{\alpha}\tilde{v}.B_1 \sim \bar{\alpha}\tilde{v}.B_2$, and also that guarding increases the index of $\sim_k$ by one.

(ii) Prove the last part of the Theorem, involving the positive label guard.

We end this section by giving some useful properties of $\sim$, in the form of equational laws. Note that Theorem 5.3 already gives many of its properties, since $\equiv$ is contained in $\sim$. Since we run the risk of bewildering the reader with a confused mass of properties, let us emphasize some structure.

In Theorem 5.3, Sum ≡ states that + and NIL form a commutative semigroup with absorption, and Res ≡, Rel ≡, Com ≡ each describe how one of the static behaviour operations $\backslash\alpha$, $[S]$, $|$ interacts with the dynamic operations +, μv and NIL. In the following theorem Com ~ states that $|$ and NIL form a commutative semigroup, while Res ~ and Rel ~ state how the static operations interact with each other. The laws of Theorem 5.5 are only concerned with the static operations- they are essentially the Laws of Flow in [MM, Mil 2] .

Theorem 5.5 (Strong congruences) The following strong congruences hold:

Com ~	(1) $B_1|B_2 \sim B_2|B_1$	(2) $B_1|(B_2|B_3) \sim (B_1|B_2)|B_3$
	(3) $B|\mathrm{NIL} \sim B$	

Res ~	(1) $B\backslash\alpha \sim B$	$(B{:}L,\ \alpha \notin \mathrm{names}(L))$
	(2) $B\backslash\alpha\backslash\beta \sim B\backslash\beta\backslash\alpha$	
	(3) $(B_1|B_2)\backslash\alpha \sim B_1\backslash\alpha|B_2\backslash\alpha$	$(B_1{:}L_1, B_2{:}L_2, \alpha \notin \mathrm{names}\ (L_1 \cap \bar{L}_2))$

Rel ~	(1) $B[I] \sim B$	($I:L \to L$ is the identity relabelling)
	(2) $B[S] \sim B[S']$	($B:L$, and $S \restriction L = S' \restriction L$)
	(3) $B[S][S'] \sim B[S' \circ S]$	
	(4) $B[S] \backslash \beta \sim B \backslash \alpha [S]$	($\beta = name(S(\alpha))$)
	(5) $(B_1 \mid B_2)[S] \sim B_1[S] \mid B_2[S]$	

Proof We give the proof of Com~(2). It is the hardest - but all the proofs are routine inductions.

We prove $\forall B_1 B_2 B_3 \,.\, B_1 \mid (B_2 \mid B_3) \sim_k (B_1 \mid B_2) \mid B_3$ by induction on k.

For $k = 0$ it's trivial.

Now for $k+1$, let $B_1 \mid (B_2 \mid B_3) \xrightarrow{\mu v} D$; we require D' such that $(B_1 \mid B_2) \mid B_3 \xrightarrow{\mu v} D' \sim_k D$.

There are several cases:

(a) $B_1 \xrightarrow{\mu v} B_1'$, and $D = B_1' \mid (B_2 \mid B_3)$ by Com→(1).
Then $(B_1 \mid B_2) \mid B_3 \xrightarrow{\mu v} (B_1' \mid B_2) \mid B_3$ by Com→(1) twice
$\sim_k D$ by induction.

(b) $B_2 \mid B_3 \xrightarrow{\mu v} C$, and $D = B_1 \mid C$ by Com→(2).

Subcases

(i) $B_2 \xrightarrow{\mu v} B_2'$, and $C = B_2' \mid B_3$ by Com→(1) ; i.e. $D = B_1 \mid (B_2' \mid B_3)$.
Then $B_1 \mid B_2 \xrightarrow{\mu v} B_1 \mid B_2'$ by Com→(2) ,
so $(B_1 \mid B_2) \mid B_3 \xrightarrow{\mu v} (B_1 \mid B_2') \mid B_3$ by Com→(1) ,
$\sim_k D$ by induction.

(ii) $B_3 \xrightarrow{\mu v} B_3'$, and $C = B_2 \mid B_3'$ by Com→(2); similar.

(iii) $B_2 \xrightarrow{\lambda u} B_2'$, $B_3 \xrightarrow{\bar{\lambda} u} B_3'$, $C = B_2' \mid B_3'$ and $\mu v = \tau$;
so $D = B_1 \mid (B_2' \mid B_3')$ by Com→(3).
Then $B_1 \mid B_2 \xrightarrow{\lambda u} B_1 \mid B_2'$ by Com→(2),
so $(B_1 \mid B_2) \mid B_3 \xrightarrow{\tau} (B_1 \mid B_2') \mid B_3'$ by Com→(3),
$\sim_k D$ by induction.

(c) $B_1 \xrightarrow{\lambda u} B_1'$, $B_2 \mid B_3 \xrightarrow{\bar{\lambda} u} C$, $D = B_1' \mid C$ and $\mu v = \tau$ by Com→(3).

Subcases

(i) $B_2 \xrightarrow{\bar{\lambda} u} B_2'$, and $C = B_2' \mid B_3$ by Com→(1) ; i.e. $D = B_1' \mid (B_2' \mid B_3)$
Then $B_1 \mid B_2 \xrightarrow{\tau} B_1' \mid B_2'$ by Com→(3) ,
so $(B_1 \mid B_2) \mid B_3 \xrightarrow{\tau} (B_1' \mid B_2') \mid B_3$ by Com→(1),
$\sim_k D$ by induction.

(ii) $B_3 \xrightarrow{\bar{\lambda} u} B_3'$, and $C = B_2 \mid B_3'$ by Com→(2) : similar.

hus we have found the required $D' \sim_k D$ in each case;
imilarly given $(B_1|B_2)|B_3 \xrightarrow{\mu v} D$, we find D' such that

$$B_1|(B_2|B_3) \xrightarrow{\mu v} D' \sim_k D \ .$$

his completes the inductive step, showing

$$B_1|(B_2|B_3) \sim_{k+1} (B_1|B_2)|B_3$$ ⊠

xercise 5.4 Prove Com~(3) and Res~(3) . For the second, you need to appeal to Proposition 5.1.

We now state and prove a theorem which we need later. It depends itically on the assumption that all behaviour identifiers are guardedly ll defined (§5.4).

heorem 5.6 Strong congruence 'satisfies its definition' in the following sense:

$B \sim C$ iff for all μ, v
(i) if $B \xrightarrow{\mu v} B'$ then for some C' , $C \xrightarrow{\mu v} C'$ and $B' \sim C'$,
(ii) if $C \xrightarrow{\mu v} C'$ then for some B', $B \xrightarrow{\mu v} B'$ and $B' \sim C'$.

roof ($\Leftarrow$) $B' \sim C'$ implies $B' \sim_k C'$ for any k ; hence from (i) and (ii) we deduce $B \sim_{k+1} C$ for all k , by definition, whence $B \sim C$.

($\Rightarrow$) Since $B \sim_{k+1} C$ for all k , we have by definition that if $B \xrightarrow{\mu v} B'$ then, for each k, $\exists C_k . C \xrightarrow{\mu v} C_k$ & $B' \sim_k C_k$. But from our assumption that all behaviour identifiers are guardedly well-defined it follows that $\{C' ; C \xrightarrow{\mu v} C'\}$ is finite (we omit the details of this argument). Hence for some C' ,

$$C \xrightarrow{\mu v} C' \text{ and } B' \sim_k C' \text{ for infinitely many } k$$

and this implies $B' \sim_k C'$ for all k , since the relations $\sim_k$ are decreasing in k , hence $B' \sim C'$.

Thus (i) is proved, and (ii) is similar. ⊠

8 Congruence of Behaviour expressions and the Expansion Theorem

Having established definitions and properties of direct equivalence d congruence of programs - behaviour expressions without free variables - are now in a position to lift the results to arbitrary behaviour expressions. All that is needed is to define $\equiv$ and $\sim$ over expressions as follows:

Definition

Let $\tilde{x}$ be the free variables occurring in B_1 or B_2 or both. Then

$B_1 \equiv B_2$ iff, for all $\tilde{v}$, $B_1\{\tilde{v}/\tilde{x}\} \equiv B_2\{\tilde{v}/\tilde{x}\}$

$B_1 \sim B_2$ iff, for all $\tilde{v}$, $B_1\{\tilde{v}/\tilde{x}\} \sim B_2\{\tilde{v}/\tilde{x}\}$

Now we clearly want to extend the results of Theorems 5.3, 5.5 to arbitrary expressions; for example, we would like to apply Com~(3) of Theorem 5.5 to replace

$$\bar{\alpha}(x+1).\, NIL|NIL \quad \text{by} \quad \bar{\alpha}(x+1).\, NIL$$

anywhere in any expression, but the law only applies at present to programs, and the expressions shown have a free variable x.

We state without proof the desired generalisation.

Theorem 5.7 The relation $\sim$ is a congruence over behaviour expressions. Moreover, the results of Theorems 5.3, 5.5 hold over arbitrary expressions with the following adjustments:

(i) In Com≡ and Ide≡ of Theorem 5.3, replace $\tilde{v}$ (a value tuple) everywhere by $\tilde{E}$ (a tuple of value expressions).

(ii) Add in Com≡ the condition that, in the first (resp.second) sum on the right-hand side, no free variable of C(resp. B) is bound by g.

We now have enough to prove the Expansion Theorem, which we used in Chapter 4.

Theorem 5.8 (The Expansion Theorem).

Let $B = (B_1|\ldots|B_m)\backslash A$, where each B_i is a sum of guards. Then

$$B \sim \sum\{g.((B_1|\ldots|B_i'\ldots|B_m)\backslash A);\ g.B_i' \text{ a summand of } B_i,\ name(g) \notin A\}$$
$$+ \sum\{\tau.((B_1|\ldots|B_i'\{\tilde{E}/\tilde{x}\}|\ldots|B_j'|\ldots|B_m)\backslash A);\ \alpha\tilde{x}.B_i' \text{ a summand of } B_i,\ \bar{\alpha}\tilde{E}.B_j' \text{ a summand of } B_j,\ i \neq j\}$$

provided that in the first term no free variable in $B_k (k \neq i)$ is bound by g.

Proof. We first show, by induction on m, that

$$B_1|\ldots|B_m \sim \sum\{g.(B_1|\ldots|B_i'|\ldots|B_m) \; ; \; g.B_i' \text{ a summand of } B_i \; , \; 1 \le i \le m\}$$
$$+ \sum\{\tau.(B_1|\ldots|B_i'\{\tilde{E}/\tilde{x}\}|\ldots|B_j'|\ldots|B_m) \; ; \; \alpha\tilde{x}.B_i' \text{ a summand of } B_i \; , \; \bar{\alpha}\tilde{E}.B_j' \text{ a summand of } B_j \; , \; i,j \in \{1,\ldots,m\}, \; i \ne j\}$$

under the proviso of the Theorem. Note first that for $m = 1$ the second term is vacuous and the result follows simply by reflexivity of $\sim$. Now assume the property for $m-1$, with right-hand side C. Then we have (by congruence)

$$B_1|\ldots|B_{m-1}|B_m \sim C|B_m$$

and we may apply Com $\equiv$, generalised as in Theorem 5.7, since each of C and B_m is a sum of guards - and moreover the side-condition for Com $\equiv$ (stated as (ii) in Theorem 5.7) follows from the proviso of the present theorem. The property for m then follows by routine, though slightly tedious, manipulations; of course we rely strongly on Com $\sim$ (2).

Finally, the theorem follows easily by repeated use of Res $\equiv$(3) and Sum $\equiv$(3). ☒

Exercise 5.5 Complete the details of the inductive step in the proof, and see exactly where the proviso of the theorem is necessary.

In summary : we now have a powerful set of laws for transforming programs and behaviour expressions while preserving their derivation pattern. (These laws are enough to prove the Expansion Theorem, Theorem 5.8, for example.)

We have prepared the way for introducing CTs, an algebra which satisfies these laws and so may be regarded as a model of CCS which is faithful to its derivation patterns.

But we should mention that observation equivalence ($\approx$) (generalised from §3.3 to admit value-passing) is a wider relation that our $\sim$, and satisfies still more equational laws.

CHAPTER 6

Communication Trees (CTs) as a model of CCS †

6.1 CTs and the Dynamic Operations

Let us review the definition of STs. An ST of sort $L \subseteq \Lambda$ is a rooted, finitely branching, unordered tree whose arcs are labelled by members of $L \cup \{\tau\}$.

Another way of saying this is that an ST of sort L is a finite collection (multiset) of pairs of form $<\mu,t>$ $(\mu \in L \cup \{\tau\})$ where each t is again an ST of sort L.

(We allow this definition to include the possiblity of infinite paths in an ST, though to state this formally requires some mathematical sophistication which we do not want to be bothered with - the idea of infinite paths is clear enough.)

Here is a typical ST:

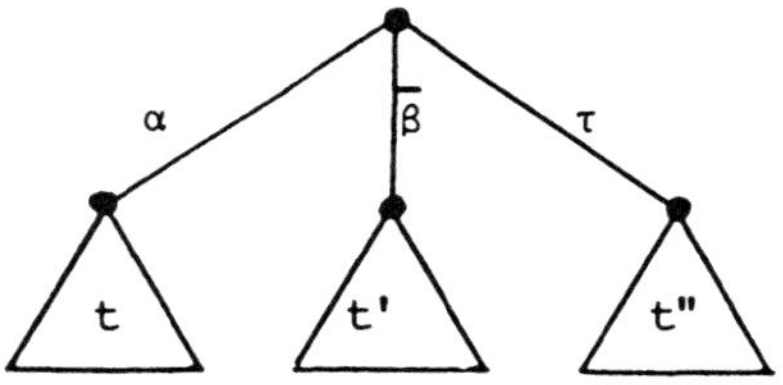

Now in the language of Chapter 5, positive labels are allowed to bind variables, and negative ones are allowed to qualify values (or value expressions). Thus, what 'happens next' after passing a positive label (= input guard) depends upon the value <u>input</u>; less critically, a value is <u>output</u> while passing a negative label (= output guard). Supposing that $\{v_0,v_1,\ldots\}$ are the values of type appropriate to α, and v is a value of type appropriate to $\bar{\beta}$, then a typical CT will look like this:

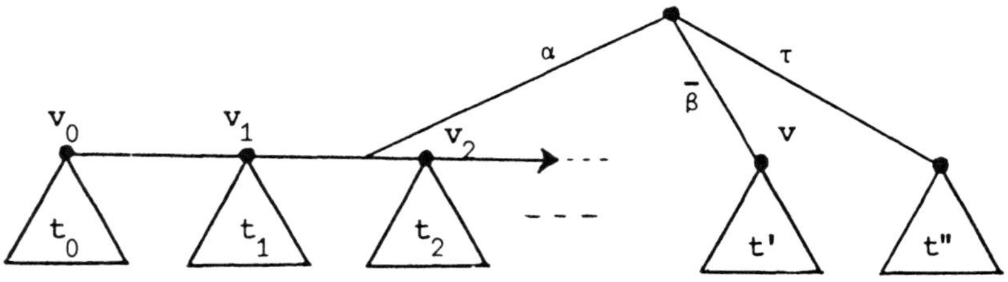

---

† This chapter is not essential to the technical development, and can be omitted. Its purpose is to assist understanding by giving the natural generalisation of STs to admit value-passing.

indicating (i) that on passing guard α, the input v_i selects t_i to 'happen next'.

(ii) that v is output on passing $\bar{\beta}$.

We expect this CT to be the interpretation of a behaviour program

$$\alpha x.B + \bar{\beta}v.B' + \tau.B''$$

where (i) the programs $B\{v_i/x\}$ stand for CTs t_i;

(ii) the programs B' and B'' stand for t' and t''.

Notice that the variable x appears nowhere in the CT; its purpose in the program is to show how B depends upon the value input, and this dependence is explicit in the CT; each t_i depends, literally, from the value v_i. (Of course, we can never draw a whole CT, in general - even to finite depth - because of infinite value domains).

More formally, then:

<u>Definition</u> A CT of sort L is a finite collection (multiset) of pairs, each of form

$\langle\alpha,f\rangle$ $(\alpha\in L)$, where f is a family of CTs of sort L indexed by the value set appropriate to α

or $\langle\bar{\beta},\langle v,t\rangle\rangle$ $(\bar{\beta}\in L)$, where v is a value appropriate to $\bar{\beta}$ and t is a CT of sort L

or $\langle\tau,t\rangle$ where t is a CT of sort L.

Let us denote by CT_L the CTs of sort L, and by V_α the set of values appropriate for α. We have, as with STs, an algebra of CTs as follows:

<u>NIL (nullary operation)</u>

NIL is the CT •

$NIL \in CT_{\emptyset}$.

<u>+ (binary operation)</u>

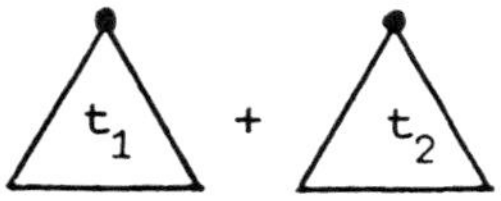

is the CT

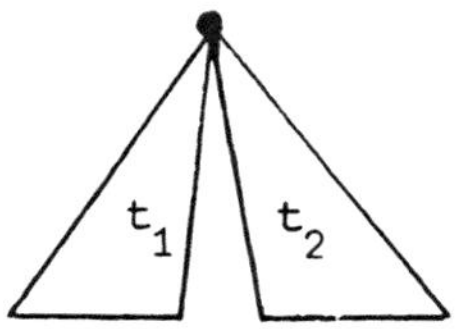

$$+ \in CT_L \times CT_M \to CT_{L\cup M} .$$

α (a "V_α-ary" operation)

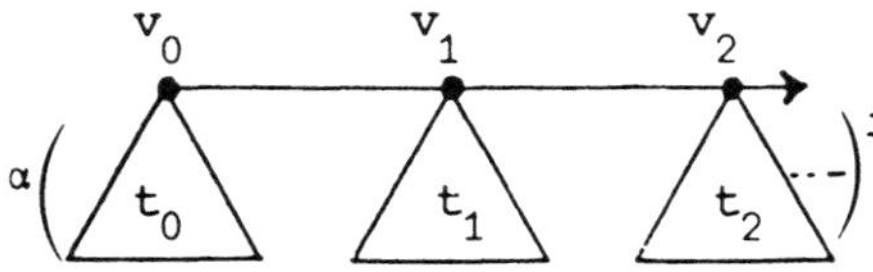

is the CT

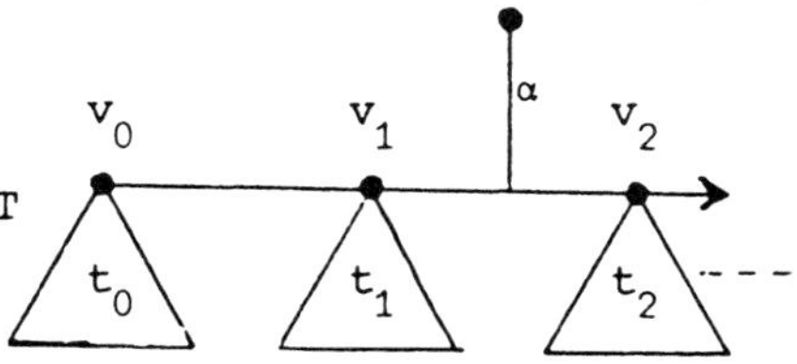

α takes a set of members of CT_L indexed by V_α, which is just a function $f: V_\alpha \to CT_L$, and gives a member of $CT_{L\cup\{\alpha\}}$; so

$$\alpha \in (V_\alpha \to CT_L) \to CT_{L\cup\{\alpha\}}.$$

This is why we called α a V_α-ary operation.

$\bar{\alpha}$ (a family of unary operations)

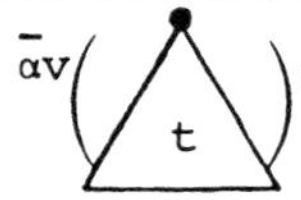

, for each $v \in V_\alpha$, is the CT

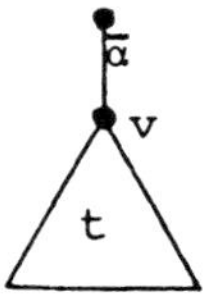

;

For each v, $\bar{\alpha}v \in CT_L \to CT_{L\cup\{\bar{\alpha}\}}$; $\quad \bar{\alpha} \in V_\alpha \to (CT_L \to CT_{L\cup\{\bar{\alpha}\}})$.

τ (unary operation)

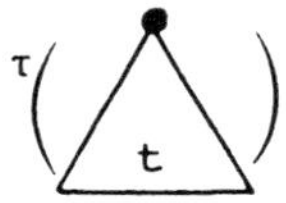

is the CT

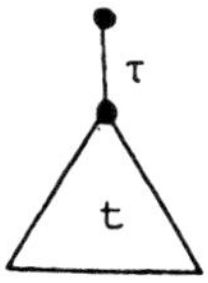

;

$$\tau \in CT_L \to CT_L.$$

Clearly there is a very close relation between CCS programs (involving only the dynamic operations) and expressions for CTs in this algebra. This is no accident!

Corresponding to programs NIL, $\bar{\alpha}v.B$, $\tau.B$, $B + B'$ we have CTs NIL, $\bar{\alpha}vt$, τt, $t + t'$. Corresponding to the program $\alpha x.B$ we have a CT αf; if we wrote the CT family f as $v \mapsto t(v)$ then we would express αf as

$$\alpha(v \mapsto t(v))$$

Of course there are many CTs which we cannot write down as expressions, because arbitrary V_α-indexed families of CTs cannot be written down finitely.

But we can, using these notations, begin to define the interpretation of CCS in the algebra of CTs. We shall write the CT which B stands for as $[\![B]\!]$. Then we have

<u>Definition</u>

$$
\begin{aligned}
[\![NIL]\!] &= NIL \\
[\![\alpha x.B]\!] &= \alpha\,(v \mapsto [\![B\{v/x\}]\!]) \\
[\![\bar{\alpha} v.B]\!] &= \bar{\alpha} v [\![B]\!] \\
[\![\tau .B]\!] &= \tau [\![B]\!] \\
[\![B + B']\!] &= [\![B]\!] + [\![B']\!]
\end{aligned}
$$

6.2 CTs and the static operations

We now show that the static operations $|$, $\backslash\alpha$, $[S]$ can be defined recursively over CTs. Recall that a CT is, formally, a multiset of elements like $<\alpha,f>$, $<\bar{\beta},<v,t>>$ or $<\tau,t>$; we shall call such elements <u>branches</u> of the CT. We shall content ourselves with a rather informal definition of $|$, $\backslash\alpha$, $[S]$ using pictures of branches, rather than defining them formally in terms of multisets.

<u>| (binary operation)</u>

$$|\in CT_L \times CT_M \to CT_{L\cup M}$$

Let $t\in CT_L$, $u\in CT_M$. Then $t|u$ has the following branches:

(i) For each branch

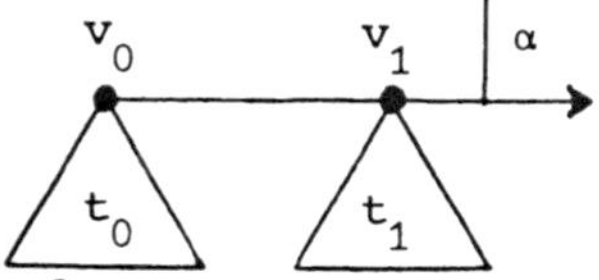

of t, a branch

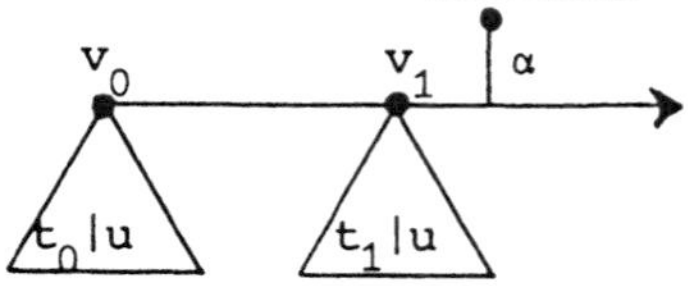

;

(ii) For each branch

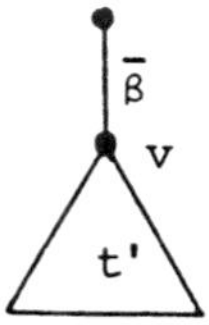

of t, a branch

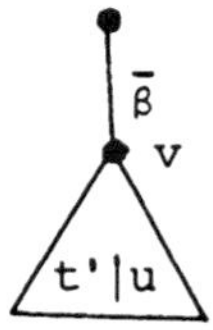

;

(iii) For each branch

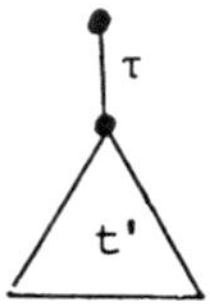

of t, a branch

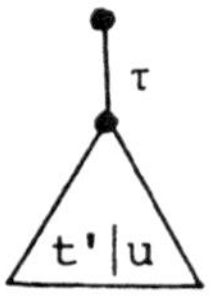

;

and similarly for the branches of u.

(iv) For each pair of branches

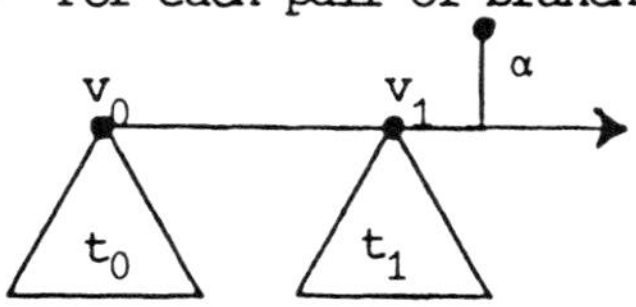

of t, and

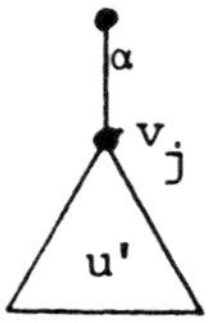

of u,

a branch

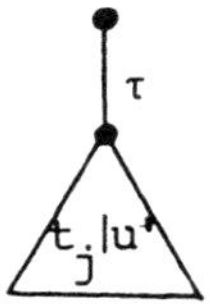

;

and similarly for branches $<\bar{\alpha},<v_j,t'>>$ of t and $<\alpha,v_i \mapsto u_i>$ of u. (Thus an output branch of u selects a member of t's complementary input branch. You should compare this definition with composition of STs in §2.3.)

<u>$\backslash\alpha$ (unary operation)</u>

$$\backslash\alpha \in CT_L \to CT_{L-\{\alpha,\bar{\alpha}\}}$$

We could give the recursive definition, but it's enough to say that $t\backslash\alpha$ is gained by pruning away all α- and $\bar{\alpha}$-branches occurring anywhere in t.

<u>[S] (unary operation)</u>

$[S]\in CT_L \to CT_M$, where $S:L \to M$ is a relabelling.

Again it's enough to say that t[S] is gained by replacing λ by $S\lambda$ everywhere in t $(\lambda\in L)$.

<u>Exercise 6.1</u> Give the recursive defintions of $\backslash\alpha$, [S] in the same style as we defined $|$.

Now of course, we can continue our definition of the interpretation of behaviour programs, as follows:

<u>Definition</u> $[\![B|B']\!] = [\![B]\!]|[\![B']\!]$

$[\![B\backslash\alpha]\!] = [\![B]\!]\backslash\alpha$

$[\![B[S]]\!] = [\![B]\!][S]$

$[\![$<u>if</u> true <u>then</u> B <u>else</u> B'$]\!] = [\![B]\!]$

$[\![$<u>if</u> false <u>then</u> B <u>else</u> B'$]\!] = [\![B']\!]$

Since our definitions of $[\![\,]\!]$ for programs look very trivial, as they should, we must remind ourselves of the purpose. We are aiming to show that when we are working with strong equivalence of programs (the congruence relation $\sim$ defined in §5.7), and using its properties as listed in theorems 5.3, 5.5 (but omitting Sum $\equiv$(4), the absorption law), then we are justified in thinking of the programs as the CTs that they denote; CTs are meant principally to be a helpful mental picture, or visual aid.

The rest of this chapter gives the appropriate justification. But first we must deal with recursively defined CTs.

6.3 CTs defined by recursion

Assume as in §5.4 that our behaviour identifies b are defined by clauses

$$b(x_1,\ldots,x_{n(b)}) \Leftarrow B_b,$$

one for each b. Here it will be convenient to suppose that $b_0, b_1, \ldots$ are the set of identifiers, with arities $n_0, n_1, \ldots$, and write B_i for B_{b_i}, so that the clauses are

$$b_i(x_1,\ldots,x_{n_i}) \Leftarrow B_i .$$

Now we intend to show that these clauses define, for each i and vector $\tilde{v} = v_1,\ldots,v_{n_i}$ of values appropriate for b_i, a unique CT as the interpretation of

$$b_i(\tilde{v}) .$$

What are these CTs to be? We will call them $[\![b_i(\tilde{v})]\!]$. When we know them, we also know the meaning of $B_i\{\tilde{v}/\tilde{x}\}$ for each i and $\tilde{v}$; this is so because, by our definitions $[\![\,]\!]$ so far, each $[\![B_i\{\tilde{v}/\tilde{x}\}]\!]$ can be rewritten as a CT expression in terms of $[\![b_j(\tilde{u})]\!]$ for various j and $\tilde{u}$. An example will make this clear. Consider the defining clause

$$b(x) \Leftarrow \underline{\text{if}}\ x = 0\ \underline{\text{then}}\ \bar{\beta}x.\text{NIL}\ \underline{\text{else}}\ \alpha y.b(y)$$

and call the right-hand side B. Then

$$[\![B\{0/x\}]\!] = [\![\bar{\beta}0.\text{NIL}]\!] = \bar{\beta}0(\text{NIL}) \quad \text{(a CT expression)}$$

while for any $v \neq 0$

$$[\![B\{v/x\}]\!] = [\![\alpha y.b(y)]\!] = \alpha(u \mapsto [\![b(y)\{u/y\}]\!]) = \alpha(u \mapsto [\![b(u)]\!]) .$$

Now we wish our CTs $b_i(\tilde{v})$, for each i and $\tilde{v}$, to be solutions of the equations over CTs

$$[\![b_i(\tilde{v})]\!] = [\![B_i\{\tilde{v}/\tilde{x}\}]\!]$$

(there are very many such equations, one for each pair i, $\tilde{v}$.)
Luckily, we can prove the following:

<u>Proposition 6.1</u> If the behaviour identifiers b_i are <u>guardedly well-defined</u> (see §5.4) then the equations

$$[\![b_i(\tilde{v})]\!] = [\![B_i\{\tilde{v}/\tilde{x}\}]\!]$$

define a <u>unique</u> CT $[\![b_i(\tilde{v})]\!]$ for each pair $(i,\tilde{v})$.

<u>Proof</u> Omitted. ⊠

We can see why this is so, for our example above, as follows.

Clearly $[\![b(0)]\!] = \bar{\beta}0(\text{NIL}) =$ 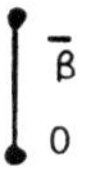 is uniquely defined.

For any $v \neq 0$ we have

$$[\![b(v)]\!] = \alpha(u \mapsto [\![b(u)]\!]) =$$

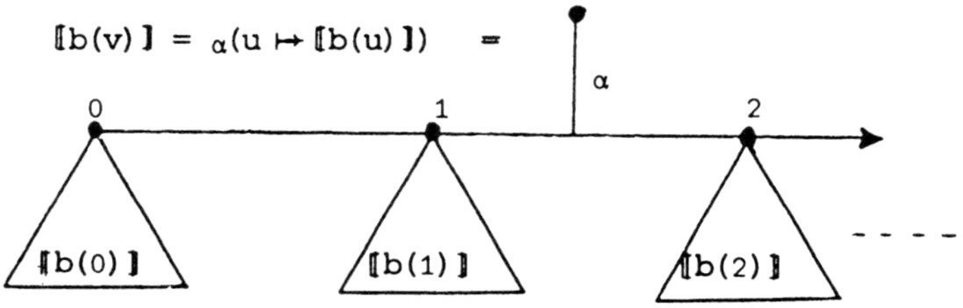

so that by using the two equations repeatedly the CT $[\![b(v)]\!]$ for any v can be developed unambiguously to any desired depth.

On the other hand, consider again the forbidden example in §5.4

$$b(x) \Leftarrow \bar{\alpha}x.\text{NIL} + b(x+1).$$

For any v (a non-negative integer) we would have

$$[\![b(v)]\!] = \bar{\alpha}v(\text{NIL}) + [\![b(v+1)]\!]$$

$=$ 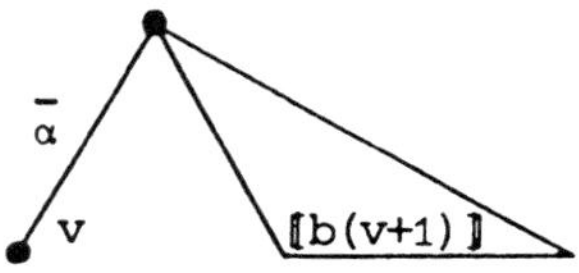

and if we develop this, we obtain the infinitely branching (forbidden!) CT for b(0):

[[b(0)]] =

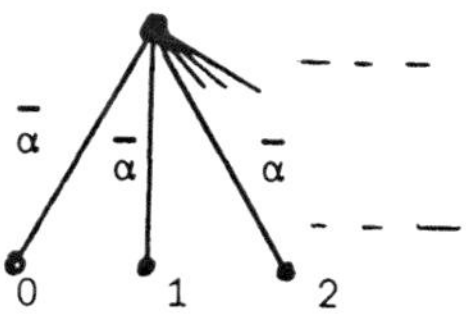

Moreover, even if we allowed infinite branching in CTs this would not be a unique solution.

<u>Exercise 6.2</u> Find another solution. (Hint: consider, if you know the theory of regular expressions, why the equation $R = SR + T$ - for given sets of strings S and T - does not have a unique solution for R as a set of strings unless $\varepsilon \notin S$, where ε is the null string.)

To sum up; we complete our interpretation of behaviour programs as CTs by defining unambiguously for each b

<u>Definition</u> $[\![b(\tilde{v})]\!] = [\![B_b\{\tilde{v}/\tilde{x}\}]\!]$

<u>Remark</u> There is a more general interpretation than CTs which makes sense of unguarded recursions, but we decided not to use it here.

6.4 Atomic actions and derivations of CTs

If we wish to think of behaviour programs as the CTs which they stand for, then - for one thing - we must be able to understand the action relations $\xrightarrow{\mu v}$ over CTs in such a way that they harmonize with the corresponding relations over programs.

We therefore start with an independent defintion of the relations $\xrightarrow{\mu v}$ over CTs. (We could use a different symbol from $\longrightarrow$ for these relations, but it will in fact always be clear whether we are talking about atomic actions of CTs or of programs.)

Definition Let t be a CT, i.e. a multiset of pairs (as defined in §6.1). Then t has the atomic actions

(i) $t \xrightarrow{\alpha v} f(v)$ for each member $\langle\alpha,f\rangle$ of t and each v of type appropriate for α;

(ii) $t \xrightarrow{\bar{\beta} v} t'$ for each member $\langle\bar{\beta},\langle v,t'\rangle\rangle$ of t;

(iii) $t \xrightarrow{\tau} t'$ for each member $\langle\tau,t'\rangle$ of t.

This states, for every t, exactly which pairs $\langle t,t'\rangle$ are in the relation $\xrightarrow{\mu v}$ for every μ and v.

Exercise 6.3 List the atomic actions of the typical CT diagrammed in §6.1.

Exercise 6.4 Prove that $t_1 + t_2 \xrightarrow{\mu v} t'$ iff either $t_1 \xrightarrow{\mu v} t'$ or $t_2 \xrightarrow{\mu v} t'$.

Exercise 6.4 gives a hint of the harmony we expect between the action relations $\xrightarrow{\mu v}$ over CTs and over programs. For if we recall the rules Sum→ of §5.3, we can rephrase them as follows:

$$B_1 + B_2 \xrightarrow{\mu v} B' \text{ iff } \underline{\text{either}}\ B_1 \xrightarrow{\mu v} B' \ \underline{\text{or}}\ B_2 \xrightarrow{\mu v} B'$$

(the 'iff' being justified by the fact that Sum→ is the only rule by which actions of $B_1 + B_2$ can be inferred).

Similarly, the CT αf, which is the multiset whose only member is $\langle\alpha,f\rangle$, has only the actions

$$\alpha f \xrightarrow{\alpha v} f(v), \text{ for each } v,$$

which we can compare with the fact, from Act→(1) in §5.3, that the program $\alpha x.B$ has only the actions

$$\alpha x.B \xrightarrow{\alpha v} B\{v/x\}, \text{ for each } v.$$

Exercise 6.5 Using the definition of | over CTs in §6.2, show that the CT $t_1|t_2$ has exactly the actions

(i) $t_1|t_2 \xrightarrow{\mu v} t_1'|t_2$ when $t_1 \xrightarrow{\mu v} t_1'$;

(ii) $t_1|t_2 \xrightarrow{\mu v} t_1|t_2'$ when $t_2 \xrightarrow{\mu v} t_2'$;

(iii) $t_1|t_2 \xrightarrow{\tau} t_1'|t_2'$ when $t_1 \xrightarrow{\lambda v} t_1'$ and $t_2 \xrightarrow{\bar{\lambda} v} t_2'$.

Compare Com→ in §5.3.

Surely then the atomic actions of B and its CT $[\![B]\!]$ are closely related. We state the relation in a theorem:

Theorem 6.2

(1) If $B \xrightarrow{\mu v} B'$ then $[\![B]\!] \xrightarrow{\mu v} [\![B']\!]$;

(2) If $[\![B]\!] \xrightarrow{\mu v} t'$, then for some B', $B \xrightarrow{\mu v} B'$ and $[\![B']\!] = t'$.

Proof Mainly by induction on the structure of B; but particular care is needed when $B = b(\tilde{v})$, and the assumption that the b's are guardedly well defined is important. ⊠

In other words, the atomic actions of $[\![B]\!]$ are exactly $[\![B]\!] \xrightarrow{\mu v} [\![B']\!]$ where $B \xrightarrow{\mu v} B'$ is an atomic action of B; this means that in considering atomic actions, it makes no difference whether we think of programs or of the CTs that they stand for.

The next step is to show that this holds too in considering strong equivalence.

6.5 Strong equivalence of CTs

We proceed in the same style; that is, we define strong equivalence (~) over CTs independently, and then show how it harmonises with strong equivalence of programs. Our definition is entirely analogous to that of ~ for programs (§5.8); we use a decreasing sequence $\sim_0, \sim_1, \dots, \sim_k, \dots$ of equivalences:

Definition $t \sim_0 u$ is always true;

$t \sim_{k+1} u$ iff for all μ, v

(i) if $t \xrightarrow{\mu v} t'$ then for some u', $u \xrightarrow{\mu v} u'$ and $t' \sim_k u'$;

(ii) if $u \xrightarrow{\mu v} u'$ then for some t', $t \xrightarrow{\mu v} t'$ and $t' \sim_k u'$.

$t \sim u$ iff $\forall k \geq 0 . t \sim_k u$.

Although we don't need it at present, we may as well state the analogue of Theorem 5.4.

Theorem 6.3 ~ is a congruence relation in the algebra of CTs. More precisely, $t_1 \sim t_2$ implies

$$t_1 + u \sim t_2 + u,\ u + t_1 \sim u + t_2$$

$$\bar{\alpha}v(t_1) \sim \bar{\alpha}v(t_2),\ \tau(t_1) \sim \tau(t_2)$$

$$t_1|u \sim t_2|u,\ u|t_1 \sim u|t_2$$

$$t_1\backslash\alpha \sim t_2\backslash\alpha,\ t_1[S] \sim t_2[S]$$

and for $f_1(v) \sim f_2(v)$ (for all v) implies $\alpha f_1 \sim \alpha f_2$.

Proof Analogous to Theorem 5.4, and omitted. ⊠

What we do need, to complete our justification of thinking of programs as CTs, is the following:

Theorem 6.4 $B_1 \sim B_2$ iff $[\![B_1]\!] \sim [\![B_2]\!]$.

Proof We must prove separately, by induction on k, that

(1) $B_1 \sim_k B_2$ implies $[\![B_1]\!] \sim_k [\![B_2]\!]$;

(2) $[\![B_1]\!] \sim_k [\![B_2]\!]$ implies $B_1 \sim_k B_2$.

We do only (1), leaving (2) as an exercise. The case $k=0$ is trivial.

Exercise 6.6 Why?

Now assume (1) at k, and assume $B_1 \sim_{k+1} B_2$, and prove $[\![B_1]\!] \sim_{k+1} [\![B_2]\!]$. Suppose $[\![B_1]\!] \xrightarrow{\mu v} t_1'$. Then by Theorem 6.2(2)

$$B_1 \xrightarrow{\mu v} B_1' \quad \text{for some } B_1', \text{ with } [\![B_1']\!] = t_1'.$$

So by assumption

$$B_2 \xrightarrow{\mu v} B_2' \quad \text{for some } B_2', \text{ with } B_1' \sim_k B_2',$$

and by Theorem 6.2(1)

$$[\![B_2]\!] \xrightarrow{\mu v} [\![B_2']\!], \text{ with } t_1' = [\![B_1']\!] \sim_k [\![B_2']\!] \text{ by inductive hypothesis.}$$

This verifies the first clause in $\sim_{k+1}$'s definition; the second clause follows by symmetry, so the inductive step for (1) is complete. ⊠

Exercise 6.7 Prove (2) by induction on k. You will again need both parts of Theorem 6.2; if you think you need only one part, then your proof is likely to be wrong.

6.6 Equality in the CT model

Can we have $B_1 \sim B_2$ but $[\![B_1]\!] \neq [\![B_2]\!]$? That is, if two programs are strongly equivalent, are their CTs perhaps always the same?

No, because for example

$$\tau.\text{NIL} + \tau.\text{NIL} \sim \tau.\text{NIL};$$

but the two CTs are 

and 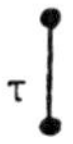

respectively.

But then perhaps the only difference between the CTs $[\![B_1]\!]$ and $[\![B_2]\!]$, when $B_1 \sim B_2$, is due to the fact that $t + t = t$ is false for CTs, because we allow the presence of identical branches.

In fact, we first thought that if we adjusted our definition of CTs to be in terms of sets rather than multisets, then all our results so far would hold, and also we would have

$$B_1 \sim B_2 \quad \text{iff} \quad [\![B_1]\!] = [\![B_2]\!] \qquad (?)$$

However, Brian Mayoh showed this to be false, with the following simple counter-example. Suppose x is a Boolean variable, and consider the two programs

$$B_1 = \alpha x.C_1 + \alpha x.C_2$$

$$B_2 = \alpha x\,(\underline{\text{if}}\ \ x\ \ \underline{\text{then}}\ C_1\ \underline{\text{else}}\ C_2) + \alpha x.\ (\underline{\text{if}}\ \ x\ \ \underline{\text{then}}\ C_2\ \ \underline{\text{else}}\ \ C_1)$$

where C_1 and C_2 do not contain x. Clearly we have only the following four actions for B :

$$B_1 \xrightarrow{\alpha v} C_i\ , \qquad v\in\{\text{true},\text{false}\} \text{ and } i\in\{1,2\}$$

and B_2 has exactly the same four actions. So $B_1 \sim B_2$. But $[\![B_1]\!]$ and $[\![B_2]\!]$ are different CTs:

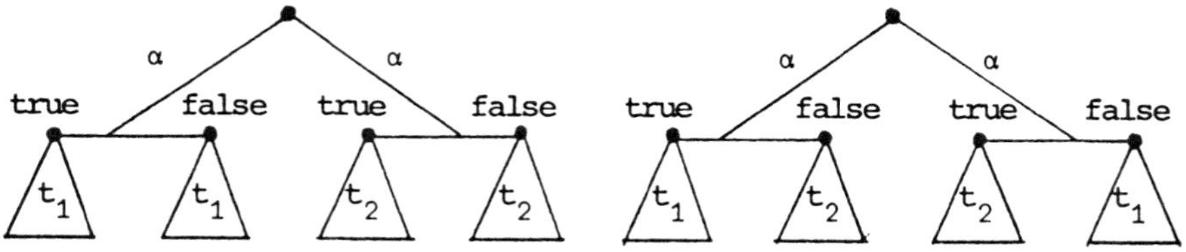

in which $t_i = [\![C_i]\!]$, $i\in\{1,2\}$. So in general $[\![B_1]\!] \neq [\![B_2]\!]$, though of course $[\![B_1]\!] \sim [\![B_2]\!]$ by Theorem 6.4.

We chose to define CTs as multisets rather than sets of branches, because it seemed that multisets are a more concrete intuitive model;

after all, to check whether two branches are identical requires an infinite amount of work! But it is very much a matter of taste.

Even in the present model, many equalities hold. In fact, if we allow ourselves to drop the semantic brackets $[\![\,]\!]$, and take a behaviour program to denote a CT without this extra formality, then we state the following:

Theorem 6.5 All the congruences of Theorems 5.3, 5.5 are identities in the CT model, except Sum≡(4) (absorption).

Proof Omitted. It is a matter of proving that the two CTs in question - for example $(B_1|B_2)\backslash\alpha$ and $(B_1\backslash\alpha)|(B_2\backslash\alpha)$ (Res~(3) in Theorem 5.5) - are identical to depth k, for arbitrary k (using induction on k). In fact, the identities of Theorem 5.3 can be proved without any induction. ☒

Exercise 6.8 Prove some of the identities of Theorem 5.3. Also prove Com~(1) of Theorem 5.5 - $B_1|B_2 = B_2|B_1$ - by induction on depth. That is, assume that $C_1|C_2$ and $C_2|C_1$ are identical to depth k for all C_1, C_2, then show that the branches of $B_1|B_2$, $B_2|B_1$ are in 1-1 correspondence, with corresponding branches identical to depth $k+1$.

6.7 Summary

In this chapter we have

(i) Constructed CTs as an intuitive model of CCS;

(ii) Shown that, in considering atomic actions and strong equivalence of programs, we are justified in considering these notions as they apply to the denoted CTs;

(iii) Shown that many useful program equivalence laws are actually identities for CTs.

We have not studied the wider relation of observation-equivalence over programs. But it turns out that, for any equivalence relation which is defined in terms of $\xrightarrow{\mu v}$ and/or ~, we can think of this also as as equivalence relation over CTs.

Exercise 6.9 After reading §7.1 and §7.2 on observation equivalence ($\approx$), define the analogous relation $\approx$ over CTs. Then investigate whether the analogue of Theorem 6.4

$$B_1 \approx B_2 \quad \text{iff} \quad [\![B_1]\!] \approx [\![B_2]\!]$$

is true, as suggested in §5.1.

One further point should be mentioned. The syntax of CCS is such that only a small subclass of CTs are expressible as programs. In particular, a CT of form $\{<\alpha,f>\}$ can only be expressed by a program $\alpha\tilde{x}.B$ for which B, considered as a function of its free variables $\tilde{x}$, expresses the family f schematically. Now there are effectively indexed CT-families f which cannot be represented by CCS expressions; consider for example the family $f = \{\bar{\gamma}_i$ 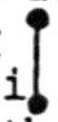 $;\ i \in N\}$, and let α bind an integer variable, so that $\{<\alpha,f>\}$ is the CT

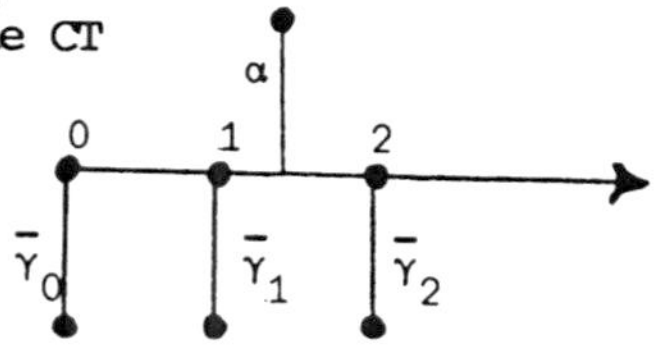

whose (infinite) sort is $\{\alpha, \bar{\gamma}_0, \bar{\gamma}_1, \bar{\gamma}_2, \ldots\}$. To express it in CCS we may wish to allow labels to be parametically dependent upon values, and write $\alpha x.\bar{\gamma}_x.\mathrm{NIL}$. In more complex cases $\bar{\gamma}_x$ could also qualify a value expression, or be replaced by a positive parametric label binding a variable. Such extensions of CCS may be of real practical value. If we wish to consider them, then the theory of CTs increases in importance since it does not commit us to any particular expressible subclass of CTs.

CHAPTER 7

Observation equivalence and its properties

7.1 Review

In Chapter 6 we studied CTs as a model of CCS; this should have given insight into the laws of strong congruence ($\sim$) stated in Theorems 5.3 and 5.5, since CTs satisfy all these laws except the absorption law $B + B \equiv B$, interpreted as identities. In spite of this slight discrepancy, it is still useful to think of programs 'as' CTs.

In §3.3 we defined a notion of Observation Equivalence ($\approx$) for STs; in our Data Flow example (§4.3) we anticipated using it in full CCS but gave no definition. We saw that its purpose was to allow unobservable actions (τ) to be absorbed into experiments.

Recall also the derivations of §4.4. We abbreviated

$B \xrightarrow{\tau^m} B'$ $(m \geq 0)$ by $B \xRightarrow{\varepsilon} B'$

$B \xrightarrow{\tau^m . \mu v . \tau^n} B'$ $(m,n \geq 0)$ by $B \xRightarrow{\mu v} B'$

More generally, we now abbreviate

$$B \xrightarrow{\tau^{m_0} . \mu_1 v_1 . \tau^{m_1} . \cdots . \mu_k v_k . \tau^{m_k}} B' \quad (k \geq 0,\ m_0, \ldots, m_k \geq 0)$$

by $B \xRightarrow{\mu_1 v_1 . \cdots . \mu_k v_k} B'$

which includes the above cases (they correspond to $k = 0$, $k = 1$). It also includes the possibility $\mu_i = \tau$, so that for example $B \xRightarrow{\tau} B'$ means $B \xrightarrow{\tau^m} B'$ for some $m > 0$, while $B \xRightarrow{\varepsilon} B'$ means $B \xrightarrow{\tau^m} B'$ for some $m \geq 0$; but usually we shall have $\mu_i \in \Lambda$.

For each $s = \lambda_1 v_1 . \cdots . \lambda_k v_k \in (\Lambda \times V)^*$, $\xRightarrow{s}$ is the <u>s-experiment relation</u>, and each instance $B \xRightarrow{s} B'$ is called a <u>s-experiment</u>. We now define Observation Equivalence $\approx$ in terms of s-experiments.

7.2 Observation equivalence in CCS

Analogous to §3.3, $\approx$ is defined for programs by a decreasing sequence of equivalences:

<u>Definition</u> $B \approx_0 C$ is always true;

$B \approx_{k+1} C$ iff for all $s \in (\Lambda \times V)^*$

(i) if $B \stackrel{s}{\Longrightarrow} B'$ then for some C', $C \stackrel{s}{\Longrightarrow} C'$ and $B' \approx_k C'$;

(ii) if $C \stackrel{s}{\Longrightarrow} C'$ then for some B', $B \stackrel{s}{\Longrightarrow} B'$ and $B' \approx_k C'$;

$B \approx C$ iff $\forall k \geq 0.\ B \approx_k C$.

<u>Remarks</u>

(1) There is a question as to whether we need to consider <u>all</u> s-experiments in this definition, or if it is enough to consider only those of length 1 - i.e. we might replace $s \in (\Lambda \times V)^*$ by $s \in \Lambda \times V$ in the definition. The relation $\approx$ thus obtained is different, but it turns out that the congruence (§7.3) which it induces is the same (assuming only that CCS includes an equality predicate over values), though we shall not prove it here. Our present definition, using $(\Lambda \times V)^*$, has somewhat nicer properties.

(2) Our definition has a property which must be pointed out. It allows the program (CTs)

τ^ω =

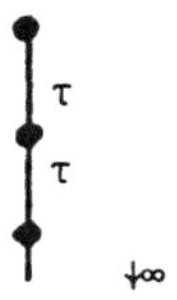

and NIL = •

to be equivalent! (τ^ω can be defined by $b \Leftarrow \tau.b$.)

<u>Exercise 7.1</u> Prove $\tau^\omega \approx_k \mathrm{NIL}$ by induction on k.

Notice that the only experiment on τ^ω is $\tau^\omega \stackrel{\varepsilon}{\Longrightarrow} \tau^\omega$ (corresponding to $\tau^\omega \stackrel{\tau^m}{\Longrightarrow} \tau^\omega$ for any m), and NIL's only experiment is $\mathrm{NIL} \stackrel{\varepsilon}{\Longrightarrow} \mathrm{NIL}$.

Thus, whenever we have proved $B \approx C$ (e.g. B may be a program and C its specification) we cannot deduce that B has no infinite unseen action, even if C has none. In one sense we can argue for our definition, since infinite unseen action is - by our rules - unobservable! But the problem is deeper; it is related to so-called <u>fairness</u>, which we discuss briefly in §11.3. In any case, there is a more refined notion of $\approx$ which respects the presence of infinite unseen action, with properties close to those we mention for the present one.

(3) Disregarding the question of which equivalence is correct, if indeed there is a single 'correct' one, the finer equivalence (under a slight further refinement) has interesting properties. Hennessy and Plotkin [HP 2] have recently found that it can be axiomatized, in a sense which we cannot explain here. Much more needs to be known before we can say which equivalence yields better proof methods; at least we can say that, if an equivalence can be proved under the refined definition, then it holds also under ours.

We now turn to the properties of $\approx$. There are many, but three are enough to give a feeling for it, and to allow you to read the first case study in Chapter 8, if you wish, before proceeding to §7.3.

The main thing which distinguishes $\approx$ from $\sim$ is the following:

Proposition 7.1 $B \approx \tau.B$

Proof We show $B \approx_k \tau.B$ by induction on k. k=0 is trivial, so we assume for k and prove for k+1:

(i) Let $B \overset{s}{\Longrightarrow} B'$. Then also $\tau.B \overset{s}{\Longrightarrow} B'$, and we know $B' \approx_k B'$ (each $\approx_k$ is an equivalence relation!)

(ii) Let $\tau.B \overset{s}{\Longrightarrow} C'$. Then

either (a) $s=\varepsilon$, and C' is $\tau.B$; but then also $B \overset{\varepsilon}{\Longrightarrow} B$, and by induction $B \approx_k \tau.B$

or (b) $\tau.B \xrightarrow{\tau} B \overset{s}{\Longrightarrow} C'$, i.e. $B \overset{s}{\Longrightarrow} C'$ also, and again $C' \approx_k C'$

This completes the inductive step, yielding $B \approx_{k+1} \tau.B$. ☒

This proposition should make you immediately suspicious of $\approx$, because we can show that it cannot be a congruence. In particular

$B \approx C$ does not imply $B + D \approx C + D$;

e.g. take B as NIL, C as τ.NIL, D as α.NIL -

then $B \approx C$ by Prop. 7.1, but $B + D \not\approx_2 C + D$.

Exercise 7.2 Show that NIL + α.NIL $\not\approx_2 \tau$.NIL + α.NIL, by observing that RHS $\overset{\varepsilon}{\Longrightarrow}$ NIL, but the only ε-experiment on LHS yields a result which is $\not\approx_1$ NIL.

Even so, Theorem 7.3 below tells us that $\approx$ is near enough a congruence for many purposes. First we need to see its relation with $\sim$.

Theorem 7.2 $B \sim C$ implies $B \approx C$.

Proof We show that $B \sim C$ implies $B \approx_k C$ by induction on k. At $k=0$ it is trivial; assume it at k (for all B and C), and prove it at $k+1$. Assume $B \sim C$:

(i) Let $B \overset{s}{\Longrightarrow} B_n$, say $B \xrightarrow{\mu_1 v_1} B \to \cdots \xrightarrow{\mu_n v_n} B_n$, where some of the $\mu_i v_i$ may be τ, while the remainder constitute s. Then by Theorem 5.6 used repeatedly, there exist $C_1, \ldots, C_n$ with

$$C \xrightarrow{\mu_1 v_1} C_1 \to \cdots \xrightarrow{\mu_n v_n} C_n, \quad \text{i.e.} \quad C \overset{s}{\Longrightarrow} C_n$$

with $B_i \sim C_i$ for all $i \le n$.
In particular $B_n \sim C_n$, so by induction $B_n \approx_k C_n$, and we have found the desired C_n.

(ii) Let $C \overset{s}{\Longrightarrow} C_n$; then similarly we find B_n with $B \overset{s}{\Longrightarrow} B_n \approx_k C_n$. ⊠

The importance of this theorem is that all laws of Theorems 5.3, 5.5 hold also for $\approx$.

Theorem 7.3 Observation equivalence is a congruence for all behaviour operations except +. More precisely:

(1) $B \approx_k C$ implies
$$\begin{cases} \overline{\alpha}\tilde{v}.B \approx_k \overline{\alpha}\tilde{v}.C, \quad \tau.B \approx_k \tau.C, \\ B|D \approx_k C|D, \\ B\backslash\alpha \approx_k C\backslash\alpha, \quad B[S] \approx_k C[S] \end{cases}$$

and $B\{\tilde{v}/\tilde{x}\} \approx_k C\{\tilde{v}/\tilde{x}\}$ for all $\tilde{v}$ implies $\alpha\tilde{x}.B \approx_k \alpha\tilde{x}.C$.

(2) Hence the same holds with the indices k removed.

Proof Let us just take the most interesting case:

$B \approx_k C$ implies $B|D \approx_k C|D$,

which we prove by induction on k. (This property is not true for the different observation equivalence suggested in Remark (1) above.) Assume at k, for all B, C, D, and assume $B \approx_{k+1} C$:

i) Let $B|D \overset{s}{\Longrightarrow} E$; then E must be $B'|D'$, with $B \overset{q}{\Longrightarrow} B'$, $D \overset{r}{\Longrightarrow} D'$ for some q,r (containing complementary members which 'merge' to form $\overset{s}{\Longrightarrow}$ in a way which we need not detail). Then for some C', $C \overset{q}{\Longrightarrow} C'$ and $B' \approx_k C'$ by assumption.

But then $C|D \overset{s}{\Longrightarrow} C'|D'$, and by the inductive hypothesis $B'|D' \approx_k C'|D'$, i.e. $E \approx_k C'|D'$.

(ii) Let $C|D \overset{s}{\Longrightarrow} E$, then similarly we find $B'|D'$ such that $B|D \overset{s}{\Longrightarrow} B'|D' \approx_k E$. ☒

The essence of Proposition 7.1 and Theorems 7.2, 7.3 is that we can use all our laws, and cancel τ's too, in proving observation equivalence - provided only that we infer nothing about the result of substituting C for B under $+$, when we only know $B \approx C$.

The next section tells us what such inferences can be made.

Exercise 7.2 Prove that $B \approx_k C$ implies $\bar{\alpha}v.B \approx_k \bar{\alpha}v.C$ by induction on k. Why is induction necessary? (Consider ε-experiments).

As we did for $\sim$, we extend $\approx$ to expressions by:

Definition Let $\tilde{x}$ be the free variables in B or C or both. Then $B \approx C$ iff for all $\tilde{v}$ $B\{\tilde{v}/\tilde{x}\} \approx C\{\tilde{v}/\tilde{x}\}$.

Then we have

Theorem 7.4 Proposition 7.1 and Theorems 7.2, 7.3 hold also for expressions.

Proof Routine. ☒

From now on, we deal with expressions.

7.3 Observation Congruence

We must now face the fact that $\approx$ is not a congruence (see Exercise 7.2). But we would like a congruence relation, because we would like to know that if B and C are equivalent, then in whatever context we replace B by C the result of the replacement will be equivalent to the original - which is only true for an equivalence relation which is a congruence. We have one congruence - strong congruence ($\sim$) - but it is too strong; for example $\alpha.\tau.\mathrm{NIL} \not\sim \alpha.\mathrm{NIL}$.

Can we find a congruence relation which is weaker than $\sim$ (so that all our laws, Theorems 5.3 and 5.5 will hold for it), and has some of the properties of $\approx$ (so that for example $\alpha.\tau.\mathrm{NIL}$ and $\alpha.\mathrm{NIL}$ will be congruent)? Let us draw the order relation (part of the lattice of equivalence relations) among our existing equivalence relations with stronger relations to the left, and square boxes representing congruences:

Equivalences over behaviour programs:

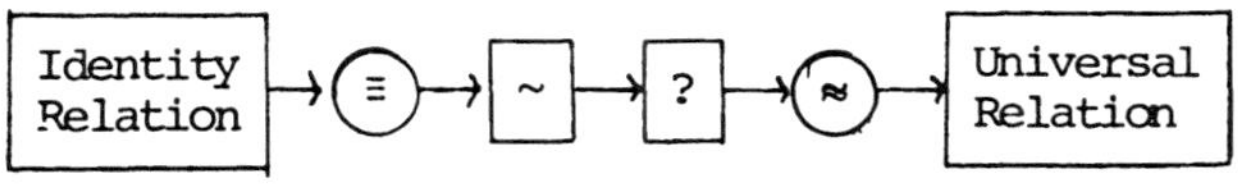

We want to fill in "?". It must be stronger than $\approx$ because we do want congruent programs to be observation equivalent. We get what we want by the following:

Definition $B \approx^c C$ (Observation congruence) iff for every expression context $\mathcal{C}[\ ]$, $\mathcal{C}[B] \approx \mathcal{C}[C]$.

Theorem 7.5

(1) $\approx^c$ is a congruence relation;

(2) If θ is a congruence and $B\,\theta\,C$ implies $B \approx C$, then $B\,\theta\,C$ implies $B \approx^c C$.

Proof Omitted; it is completely standard, and has nothing to do with particular properties of the equivalence $\approx$. ∎

Our Theorem says that $\overset{c}{\approx}$ is the weakest congruence stronger than (smaller than) $\approx$.

Corollary 7.6 $B \sim C$ implies $B \overset{c}{\approx} C$ implies $B \approx C$.

Proof Immediate. ☒

It is one thing to define a congruence, another to know its properties. We first find out more about the relation of $\overset{c}{\approx}$ to $\approx$; in the next section we find some laws satisfied by $\overset{c}{\approx}$.

We saw earlier that sum contexts were critical for $\approx$, because $B \approx C$ does not imply $B + D \approx C + D$. This leads us to explore a new equivalence relation $\overset{+}{\approx}$:

Definition $B \overset{+}{\approx} C$ iff $\forall D.\ B + D \approx C + D$.
(equivalence in all sum contexts.)

Now the critical result is the following:

Theorem 7.7 $\overset{+}{\approx}$ is a congruence.

Proof See §7.6. This proof is not standard, but depends strongly on the definition of $\approx$; it is not true for the alternative in Remark (1) of §7.2 and that is why we chose our definition. Theorem 7.3 is critical. ☒

From this we get, fortunately:

Theorem 7.8 $\overset{c}{\approx}$ and $\overset{+}{\approx}$ are the same congruence.

Proof
(i) $B \overset{+}{\approx} C$ implies $B \overset{c}{\approx} C$ by Theorems 7.5(2) and 7.7, since $\overset{+}{\approx}$ is stronger than $\approx$ (take D to be NIL in the definition).
(ii) $B \overset{c}{\approx} C$ implies $B \overset{+}{\approx} C$, since [ ]+ D is just a special kind of context. ☒

Now we know that we preserve $\approx$ by substitution except in '+' contexts. What do we do if we have $B \approx C$ and wish to know something about $B + D$ and $C + D$? Luckily, for an important class of expressions B and C we can infer from $B \approx C$ that $B \overset{c}{\approx} C$, and then infer that $B + D \overset{c}{\approx} C + D$.

Definition B is stable iff $B \xrightarrow{\tau} B'$ is impossible for any B'.

Thus a stable behaviour is one which cannot 'move' unless you observe it. Stability is important in practice; one reason why our scheduler in Chapter 3 works, for example, is that it will always reach a stable state if it is deprived of external communication for long enough. Compare the notion of "rigid" in Chapter 1; we may define a rigid program to be one whose derivatives, including itself, are all stable.

There are two main propositions about stability; first we prove a
mma in a slightly more general form than we need for the propositions
: the general form helps in the proof of Theorem 7.7 (skip the lemma
you are only interested in main results, not proofs).

mma 7.9 If $B \approx^{+} C$ and $B \xrightarrow{\tau} B'$, then for each k there is a C' such at $C \xRightarrow{\tau} C'$ and $B' \approx_k C'$.

oof Suppose C' does not exist; we find D such that $B + D \not\approx_k C + D$, ntrary to assumption. Take D to be $\lambda_o.\mathrm{NIL}$, where λ_o is not in the rt of B or C. Now since $B \xrightarrow{\tau} B'$, we have $B + D \xRightarrow{\varepsilon} B'$. But if $D \xRightarrow{\varepsilon} E$ then either (i) E is $C + D$, $\not\approx B'$ since $C + D \xrightarrow{\lambda_o} \mathrm{NIL}$, but $\not\xRightarrow{\lambda_o}$; or (ii) $C \xRightarrow{\tau} E$, $\not\approx_k B'$ by supposition; or (iii) $D \xRightarrow{\tau} E$ - ossible since D is stable.

Hence $B+D \not\approx C+D$, contradicting $B \approx^{+} C$. ☒

position 7.10 If $B \approx^{c} C$ then either both are stable or neither is.

oof Direct from Lemma 7.9 ($B' \approx_k C'$ not needed). ☒

More important, for proof methods, is the following:

position 7.11 If B and C are stable, and $B \approx C$, then $B \approx^{c} C$.

oof It is enough to show that $B + D \approx_k C + D$ for arbitrary D, by duction on k. We do the inductive step.

Let $B+D \xRightarrow{s} E$:

If $s = \varepsilon$ then either E is $B + D$, and then $C + D \xRightarrow{\varepsilon} C + D, \approx_k B + D$ by induction, or $D \xRightarrow{\tau} E$, and then $C + D \xRightarrow{\varepsilon} E$ also ($B \xRightarrow{\tau} E$ impossible by stability).

i) Otherwise either $D \xRightarrow{s} E$, and then $C + D \xRightarrow{s} E$ also, or $B \xRightarrow{s} E$, whence $C \xRightarrow{s} F \approx_k E$ (because $B \approx C$), whence also $C + D \xRightarrow{s} F \approx_k E$.
us we have found in each case an F s.t. $C + D \xRightarrow{s} F \approx_k E$. The converse gument is similar, so $B + D \approx_{k+1} C + D$. ☒

Now for any guard $g \neq \tau$, we can deduce from $B \approx C$ (for any B,C) at $g.B \approx g.C$ (Theorem 7.3), and hence $g.B \approx^{c} g.C$ since both are stable.

This implication holds in fact for any guard, by the following position (which is essential in the proofs of Chapter 8):

position 7.12 For any guard g,

$B \approx C$ implies $g.B \approx^{c} g.C$.

Proof By the above remarks we need only consider $g = \tau$. We prove $\tau.B + D \approx_k \tau.C + D$ for arbitrary D, by induction on k. Inductive step:

Let $\tau.B + D \overset{s}{\Longrightarrow} E$. Then

(i) If $s=\varepsilon$ then either E is $\tau.B + D$, and then $\tau.C + D \overset{\varepsilon}{\Longrightarrow} \tau.C + D \approx_k E$ by induction, or $D \overset{\tau}{\Longrightarrow} E$, and then $\tau.C + D \overset{\varepsilon}{\Longrightarrow} E$ also, or $\tau.B \overset{\tau}{\Longrightarrow} E$, and then $B \overset{\varepsilon}{\Longrightarrow} E$, whence $C \overset{\varepsilon}{\Longrightarrow} F \approx_k E$ (since $B \approx C$), whence also $\tau.C + D \overset{\varepsilon}{\Longrightarrow} F \approx_k E$.

(ii) Otherwise either $D \overset{s}{\Longrightarrow} E$, and then $C + D \overset{s}{\Longrightarrow} E$ also, or $B \overset{s}{\Longrightarrow} E$, whence $C \overset{s}{\Longrightarrow} F \approx_k E$ (since $B \approx C$), whence also $\tau.C + D \overset{s}{\Longrightarrow} F \approx_k E$.

As in Prop. 7.11, this completes the proof. ⊠

By now these inductive proofs of $\approx_k$, appealing to the inductive hypothesis only when ε-experiments are considered, are becoming familiar; we shall leave them as exercises in future.

7.4 Laws of Observation Congruence

We are going to prove three laws, for which we have strong evidence that they say all that needs to be said about the strange invisible τ under $\overset{c}{\approx}$; this suggests that the apparently never-ending stream of laws is drawing to a close! The evidence is that these new laws, together with those of Theorem 5.3, have been shown to be complete for CCS without recursion and value-passing. This means that any true statement $B \overset{c}{\approx} C$ (in this restricted language) can be proved from the laws; in fact the laws of Theorem 5.3 are quite a lot simpler without value-passing, and those of Theorem 5.5 are unnecessary without recursion.

One would expect to have to add some induction principle in the presence of recursion; what needs to be added for value-passing is less obvious (but in several more-or-less natural examples, including those in Chapter 8, we have not needed more than we have already).

Theorem 7.13 (τ laws)

(1) $g.\tau.B \overset{c}{\approx} g.B$

(2) $B + \tau.B \overset{c}{\approx} \tau.B$

(3) $g.(B + \tau.C) + g.C \overset{c}{\approx} g.(B + \tau.C)$

Proof (1) follows directly from Prop. 7.1 ($\tau.B \approx B$) and Prop 7.12. For (2), we must prove for arbitrary D,k

$$B + \tau.B + D \approx_k \tau.B + D$$

and this follows the pattern of Props. 7.11, 7.12.

For (3) similarly, we need

$$g.(B + \tau.C) + g.C + D \approx g.(B + \tau.C) + D$$

which follows the same pattern, but needs the extra easy fact that for $s \neq \varepsilon$, if $g.C \stackrel{s}{\Longrightarrow} E$ then also $g.(B + \tau.C) \stackrel{s}{\Longrightarrow} E$. ⊠

Exercise 7.3 Complete the proofs of (2) and (3).

A more useful form of (2) is the following:

Corollary 7.14 $B + \tau.(B + C) \stackrel{c}{\approx} \tau.(B + C)$.

Proof

Exercise 7.4 Prove this, by first applying (2) to $\tau.(B+C)$; you will need another law of +. ⊠

One may justify the laws intuitively by thinking of any behaviour B as a collection of action capabilities (the branches of its CT), including perhaps some τ-actions (the τ-branches) which are capable of rejecting the other capabilities.

Law (1) may then be explained by saying that, under the guard g, the τ-action of $\tau.B$ rejects no other capabilities and therefore has no effect. For Law (2), the capabilities represented by B are again present after the τ-action of $\tau.B$ in the context $B + \tau.B$, so $\tau.B$ itself has all the power of $B + \tau.B$. For Law (3), an observation of the left side may reject B by passing the guard g in g.C, but this rejection is already represented in $g.(B + \tau.C)$. But such wordy justifications badly need support; observation equivalence is what gives them support here.

Laws (2) and (3) are absorption laws; they yield many other absorptions.

Exercise 7.5 Prove, directly from the laws, that

(i) $\tau.(B_1 + \tau.(B_2 + \tau.B_3)) + B_3 \stackrel{c}{\approx} \tau.(B_1 + \tau.(B_2 + \tau.B_3))$

(ii) $\tau.(B_1 + \tau.(B_2 + B_3)) + B_3 \stackrel{c}{\approx} \tau.(B_1 + \tau.(B_2 + B_3))$

(iii) $\tau.(B_1 + \alpha.(B_2 + \tau.B_3)) + \alpha.B_3 \stackrel{c}{\approx} \tau.(B_1 + \alpha.(B_2 + \tau.B_3))$

and consider how they generalise. On the other hand, disprove

$$\alpha.(B + C) + \alpha.C \stackrel{c}{\approx} \alpha.(B + \tau.C)$$

by finding B,C which make them not $\approx$.

7.5 Proof Techniques

In conducting proofs, we may take the liberty of using "=" in place of "$\sim$" or "$\stackrel{c}{\approx}$", adopting the familiar tradition that "=" means equality in the intended interpretation; this helps us to highlight our uses of $\approx$, for which care is needed because it is not a congruence. With this convention, let us summarise the important properties.

(i) The laws of $\sim$ (Chapter 5);

(ii) $B \approx \tau.B$ (Proposition 7.1);

(iii) $B = C$ implies $B \approx C$ (Corollary 7.6);

(iv) $\approx$ is preserved by all operations except $+$ (Theorem 7.3);

(v) $B \approx C$ implies $B=C$ when both stable (Proposition 7.11);

(vi) $B \approx C$ implies $g.B=g.C$ (Proposition 7.12);

(vii) The τ laws (Theorem 7.13).

Since we mentioned that the τ laws have a completeness property, why bother with $\approx$ in proofs? The reason is to do with stability. We can often show that a behaviour B of interest, not stable itself, satisfies

$$B = \tau.B^*$$

for some stable B^*; so of course $B \approx B^*$ (but $B \not\approx^c B^*$, by Proposition 7.10! This expresses that B stabilises. Stable behaviours are often easier to handle, and the constrained substitutivity of $\approx$ often allows us to conduct our proofs mainly in terms of stable behaviours. Chapter 8 should make this point clear.

Many proofs can be done with our laws without using any induction principle, though the laws are established using induction on $\approx_k$. There is, however, a powerful induction principle - Computation Induction - due to Scott, which we cannot use at present since it involves a partial order over behaviours. We believe that this principle can be invoked for the finer notion of observation equivalence alluded to in §7.2, Remark(2); it remains to be seen how important its use will be.

7.6 Proof of Theorem 7.7

Theorem 7.7 $\overset{+}{\approx}$ is a congruence.

Proof First, we show that $B \overset{+}{\approx} C$ implies $B + D \overset{+}{\approx} C + D$; that is, we require $(B + D) + E \approx (C + D) + E$ for arbitrary E.

But $(B + D) + E \approx B + (D + E)$ (Theorem 5.3)

$\approx C + (D + E)$ (since $B \overset{+}{\approx} C$)

$\approx (C + D) + E$.

Next we require that $B \overset{+}{\approx} C$ implies
$$\begin{cases} g.B \overset{+}{\approx} g.C , \\ B\backslash\alpha \overset{+}{\approx} C\backslash\alpha , \\ B[S] \overset{+}{\approx} C[S] ; \end{cases}$$

e.g. we want $g.B + E \approx g.C + E$ for any E. In each case the proof follows the pattern of proof in Propositions 7.11, 7.12 (these Propositions are stated in terms of $\approx^c$, but the proofs are entirely in terms of $\approx$).

The critical case is $B \overset{+}{\approx} C$ implies $B|D \overset{+}{\approx} C|D$. Assume $B \overset{+}{\approx} C$ and prove $B|D + E \approx_k C|D + E$, for arbitrary E, by induction on k.
Inductive Step: Let $B|D + E \overset{s}{\Longrightarrow} E$;

(i) If $s \neq \varepsilon$, then either $E \overset{s}{\Longrightarrow} E'$, and then $C|D + E \overset{s}{\Longrightarrow} E'$ also, or $B|D \overset{s}{\Longrightarrow} E'$, and then $C|D \overset{s}{\Longrightarrow} F' \approx_k E'$ for some F' (since $B \approx C$ so $B|D \approx C|D$ by Theorem 7.3), whence $C|D + E \overset{s}{\Longrightarrow} F' \approx_k E'$ also.

(ii) If $s = \varepsilon$, then either E' is $B|D + E$ itself, and then $C|D + E \overset{\varepsilon}{\Longrightarrow} C|D + E, \approx_k B|D + E$ by induction, or $E \overset{\tau}{\Longrightarrow} E'$, and then $C|D + E \overset{\tau}{\Longrightarrow} E'$ also, or $B|D \overset{\tau}{\longrightarrow} B'|D' \overset{\varepsilon}{\Longrightarrow} E'$. These are now the three cases:

(a) B' is B, and $D \overset{\tau}{\longrightarrow} D'$; then $C|D \overset{\tau}{\longrightarrow} C|D'$ and $B|D' \approx C|D'$ by Theorem 7.3 so $C|D' \overset{\varepsilon}{\Longrightarrow} F' \approx_k E'$ for some F', whence $C|D + E \overset{\varepsilon}{\Longrightarrow} F' \approx_k E'$ as required.

(b) D' is D and $B \overset{\tau}{\longrightarrow} B'$; then by Lemma 7.9 $C \overset{\tau}{\Longrightarrow} C' \approx_{k+1} B'$ for some C' (this is the only use of $B \overset{+}{\approx} C$ - elsewhere $B \approx C$ is all that is needed), and we also have $B'|D \approx_{k+1} C'|D$ from Theorem 7.3, so since $B'|D \overset{\varepsilon}{\Longrightarrow} E'$, $C'|D \overset{\varepsilon}{\Longrightarrow} F' \approx_k E'$ for some F'. So finally $C|D + E \overset{\tau}{\Longrightarrow} C'|D \overset{\varepsilon}{\Longrightarrow} F' \approx_k E'$.

(c) $B \overset{\lambda v}{\longrightarrow} B'$ and $D \overset{\bar{\lambda} v}{\longrightarrow} D'$; then $C \overset{\lambda v}{\Longrightarrow} C' \approx_{k+1} B'$ for some C', whence $C|D \overset{\tau}{\Longrightarrow} C'|D' \approx_{k+1} B'|D'$ by Theorem 7.3, whence $C'|D' \overset{\varepsilon}{\Longrightarrow} F' \approx_k E'$ for some F', whence also $C|D + E \overset{\varepsilon}{\Longrightarrow} F' \approx_k E'$.

Thus we have found F' in every case so that $C|D + E \overset{\varepsilon}{\Longrightarrow} F' \approx_k E'$; by symmetry, we have $B|D + E \approx_{k+1} C|D + E$ which completes the induction.

⊠

7.7 Further exercises

We end this Chapter with some harder exercises, for readers interested in the theoretical development.

Exercise 7.6 (Hennessy). Prove the following result, which further clarifies the relation between $\approx$ and $\approx^c$:

$$B \approx C \text{ iff } (B \approx^c C \text{ or } B \approx^c \tau.C \text{ or } \tau.B \approx^c C) .$$

Exercise 7.7 We would like to know that if $b \Leftarrow \alpha.b$ and $B \overset{c}{\approx} \alpha.B$ then $b \overset{c}{\approx} B$; this states that, up to $\overset{c}{\approx}$, the recursive definition $b \Leftarrow \alpha.b$ has a unique solution. The argument in §3.4, proving the scheduler correct, used a mild generalisation of this result. The following exercises lead to a more general theorem (for simplicity, work without value passing).

(i) Prove: if $B \approx \alpha.B$ and $C \approx \alpha.C$ then $B \approx C$.

(ii) Deduce: if $B \overset{c}{\approx} \alpha.B$ and $C \overset{c}{\approx} \alpha.C$ then $B \overset{c}{\approx} C$.

More generally, let $\mathcal{C}[\ ]$ be of form

$$D_1 + \mu_1.(D_2 + \mu_2.(\ldots\ldots(D_m + \mu_m.[\,])\ldots))$$

for $m \geq 1$, where at least one μ_i is not τ.

(iii) Prove: if $B \approx \mathcal{C}[B]$ and $C \approx \mathcal{C}[C]$ then $B \approx C$.

(iv) Deduce: if $B \overset{c}{\approx} \mathcal{C}[B]$ and $C \overset{c}{\approx} \mathcal{C}[C]$ then $B \overset{c}{\approx} C$.

(v) Deduce: if $b \Leftarrow \mathcal{C}[b]$ and $B \overset{c}{\approx} \mathcal{C}[B]$ then $b \overset{c}{\approx} B$.

Exercise 7.8 Consider a different definition of observation equivalence. First, define a decreasing sequence of pre-orders $\lesssim_0, \lesssim_1, \ldots, \lesssim_k, \ldots$:

$B \lesssim_0 C$ is always true ;

$B \lesssim_{k+1} C$ iff, for all s ,

if $B \overset{s}{\Longrightarrow} B'$ then for some C', $C \overset{s}{\Longrightarrow} C'$ and $B' \lesssim_k C'$.

Thus we take only the first clause of the definition of $\approx_{k+1}$. Then;

$B \lesssim C$ iff $\forall k.\ B \lesssim_k C$; $B \eqsim C$ iff $B \lesssim C$ and $C \lesssim B$.

We may take $\eqsim$ as a candidate for observation equivalence.

(i) Prove that $\lesssim_k, \lesssim$ are preorders, that $\eqsim$ is an equivalence, and that $B \approx C$ implies $B \eqsim C$.

(ii) Prove that $\eqsim$ is a congruence; in particular, that $B \eqsim C$ implies $\forall D.\ B+D \eqsim C+D$ (first show that each $\lesssim_k$ has this property). Thus $\eqsim$ and $\approx$ differ, since the latter is not a congruence.

(iii) Find a simple example in which $B \eqsim C$ but $B \not\approx C$. Also show (by a similar example) that $\eqsim$ does not respect deadlock properties in the sense of Exercise 3.6.

This is why we rejected $\eqsim$ as our notion of observation equivalence, in spite of its somewhat simpler theory.

CHAPTER 8

Some proofs about data structures

8.1 Introduction

We have already shown some not quite trivial algorithms and systems expressed in CCS. The point of this chapter is twofold. First we want to show that familiar data structures, as well as algorithms, find natural expression in CCS; second, we want to illustrate how the properties of observation equivalence and congruence allow us to prove that systems work properly. The data structures here give good proof examples. To what extent they correspond to hardware realisations must be left open, but it does not appear unreasonable that at least some hardware structures can be faithfully represented in CCS.

8.2 Registers and memories

The simplest shared resource, which may be the means of interaction between otherwise independent agents, is probably a single memory register. Many concurrent algorithms have been represented in languages which permit agents to interact only through 'shared variables' (usually 'writeable' as well as 'readable'). We argued in §4.5 that algorithms are not always best expressed this way - many people have recently made this point.

But if we do want a register, readable and writeable by one or more agents, its behaviour may be well represented by $REG(v):\{\alpha,\bar{\gamma}\}$ defined by:

$$REG(v) \Leftarrow \alpha x.REG(x) + \bar{\gamma}v.REG(v)$$

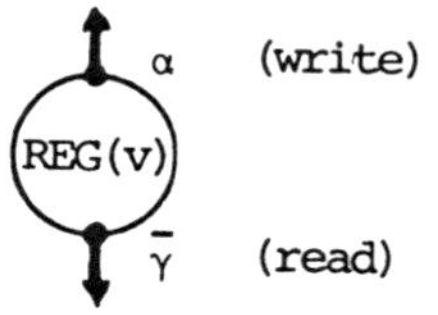

Two kinds of atomic experiment are possible:

$$REG(v) \xrightarrow{\alpha u} REG(u) \qquad \text{(write u)}$$
$$REG(v) \xrightarrow{\bar{\gamma}v} REG(v) \qquad \text{(read v)}$$

We may also find it useful to define

$$LOC \Leftarrow \alpha x.REG(x)$$

- a register without initial content, which at first admits only writing.

If we define relabellings $S_i = \alpha_i\gamma_i/\alpha\gamma$ $(1\le i\le n)$ where the α_i,γ_i are all distinct names, then we can define a memory of sort $\{\alpha_1,\gamma_1, \ldots,\alpha_n,\gamma_n\}$ by

$$MEMORY_n = LOC[S_1] \mid \ldots \mid LOC[S_n]$$

or, using Π to represent multiple composition:

$$\text{MEMORY}_n = \prod_{1\le i\le n} \text{LOC}[S_i]$$

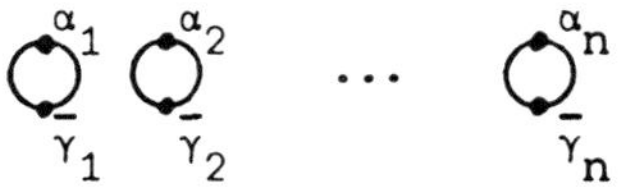

Note that this use of composition just places the registers side by side; they don't communicate with each other!

Let us now suppose, more realistically, that we want to build a memory of size 2^k with just three ports:

(i) At α, it receives in sequence the k bits $a_{k-1}, \ldots, a_0$ of a memory address m, $0 \le m < 2^k$;

(ii) At β it receives a value to be written at address m;

(iii) At $\overline{\gamma}$ it delivers the value stored at address m.

Let us call the memory, storing values $\tilde{v} = (v_0, \ldots, v_{2^k-1})$, $M_k(\tilde{v}):\{\alpha,\beta,\overline{\gamma}\}$. We shall adopt a convention which is in fact a reality for magnetic core memories; destructive reading. To <u>write</u> a new value u into address m in $M_k(\tilde{v})$, the environment will perform

$$\overline{\alpha}m_{k-1}. \ldots .\overline{\alpha}m_0.\overline{\beta}u.\gamma x. \ldots$$

and ignore the value received at γ (which is bound to x); this value will actually be v_m. Thus to <u>read</u> the memory at m, the environment first writes an arbitrary value (say 0) to m, receives and holds v_m, and writes v_m back at m; it performs

$$\overline{\alpha}m_{k-1}. \ldots .\overline{\alpha}m_0.\overline{\beta}0.\gamma x.\overline{\alpha}m_{k-1}. \ldots .\overline{\alpha}m_0.\overline{\beta}x.\gamma y.\ B$$

where B (the continuing environment behaviour) will use x somehow, but ignore y.

In summary then, we can express how we want M_k to behave by saying that for any environment expression B of form

$$\overline{\alpha}m_{k-1}. \ldots .\overline{\alpha}m_0.\overline{\beta}u.\gamma x.\ B' \qquad (1)$$

the following observation equivalence must hold:

$$(\ M_k(\tilde{v})\ |\ B\ )\backslash\alpha\backslash\beta\backslash\gamma \ \approx\ (\ M_k(\tilde{v}(u/m))\ |\ B'\{v_m/x\}\ )\backslash\alpha\backslash\beta\backslash\gamma \qquad (2)$$

where $\tilde{v}(u/m)$ means $(v_0, \ldots, v_{m-1}, u, v_{m+1}, \ldots, v_{2^k-1})$.

This requirement is an example of incomplete specification; we do not specify what happens if B supplies too few or too many address bits, or acts strangely in some other way. It is a natural incompleteness, ecause we might naturally compose M_k with a 'front end' agent whose job s to receive integer addresses, decode them into bit-sequences of length (complaining if the integer received is outside the range $[0,2^k-1]$) nd conduct the correct reading and writing sequences with M_k . Also, he incomplete specification actually makes the design of M_k easy, as we hall see.

A specification which would be too incomplete would be to demand merely hat

$$M_k(\tilde{v}) \xRightarrow{\alpha m_{k-1}.\ \dots\ .\alpha m_0.\beta u.\bar{\gamma} v_m} M_k(\tilde{v}(u/m)) \quad ;$$

ertainly $M_k(\tilde{v})$ must have this derivation for every $m = m_{k-1},\dots,m_0$ nd every u , but this would not exclude unwanted derivations like

$$M_k(\tilde{v}) \xRightarrow{\varepsilon} NIL$$

deadlock!

Now let us abbreviate $\{\alpha,\beta,\bar{\gamma}\}$ by L , and define arbitrary sorts $_0 = \{\alpha_0,\beta_0,\bar{\gamma}_0\}$, $L_1 = \{\alpha_1,\beta_1,\bar{\gamma}_1\}$, asking only that all these names $,\dots,\gamma_1$ are distinct and that $\alpha_0,\beta_0,\gamma_0,\alpha_1,\beta_1,\gamma_1$ don't appear in L_B , he sort of B . We will also abbreviate $\backslash\alpha\backslash\beta\backslash\gamma$ by $\backslash L$, $\backslash\alpha_0\backslash\beta_0\backslash\gamma_0$ y $\backslash L_0$, etc., and set $S_i = \alpha_i\beta_i\gamma_i/\alpha\beta\gamma$, $i = 0,1$.

First we can see that the specification (2) is equivalent to demanding

$$(\ M_k(\tilde{v})[S_0]\ |\ B_0)\backslash L_0 \approx (\ M_k(\tilde{v}(u/m))[S_0]\ |\ B'_0\{v_m/x\}\ )\backslash L_0 \qquad (3)$$

or any B_0 of form $\bar{\alpha}_0 m_{k-1}.\ \dots\ .\bar{\alpha}_0 m_0.\bar{\beta}_0 u.\gamma_0 x.\ B'_0$; to deduce (2) from 3) we note that

$$\begin{aligned} (\ M_k(\tilde{v})\ \ |\ B\ )\backslash L &= (\ M_k(\tilde{v})\ \ |\ B\ )[S_0]\backslash L_0 && (\underline{\text{Rel}\sim}(1),(2),(4)\ ) \\ &= (\ M_k(\tilde{v})\ \ [S_0]\ |\ B[S_0]\ )\backslash L_0 && (\underline{\text{Rel}\sim}(5)\ ) \\ &= (\ M_k(\tilde{v})[S_0]\ |\ B_0\ )\backslash L_0 && (\underline{\text{Rel}\equiv}(3)\ ) \\ &\qquad \text{with } B'_0 = B'[S_0]\ ; \end{aligned}$$

he other side of (2) transforms similarly, and (3) can be used to get (2). onversely to deduce (3) from (2) we work with $R_0 = \alpha\beta\gamma/\alpha_0\beta_0\gamma_0$, the nverse relabelling to S_0 , and use Rel~(1),(3) knowing that $R_0 \circ S_0 = I$, he identity relabelling. Such manipulations should become routine!

We now come to the design of M_k . $M_0(v)$, the memory of size 1 conaining v , is given by

$$M_0(v) \quad = \quad CELL(v) \ , \quad \text{where } CELL(x) \Leftarrow \beta y.\bar{\gamma}x.\ CELL(y) \qquad (4)$$

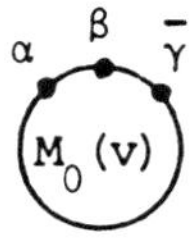

(The α port is not used.)

We build $M_{k+1}(\tilde{v}:\tilde{w})$ ($\tilde{v},\tilde{w}$ each of length 2^k; $\tilde{v}:\tilde{w}$ is their concatenation) out of $M_k(\tilde{v})$ and $M_k(\tilde{w})$ by composing them with NODE: $L \cup \bar{L}_0 \cup \bar{L}_1$, whose job is to inspect the first address bit z which it receives and - roughly - transmit the rest of the communication to $M_k(\tilde{v})$ or $M_k(\tilde{w})$ according as $z = 0$ or 1. Precisely:

$$\begin{array}{lll} \text{NODE} & \Leftarrow & \alpha z.\ \text{NODE}_z \\ \text{NODE}_i & \Leftarrow & \alpha z.\bar{\alpha}_i z.\ \text{NODE}_i + \beta x.\bar{\beta}_i x.\gamma_i y.\bar{\gamma} y.\ \text{NODE} \quad (i=0,1) \end{array} \tag{5}$$

and

$$M_{k+1}(\tilde{v}:\tilde{w}) = (\ M_k(\tilde{v})[S_0] \mid M_k(\tilde{w})[S_1] \mid \text{NODE}\ )\backslash L_0 \backslash L_1 \tag{6}$$

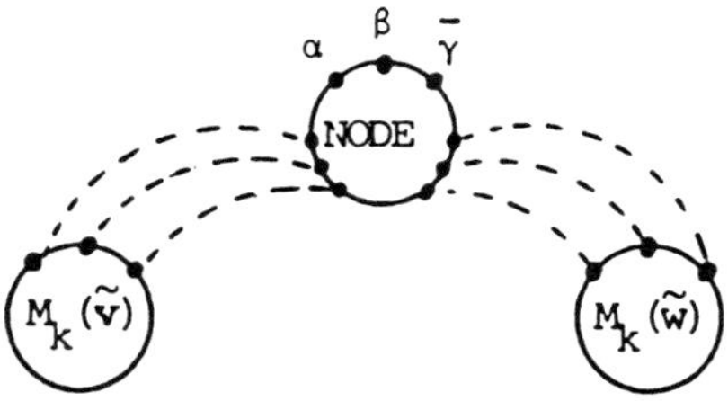

Notice that NODE_i does not know how many bits to receive; it must be ready for an address bit <u>or</u> a value, and act accordingly.

The diagram on the next page shows $M_3(\tilde{v})$, with arrows indicating the initial capabilities of the components. By swinging arrows about on it, you can convince yourself that it works - and that 'wrong' sequences deadlock; e.g. $M_3(\tilde{v}) \xRightarrow{\alpha 0.\alpha 1.\beta u} \text{NIL}$.

(The idea to use as an example a memory built of nodes which 'use the first bit to direct traffic' came from a talk with Nigel Derrett, who told me that this method is used in practice.)

Having now defined M_k rather succinctly by (4) - (6), and specified its intended behaviour by (1) and (2), we proceed to prove that it meets its specification.

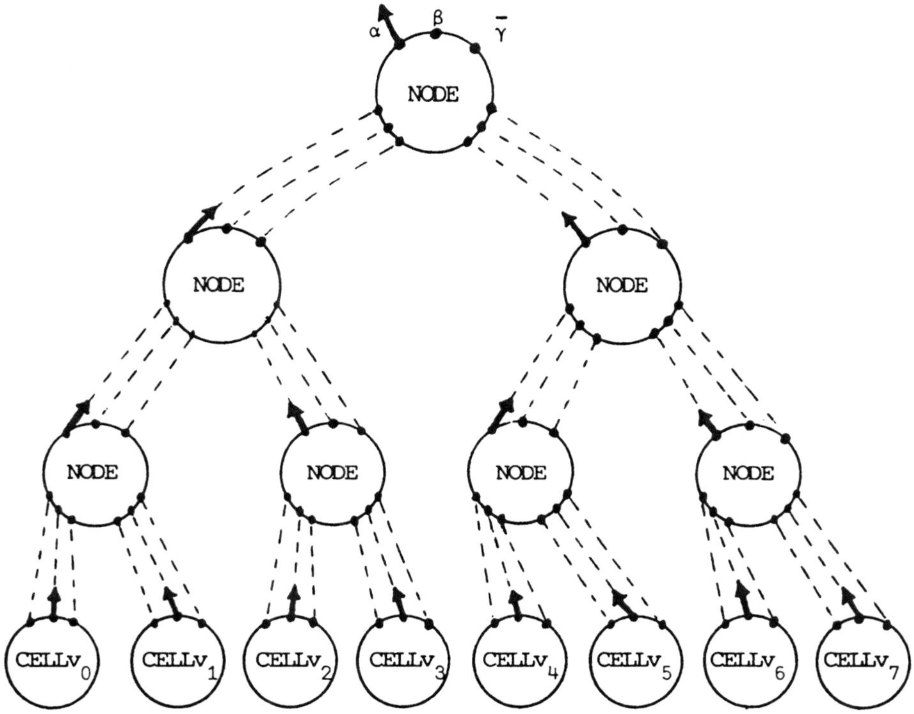

Diagram of $M_3(\tilde{v})$,
showing initial action capabilities .

<u>Theorem 8.1</u> For any B of form $\bar{\alpha}m_{k-1}.\ \cdots\ .\bar{\alpha}m_0.\bar{\beta}u.\gamma x.\ B'$,

$$(\ M_k(\tilde{v})\ \mid\ B\ )\backslash L\ \approx\ (\ M_k(\tilde{v}(u/m))\ \mid\ B'\{v_m/x\}\ )\backslash L\ .$$

<u>Proof</u> For $k = 0$ we have, since $\tilde{v} = (v_0)$,

$$\begin{aligned}(\ M_0(\tilde{v})\ \mid\ B\ )\backslash L\ &=\ (\ \beta y.\bar{\gamma}v_0.\ CELL(y)\ \mid\ \bar{\beta}u.\gamma x.\ B'\ )\backslash L \\ &=\ \tau.\tau.(\ CELL(u)\ \mid\ B'\{v_0/x\}\ )\backslash L \qquad \text{(Expansion)} \\ &\approx\ (\ M_0(\tilde{v}(u/0))\ \mid\ B'\{v_0/x\}\ )\backslash L \qquad \text{(Proposition 7.1)}\end{aligned}$$

as required. Now assume the theorem for k . Take B of form

$$\bar{\alpha}m_k.\bar{\alpha}m_{k-1}.\ \cdots\ .\bar{\alpha}m_0.\bar{\beta}u.\gamma x.\ B'$$

and consider $M_k(\tilde{v}:\tilde{w})$, where $\tilde{v},\tilde{w}$ are of length 2^k . We want

$$(\ M_{k+1}(\tilde{v}:\tilde{w})\ \mid\ B\ )\backslash L \approx (\ M_{k+1}((\tilde{v}:\tilde{w})(u/m_k m))\ \mid\ B'\{(\tilde{v}:\tilde{w})_{m_k m}/x\}\ )\backslash L$$

where $m = m_{k-1},\ldots,m_0$. By symmetry it will be enough to prove this for the case $m_k=0$, which is to say we want

$$(\ M_{k+1}(\tilde{v}:\tilde{w})\ \mid\ B\ )\backslash L \approx (\ M_{k+1}(\tilde{v}(u/m):\tilde{w})\ \mid\ B'\{v_m/x\}\ )\backslash L\ .$$

The left-hand side is, by (6),

$$(\ (\ \underbrace{M_k(\tilde{v})[S_0]}_{L_0}\ \mid\ \underbrace{M_k(\tilde{w})[S_1]}_{L_1}\ \mid\ \underbrace{NODE}_{L\cup\bar{L}_0\cup\bar{L}_1}\ )\backslash L_0\backslash L_1\ \mid\ \underbrace{B}_{L_B}\ )\backslash L$$

(writing sorts below)

$$=\ (\ M_k(\tilde{w})[S_1]\ \mid\ (\ M_k(\tilde{v})[S_0]\ \mid\ (NODE|B)\backslash L\ )\backslash L_0\ )\backslash L_1 \tag{7}$$

where we have regrouped by repeated use of <u>Res~</u> and by <u>Com~</u>(1), remembering that $L_0\cap\bar{L}_B = L_1\cap\bar{L}_B = \emptyset$.

Now recalling $m_k=0$, by the Expansion Theorem

$$\begin{aligned}(NODE|B)\backslash L &= \tau.(\ NODE_0\ \mid\ \bar{\alpha}m_{k-1}.\ \cdots\ .\bar{\alpha}m_0.\bar{\beta}u.\gamma x.\ B'\ )\backslash L\ , \\ &\approx\ \bar{\alpha}_0 m_{k-1}.\ \cdots\ .\bar{\alpha}_0 m_0.\bar{\beta}_0 u.\gamma_0 x.(NODE|B')\backslash L\end{aligned}$$

by Proposition 7.1 and Theorem 7.3 . But this is a B_0 of the form needed for (3), which we showed equivalent to the theorem at k (which we're assuming); so recalling Theorem 7.3 - that $\approx$ can be substituted except under + - we can rewrite (7) as

$$\approx\ (\ M_k(\tilde{w})[S_1]\ \mid\ (\ M_k(\tilde{v}(u/m))[S_0]\ \mid\ B_0'\{v_m/x\}\ )\backslash L_0\ )\backslash L_1$$

where $B_0' = (NODE|B')\backslash L$, so $B_0'\{v_m/x\} = (NODE|B'\{v_m/x\})\backslash L$ since x is not a free variable in NODE . Now we can regroup, just reversing the operations by which we got the form (7), to get

$$\begin{aligned}&=\ (\ (\ M_k(\tilde{v}(u/m))[S_0]\ \mid\ M_k(\tilde{w})[S_1]\ \mid\ NODE\ )\backslash L_0\backslash L_1\ \mid\ B'\{v_m/x\}\ )\backslash L \\ &=\ (\ M_{k+1}(\tilde{v}(u/m):\tilde{w})\ \mid\ B'\{v_m/x\}\ )\backslash L \qquad \text{as required.}\end{aligned}$$

⊠

Exercise 8.1 Suppose you have available a decoder, which accepts an integer (assumed to be in the range $[0,2^k-1]$ for some fixed k) and decodes it into its bit sequence. That is:

$$DECODE \Leftarrow \delta m.\bar{\alpha}m_{k-1}. \ \ldots \ .\bar{\alpha}m_0.\bar{\zeta}.\ DECODE \quad :\{\delta,\bar{\alpha},\bar{\zeta}\}\ .$$

The integer comes in at δ, the bits go out at $\bar{\alpha}$, and $\bar{\zeta}$ signals completion.

Design another agent, called FRONTEND, so that when you compose DECODE, FRONTEND and $M_k(\tilde{v})$ with appropriate relabellings and restrictions you get a system $MEM_k(\tilde{v}) : \{\alpha,\beta,\bar{\gamma}\}$ satisfying

$$MEM_k(\tilde{v}) \approx \alpha m.\ (\beta x.MEM(\tilde{v}(x/m)) + \bar{\gamma}v_m.MEM_k(\tilde{v}))\ .$$

(To write value u at address m, the user performs $\bar{\alpha}m.\bar{\beta}u.\ \ldots$; to read the memory at m and bind the received value to y he performs $\bar{\alpha}m.\gamma y.\ \ldots\ .$) Prove the desired equivalence.

Hint: FRONTEND and DECODE must cooperate to produce expressions of the form B, so that you can use Theorem 8.1 about $M_k(\tilde{v})$.

Exercise 8.2 Can you think of a way to redesign $M_k(\tilde{v})$ so that the outgoing value doesn't have to travel up the binary tree?

8.3 Chaining operations

Suppose we have agents B_1 and B_2

and wish to join them like this:

It is natural to define a binary operation $\frown$ for this purpose.

Definition Let $B_1{:}L_1$, $B_2{:}L_2$ and $\beta\neq\alpha$; then

$$B_1 \frown B_2 = (B_1[\delta/\beta] \mid B_2[\delta/\alpha])\backslash\delta \quad \text{where } \delta \notin names(L_1 \cup L_2)\ .$$

Note that the definition is specific to $\bar{\beta}$ and α ; perhaps we should write $B_1\ \bar{\beta}\frown\alpha\ B_2$.

We need to justify our definition by showing that the choice of δ doesn't affect it. To see this, suppose that $\delta' \notin \text{names}(L_1 \cup L_2)$, $\delta' \neq \delta$. Then

$$
\begin{aligned}
&(B_1[\delta'/\beta] \,|\, B_2[\delta'/\alpha])\backslash\delta' \\
&\quad = (B_1[\delta'/\beta] \,|\, B_2[\delta'/\alpha])\backslash\delta'[\delta/\delta'] \quad \text{by } \underline{\text{Rel}\sim}(1),(2) \\
&\quad = (B_1[\delta'/\beta][\delta/\delta'] \,|\, B_2[\delta'/\alpha][\delta/\delta'])\backslash\delta \quad \text{by } \underline{\text{Rel}\sim}(4),(5) \\
&\quad = (B_1[\delta/\beta] \,|\, B_2[\delta/\alpha])\backslash\delta \quad \text{by } \underline{\text{Rel}\sim}(3) .
\end{aligned}
$$

Note that $B_1 \frown B_2$ may form other links, depending on L_1 and L_2 ; this doesn't affect our argument, but we are mainly interested in the case $L_1 \cap \bar{L}_2 = \emptyset$.

The importance of $\frown$ is that it is <u>associative</u>; this property is helpful when we need to chain several agents together. Let us prove associativity. Suppose $B_1{:}L_1$, $B_2{:}L_2$, $B_3{:}L_3$.

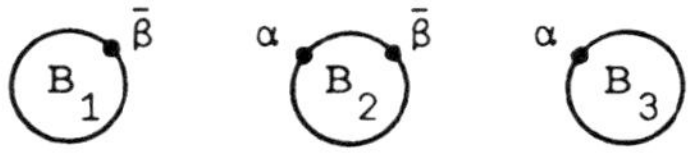

Then

$$(B_1 \frown B_2) \frown B_3 = (\ (B_1[\delta/\beta] \,|\, B_2[\delta/\alpha])\backslash\delta[\zeta/\beta] \ \,|\, B_3[\zeta/\alpha]\ )\backslash\zeta$$

choosing $\delta, \zeta \notin \text{names}(L_1 \cup L_2 \cup L_3)$ and $\delta \neq \zeta$;

$$= (\ (B_1[\delta/\beta] \,|\, B_2[\delta/\alpha])[\zeta/\beta]\backslash\delta \ \,|\, B_3[\zeta/\alpha]\backslash\delta\ )\backslash\zeta$$

by <u>Rel~</u>(4) and <u>Res~</u>(1) (we are pushing relabellings <u>inwards</u>, pulling restrictions <u>outwards</u>) ;

$$= (B_1[\delta/\beta][\zeta/\beta] \,|\, B_2[\delta/\alpha][\zeta/\beta] \,|\, B_3[\zeta/\alpha])\backslash\delta\backslash\zeta$$

by <u>Rel~</u>(5) and <u>Res~</u>(3) (check its side condition!) ;

$$= (B_1[\delta/\beta] \,|\, B_2[\delta\zeta/\alpha\beta] \,|\, B_3[\zeta/\alpha])\backslash\zeta\backslash\delta$$

by <u>Rel~</u>(3) and <u>Res~</u>(2) ;

$$= B_1 \frown (B_2 \frown B_3) \quad \text{by symmetry.}$$

Exactly the same can be done for double chaining; given two agents

we want to join them together to give

.

<u>Definition</u> Let $B_1:L_1$, $B_2:L_2$ and let $\alpha,\beta,\gamma,\delta$ be distinct. Then

$$B_1 \supset B_2 = (B_1[\eta/\beta,\theta/\delta] \mid B_2[\eta/\alpha,\theta/\gamma])\backslash\theta\backslash\eta$$

where $\eta,\theta \notin \text{names}(L_1 \cup L_2)$ and $\eta \neq \theta$.

It is easy but tedious to check the associativity of $\supset$. We shall use this operation in the next section.

Both $\frown$ and $\supset$ give us special cases of Theorem 5.8, the Expansion Theorem; we just state it for $\frown$, in the simple case where $B_1,\ldots,B_n : \{\alpha,\bar{\beta}\}$, i.e. no labels are present except the chaining labels.

<u>Expansion Theorem for $\frown$</u> If $B_1,\ldots,B_n : \{\alpha,\bar{\beta}\}$, and each is a sum of guards, then

$$\begin{aligned} B_1 \frown B_2 \frown \cdots \frown B_n = \\ &\textstyle\sum\{\alpha\tilde{x}.(B_1' \frown B_2 \frown \cdots \frown B_n) \;;\; \alpha\tilde{x}.B_1' \text{ a summand of } B_1\} \\ &+ \textstyle\sum\{\bar{\beta}\tilde{v}.(B_1 \frown B_2 \frown \cdots \frown B_n') \;;\; \bar{\beta}\tilde{v}.B_n' \text{ a summand of } B_n\} \\ &+ \textstyle\sum\{\tau.(B_1 \frown \cdots \frown B_i' \frown B_{i+1}'\{\tilde{v}/\tilde{x}\} \frown \cdots \frown B_n) \;; \\ &\qquad \bar{\beta}\tilde{v}.B_i' \text{ a summand of } B_i \;,\; \alpha\tilde{x}.B_{i+1}' \text{ a summand of } B_{i+1}\} \end{aligned}$$

All that this says is that the only <u>external</u> actions occur at the ends of the chain, and the only <u>internal</u> actions occur between neighbours. We will use the corresponding theorem for $\supset$; it's obvious enough, so we do not write it down.

<u>8.4 Pushdowns and queues</u>

Let V be a value set; we use s to range over V^* .
What should be the behaviour $PD(s) : \{\alpha,\bar{\gamma}\}$ of a pushdown store in which values are pushed in at α and popped out at $\bar{\gamma}$? A reasonable suggestion is

$$\begin{aligned} PD(s) \Leftarrow\;& \alpha x.\,PD(x{:}s) \;+ \\ & \underline{\text{if}}\; s{=}\varepsilon \;\underline{\text{then}}\; \bar{\gamma}\$.\,PD(\varepsilon) \;\underline{\text{else}}\; \bar{\gamma}(\text{first } s).PD(\text{rest } s) \end{aligned} \qquad (1)$$

Here ':' is the prefixing operation over V^* , and '\$' indicates emptiness; we test the pushdown for emptiness by popping and testing the value popped.

Thus we want to build PD(s) to satisfy

$$\begin{aligned} PD(\varepsilon) &= \alpha x.\ PD(x{:}\varepsilon) + \bar{\gamma}\$.\ PD(\varepsilon) \\ PD(v{:}s) &= \alpha x.\ PD(x{:}v{:}s) + \bar{\gamma}v.\ PD(s) \end{aligned} \qquad (2)$$

What we shall actually build is $PUSH(s) : \{\alpha,\bar{\gamma}\}$ to satisfy

$$\begin{aligned} PUSH(\varepsilon) &= \alpha x.\ PUSH(x{:}\varepsilon) + \bar{\gamma}\$.\ NIL \\ PUSH(v{:}s) &= \alpha x.\ PUSH(x{:}v{:}s) + \bar{\gamma}v.\ PUSH(s) \end{aligned} \qquad (3)$$

the only difference being that $PUSH(\varepsilon)$, when popped, degenerates to NIL . This is easier to build, and it's also easy to build a special front end, FRONT , so that (2) is satisfied by

$$PD(s) = FRONT \supset PUSH(s) \quad .$$

We build PUSH as a chain of cells, each of which can hold 0, 1 or 2 values, terminated by an end cell holding \$. A cell holding y is

<u>$CELL_1(y) : \{\alpha,\bar{\beta},\bar{\gamma},\delta\}$</u>

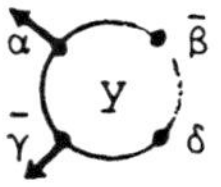

$$CELL_1(y) \Leftarrow \alpha x.\ CELL_2(x,y) + \bar{\gamma}y.\ CELL_0 \qquad (4)$$

Then the rest of the definition is

<u>$CELL_2(x,y) : \{\alpha,\bar{\beta},\bar{\gamma},\delta\}$</u>

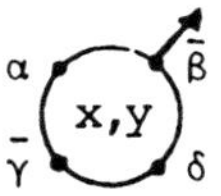

$$CELL_2(x,y) \Leftarrow \bar{\beta}y.\ CELL_1(x) \qquad (5)$$

<u>$CELL_0 : \{\alpha,\bar{\beta},\bar{\gamma},\delta\}$</u>

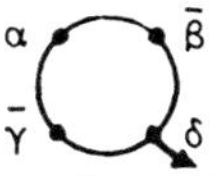

$$CELL_0 \Leftarrow \delta x.(\underline{if}\ \ x{=}\$\ \ \underline{then}\ \ CELL_\$\ \ \underline{else}\ \ CELL_1(x)) \qquad (6)$$

<u>$CELL_\$: \{\alpha,\bar{\gamma}\}$</u>

$$CELL_\$ \Leftarrow \alpha x.(CELL_1(x) \supset CELL_\$) + \bar{\gamma}\$.\ NIL \qquad (7)$$

We show the successive configurations of a typical derivation, starting from $CELL_\$$, in the diagram below.

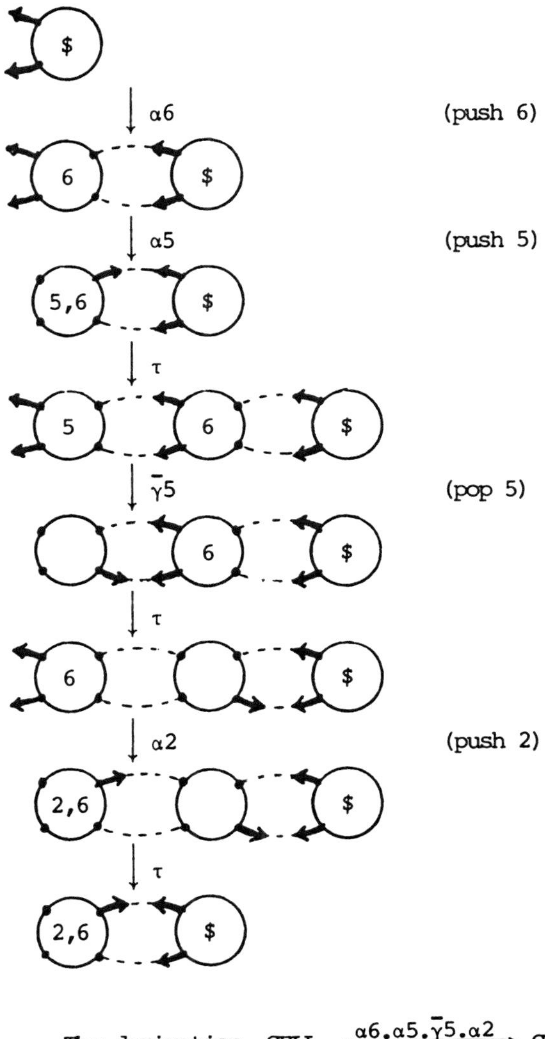

(8)

The derivation $CELL_{\$} \xrightarrow{\alpha 6.\alpha 5.\bar{\gamma}5.\alpha 2} CELL_2(2,6) \frown CELL_{\$}$.

Now for any $s = (v_1,\ldots,v_n)$ let us define

$$PUSH(s) = CELL_1(v_1) \frown \ldots \frown CELL_1(v_n) \frown CELL_{\$} \quad . \tag{9}$$

Clearly PUSH(s) is <u>stable</u>; the fourth configuration in the diagram shows you that no τ-actions are possible. It is also reasonably clear that every configuration will stabilise, given time, but that external communication can occur before stability is reached.

Let us see what we need to prove (3), which is our aim. From (9), by the Expansion Theorem, we get

$$\begin{aligned} PUSH(\varepsilon) = CELL_{\$} &= \alpha x.(CELL_1(x) \frown CELL_{\$}) + \bar{\gamma}\$.NIL \\ &= \alpha x.\ PUSH(x:\varepsilon) + \bar{\gamma}\$.\ NIL \end{aligned}$$

so the first part of (3) is done. (Recall that we allow ourselves to write '=' whenever we use a congruence, '$\sim$' or '$\approx^c$', and that '=' always implies '$\approx$'.) We also get

$$\begin{aligned} PUSH(v:s) &= CELL_1(v) \frown PUSH(s) \\ &= \alpha x.(CELL_2(x,v) \frown PUSH(s)) + \bar{\gamma}v.(CELL_0 \frown PUSH(s)) \ . \end{aligned}$$

We therefore propose to prove

$$CELL_2(u,v) \frown PUSH(s) \approx PUSH(u:v:s) \qquad (10)$$

$$CELL_0 \frown PUSH(s) \approx PUSH(s)\ . \qquad (11)$$

These cannot be congruences ($\approx^c$) since the left-hand side is unstable in each case. But '$\approx$' is strengthened to '=' by a guard (Proposition 7.12), so for example from (11) we deduce

$$\bar{\gamma}v.(CELL_0 \frown PUSH(s)) = \bar{\gamma}v.PUSH(s) \quad ;$$

applying the same technique to (10) we finally reach (3). We have achieved equality (=) before substituting under '+'.

To prove (10) and (11) we only need four little lemmas, grouped together:

<u>Lemma 8.2</u>

(1) $CELL_2(u,v) \frown CELL_1(w) \approx CELL_1(u) \frown CELL_2(v,w)$

(2) $CELL_2(u,v) \frown CELL_{\$} \approx CELL_1(u) \frown CELL_1(v) \frown CELL_{\$}$

(3) $CELL_0 \frown CELL_1(w) \approx CELL_1(w) \frown CELL_0$

(4) $CELL_0 \frown CELL_{\$} \approx CELL_{\$}$.

<u>Proof</u> All by the Expansion Theorem; we need only consider the first in detail.

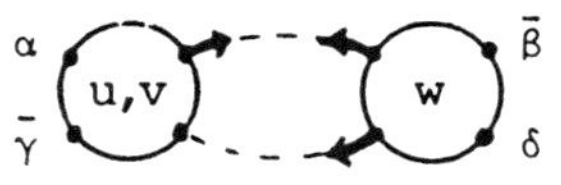

We have

$$CELL_2(u,v) \frown CELL_1(w) = \tau.(CELL_1(u) \frown CELL_2(v,w))$$
$$\approx CELL_1(u) \frown CELL_2(v,w) \quad \text{by Theorem 7.1 .}$$

For the last, we need the fact that $CELL_\$ \frown NIL = CELL_\$$.

Exercise 8.3 Prove this simple fact. ☒

Now (10) and (11) follow:

Lemma 8.3

(1) $CELL_2(u,v) \frown PUSH(s) \approx PUSH(u:v:s)$

(2) $CELL_0 \frown PUSH(s) \approx PUSH(s)$.

Proof Let $s = w_1,\ldots,w_n$; to get (1), use the definition of PUSH, and apply Lemma 8.2(1) repeatedly, then Lemma 8.2(2). To get (2), use Lemma 8.2(3),(4) similarly. Note that $\approx$ is preserved by $\frown$ since the latter is defined without using + . ☒

So by what we did before, we have settled

Theorem 8.4

$$PUSH(\varepsilon) = \alpha x.\ PUSH(x:\varepsilon) + \bar{\gamma}\$.\ NIL$$

$$PUSH(v:s) = \alpha x.\ PUSH(x:v:s) + \bar{\gamma}v.\ PUSH(s) \quad .$$

☒

Exercise 8.4 Analogous to (3), we may specify a queue by

$$QUEUE(\varepsilon) = \alpha x.\ QUEUE(x:\varepsilon) + \bar{\gamma}\$.\ NIL$$
$$QUEUE(v:s) = \alpha x.\ QUEUE(v:s:x) + \bar{\gamma}v.\ QUEUE(s) \quad .$$

(Note that ':' is being used to postfix elements to sequences, as well as for prefixing.) Make a very small change to the behaviour of $CELL_2(x,y)$ (5), and adjust the Lemmas to show that

$$QUEUE(s) = CELL_1(v_1) \frown \ldots \frown CELL_1(v_n) \frown CELL_\$ \qquad (\text{for } s = v_1,\ldots,v_n)$$

satisfies the above equations.

Exercise 8.5 Design $FRONT : \{\alpha,\bar{\beta},\bar{\gamma},\delta\}$ so that

$$FRONT \frown PUSH(s)$$

satisfies the equations (2) for PD(s) .

We were rather careful in our definition (5) of $CELL_2(x,y)$; it must push y down before it can pop x . Was this necessary? By considering diagram (8) and similar derivations you can probably satisfy yourself that $CELL_2(x,y)$ <u>can</u> be allowed to pop x . What happens to our proof though? Let us redefine

$$CELL_2(x,y) \Leftarrow \bar{\gamma}x.\ CELL_1(y) + \bar{\beta}y.\ CELL_1(x)\ .$$

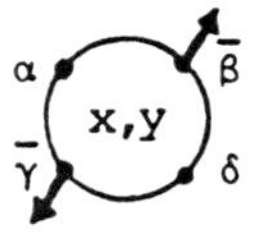

We need only make sure that Lemma 8.2(1),(2) still hold. For the first, we have by expansion

$$CELL_2(u,v) \supset CELL_1(w) =$$
$$\bar{\gamma}u.(CELL_1(v) \supset CELL_1(w)) + \tau.(CELL_1(u) \supset CELL_2(v,w)) \qquad (12)$$

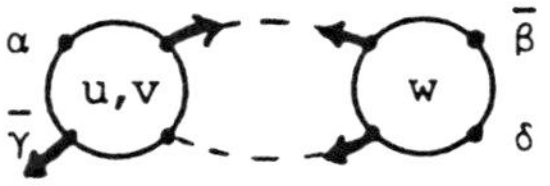

which does not look right. But can the first term be absorbed into the second? By Corollary 7.14 - a derived absorption law - we must show

$$CELL_1(u) \supset CELL_2(v,w) = \bar{\gamma}u.(CELL_1(v) \supset CELL_1(w)) + B \qquad (13)$$

for some B . Expanding the left-hand side gives

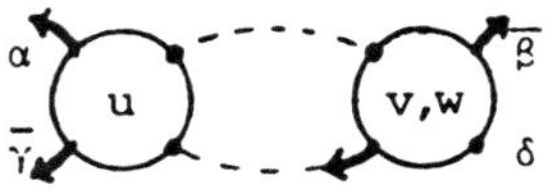

$$CELL_1(u) \supset CELL_2(v,w) = \bar{\gamma}u.(CELL_0 \supset CELL_2(v,w)) + B_1 \qquad (14)$$

while expanding part of this gives

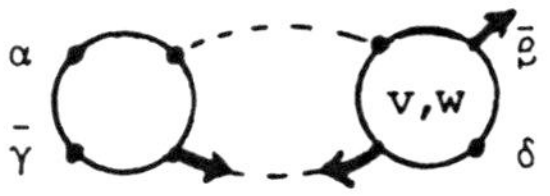

$$CELL_0 \supset CELL_2(v,w) = \tau.(CELL_1(v) \supset CELL_1(w)) + B_2\ . \qquad (15)$$

Now put (14) and (15) together:

$$\begin{aligned} &CELL_1(u) \supset CELL_2(v,w) \\ &\quad = \bar{\gamma}u.(\tau.(CELL_1(v) \supset CELL_1(w)) + B_2) + B_1\ ,\ = B \text{ say,} \\ &\quad = \bar{\gamma}u.(CELL_1(v) \supset CELL_1(w)) + B \quad \text{by Theorem 7.13(3)} \end{aligned}$$

which is what we wanted! We now have (13), and this justifies the step from (12) to

$$CELL_2(u,v) \supset CELL_1(w) = \tau.(CELL_1(u) \supset CELL_2(v,w))\ ,$$

so we still have Lemma 8.2(1).

Exercise 8.5 Show that Lemma 8.2(2) still holds, too.

Exercise 8.6 Give $CELL_0$ some extra freedom as well, and show that all of Lemma 8.2 still holds. Why does extra freedom for $CELL_0$ have no effect on the deduction (12)-(15) above?

Exercise 8.7 Complete the proof of the scheduler, half of which was done in §3.4; it remains to show that the second constraint in Method 1, §3.1, is satisfied. You will almost certainly need the derived absorption law, Corollary 7.14.

Exercise 8.8 Re-examine Exercises 4.3 and 4.4, in the light of our proof techniques.

As a deeper exercise, investigate what happens if the two GATEs in the CONTROL part of the net are removed. CONTROL will not satisfy the same equation, but the whole system may still function as specified. If so, can you prove it?

Exercise 8.9 We can get rid of $CELL_2$ completely from the definition of PUSH by defining

$$CELL_1(y) \Leftarrow \alpha x.(CELL_1(x) \frown CELL_1(y)) + \bar{\gamma} y.\, CELL_0 \quad .$$

(Notice that we could not then adapt our system to form a queue, as in Exercise 8.4!) Carry out the proof for this changed system.

CHAPTER 9

Translation into CCS

9.1 Discussion

Many concurrent algorithms can be expressed in CCS with some lucidity. On the other hand, the aim in designing a high level concurrent language is (in part) to provide and enforce a discipline in the way in which component communicate and share their resources, partly to protect the programmer from unwanted deadlocks. This often restricts (usefully) the behaviours which may be expressed.

If such a language can be translated into CCS, its meaning is thereby determined; we also obtain a way of reasoning about the language. For example, observation equivalences among its programs can be established, and these may yield useful laws for program transformation.

In this chapter we give a translation for a rather simple language. It is a subset of various languages in use; also Hennessy and Plotkin [HP 1] have specified its semantics in detail, in a very different way.

Our translation is quite straightforward; the main reason for this is that the scoping of program variables, which often requires the use of a notion of environment in semantic specifications, is for us represented directly by the restriction operation of CCS. However, when we examine how to translate an enrichment of the language in which procedures may be defined, and each procedure is supposed to admit several concurrent activations, we discover a limitation of CCS in its present form (we can handle a procedure which cannot be concurrently activated, however).

The translation will be seen to be phrase-by-phrase; each phrase of the language becomes a behaviour program which is totally independent of the context of the phrase. (Such translations are sometimes called macro-expansions.) We shall write $[\![C]\!]$ to mean the translation of phrase C. For example

$$[\![\text{IF}\ \ E\ \ \text{THEN}\ \ C\ \ \text{ELSE}\ \ C']\!]$$

will be constructed uniquely from $[\![E]\!]$, $[\![C]\!]$ and $[\![C']\!]$. This means that the construct "IF-THEN-ELSE-" in the source language can be thought of just as a derived ternary behaviour operation. We can then think of the entire source language as a derived behaviour algebra.

.2 The language P

Programs of P are built from expressions E and commands C, using ssignable program variables X. We suppose a fixed set of function symbols ', standing for functions f. A constant symbol is just a nullary function ymbol. We do not specify the value types of expressions.

The syntax of expressions is just

E::= X | F(E,...,E)

(This includes e.g. "+(X,1())" which is written "X+1").

he syntax of commands is

C::=	X:=E	(Assignment)
|	C;C	(Sequential composition)
|	IF E THEN C ELSE C	(Conditional)
|	WHILE E DO C	(Iteration)
|	BEGIN X; C END	(Declaration)
|	C PAR C	(Parallel composition)
|	INPUT X	(Input)
|	OUTPUT E	(Output)
|	SKIP	(No action)

(Parentheses are used to avoid parsing ambiguities).

The main doubt about the meaning of P is to do with PAR. For xample, can the 'concurrent' assignments in the program

X:=0 ;

X:=X+1 PAR X:=X+1

overlap in time? If so, the resulting value of X could be 1 or 2; it not, it must be 2. Our first translation will yield the former; we see how to get the latter afterwards.

.3 Sorts and auxiliary definitions

Each variable X will be represented by a register (§8.2) of sort $\{\alpha_X,\bar{\gamma}_X\}$. Recalling §8.2, we define

$$\text{LOC} \quad :\{\alpha,\bar{\gamma}\} \Leftarrow \alpha x.\text{REG}(x)$$
$$\text{REG}(y):\{\alpha,\bar{\gamma}\} \Leftarrow \alpha x.\text{REG}(x)+\bar{\gamma}y.\text{REG}(y)$$

Thus for X we will have $\text{LOC}_X = \text{LOC}[\alpha_X\gamma_X\backslash\alpha\gamma]$;
we will abbreviate $\text{REG}(y)[\alpha_X\gamma_X\backslash\alpha\gamma]$ by $\text{REG}_X(y)$.

We use $L_X = \{\bar{\alpha}_X, \gamma_X\}$ - the <u>complement</u> of the sort of LOC_X - in defining the sorts of commands and expressions; we call it the <u>access sort</u> of X.

Each n-ary function symbol F (denoting function f) will be represented by

$$b_f \Leftarrow \rho_1 x_1 . \ldots . \rho_n x_n . \bar{\rho}(f(x_1,\ldots,x_n)). \text{NIL}$$

whose sort is $\{\rho_1,\ldots,\rho_n,\bar{\rho}\}$. So for a constant symbol - e.g. 2 - we have $b_2 \Leftarrow \bar{\rho}2.\text{NIL}$.

Each expression E with variables $X_1,\ldots,X_k$ will be represented by a behaviour program of sort $\{\gamma_{X_1},\ldots,\gamma_{X_k},\bar{\rho}\}$. Thus expressions deliver their result at $\bar{\rho}$, and then die; this means that if $[\![E]\!]$ is the translation of E it has the property

$$[\![E]\!] \overset{\ldots.\bar{\rho}v}{\Longrightarrow} B \text{ implies } B = \text{NIL}.$$

In translating commands we often write, for some B,

$$([\![E]\!] \mid \rho x.B)\backslash\rho$$

which we abbreviate to $[\![E]\!]$ result $(\rho x.B)$, defining the behaviour operation <u>result</u> by

$$B_1 \text{ result } B_2 = (B_1 | B_2)\backslash\rho.$$

Each command C with <u>global</u> variables $X_1,\ldots,X_k$ will be represented by a behaviour program of sort $L_{X_1} \cup \ldots \cup L_{X_k} \cup \{\iota,\bar{o},\bar{\delta}\}$. We call this program [it uses $\iota,\bar{o}$ for input and output and signals its completion at $\bar{\delta}$. It then di

so $[\![C]\!] \overset{\ldots.\bar{\delta}}{\Longrightarrow} B$ implies $B = \text{NIL}$

Some auxiliary behaviour operations are useful in defining $[\![C]\!]$;

$$\text{done} = \bar{\delta}.\text{NIL}$$

$$B_1 \text{ before } B_2 = (B_1[\beta/\delta] \mid \beta.B_2)\backslash\beta \qquad (\beta \text{ new})$$

$$B_1 \text{ par } B_2 = (B_1[\delta_1/\delta] \mid B_2[\delta_2/\delta] \mid (\delta_1.\delta_2.\text{done} + \delta_2.\delta_1.\text{done})\backslash\delta_1\backslash\delta_2$$

$$(\delta_1,\delta_2 \text{ new})$$

<u>Exercise 9.1</u> Use the laws of Theorems 5.3, 5.5 and 7.13 to show that <u>before</u> and <u>par</u> are associative, and <u>par</u> is commutative.

We now have all we need to define the translations $[\![E]\!]$ and $[\![C]\!]$ inductively on the structure of phrases.

Exercise 9.2 Prove, by induction on the structure of expressions and commands, that

(i) If E contains variables $X_1,\ldots,X_k$ then $[\![E]\!]$ has the sort $L_{X_1}\cup\ldots\cup L_{X_k}\cup\{\bar{\rho}\}$.

(ii) If the non-local (free) variables of C are $X_1,\ldots,X_k$ then $[\![C]\!]$ has the sort $L_{X_1}\cup\ldots\cup L_{X_k}\cup\{\iota,\bar{o},\bar{\delta}\}$. (Note that X is local (bound) in BEGIN X; C END.)

Many simple equivalences over P can be shown from the translation. Here are a few as exercises.

Exercise 9.3

(i) Prove $[\![\text{SKIP;C}]\!] \approx [\![\text{C}]\!]$

(ii) Prove $[\![\text{WHILE E DO C}]\!] \sim [\![\text{IF E THEN (C; WHILE E DO C) ELSE SKIP}]\!]$

(iii) If X is not a free variable of C, prove

$[\![\text{BEGIN X; C END}]\!] \sim [\![\text{C}]\!]$

$[\![\text{BEGIN X; C; C' END}]\!] \sim [\![\text{C; BEGIN X; C' END}]\!]$

$[\![\text{BEGIN X; C PAR C' END}]\!] \sim [\![\text{C PAR (BEGIN X; C' END)}]\!]$

(iv) If X is not in E, prove

$[\![\text{BEGIN X; IF E THEN C ELSE C' END}]\!] \sim$

$[\![\text{IF E THEN (BEGIN X; C END) ELSE (BEGIN X; C' END)}]\!]$

and investigate

? $[\![\text{BEGIN X; WHILE E DO C END}]\!] \sim [\![\text{WHILE E DO BEGIN X; C END}]\!]$?

(v) What can you conclude from Exercise 9.1?

Exercise 9.4 Show that $[\![X:=X+1]\!] \overset{c}{\approx} \gamma_X x.\bar{\alpha}_X(x+1).\text{done}$. Simplify $[\![X:=0]\!]$ similarly. Now show, by brute force and expansion, that

$[\![\text{BEGIN X; X:=0; (X:=X + 1 PAR X:=X + 1); OUTPUT X END}]\!]$

$\approx [\![\text{OUTPUT 1}]\!] + [\![\text{OUTPUT 2}]\!]$

(Recall the properties of $\approx$ and $\overset{c}{\approx}$, listed in §7.5)

9.3 Translation of P

For expressions:

$$[\![X]\!] = \gamma_X x.\bar{\rho}x.\mathrm{NIL}$$

$$[\![F(E_1,\ldots,E_n)]\!] = ([\![E_1]\!][\rho_1/\rho]|\ldots|[\![E_n]\!][\rho_n/\rho]|b_f)\backslash\rho_1\ldots\backslash\rho_n$$

For commands:

$[\![X:=E]\!] = [\![E]\!]$ result $(\rho x.\bar{\alpha}_X x.\mathrm{done})$

$[\![C;C']\!] = [\![C]\!]$ before $[\![C']\!]$

$[\![$IF E THEN C ELSE C'$]\!] =$

$[\![E]\!]$ result $\rho x.($<u>if</u> x <u>then</u> $[\![C]\!]$ <u>else</u> $[\![C']\!])$

$[\![$WHILE E DO C$]\!] =$ w, a new behaviour identifier,

with w $\Leftarrow [\![E]\!]$ result $(\rho x.$ <u>if</u> x <u>then</u> $([\![C]\!]$ before w) <u>else</u> done)

$[\![$BEGIN X; C END$]\!] = (\mathrm{LOC}_X|[\![C]\!])\backslash L_X$

$[\![$C PAR C'$]\!] = [\![C]\!]$ par $[\![C']\!]$

$[\![$INPUT X$]\!] = \iota x.\bar{\alpha}_X x.\mathrm{done}$

$[\![$OUTPUT E$]\!] = [\![E]\!]$ result $(\rho x.\bar{o}x.\mathrm{done})$

$[\![$SKIP$]\!] =$ done

<u>Remarks</u>

(1) We are using $\backslash L_X$ to abbreviate $\backslash\alpha_X\backslash\gamma_X$, as was done in §8.2.

(2) The identifier w for the WHILE command must be different for every such command translated. A minor extension to CCS, adding expressions of the form

fix b.B

(in which b is a behaviour identifier bound by the prefix "fix") would avoid this inelegance. Such an expression may be understood as

b, where b $\Leftarrow$ B

where the identifier chosen is distinct from all others used. (The notation can be extended to match the definition of parameterised behaviour identifiers.) With the "fix" notation, we would write

$[\![$WHILE E DO C$]\!] =$ fix w. $[\![E]\!]$ result (...) .

.4 Adding procedures to P

The block BEGIN X; C END creates a resource X for use by C;
ıe resource X is represented by a behaviour, accessed through the sort
$_X$.

Procedures (of many different kinds) are examples of other resources
› create. Let us add a new syntax class of declarations D to our
anguage, with the understanding that each declaration D is to be
ccessed through an access sort L_D. Then we generalise the syntax of
lock commands to

BEGIN D; C END

ıd begin the syntactic definition of declarations by

D ::= VAR X | ....

ıe uniform translation of blocks will be

$$[\![\text{BEGIN D; C END}]\!] = ([\![D]\!] \mid [\![C]\!])\backslash L_D$$

nd the translation of variable declarations is now

$$[\![\text{VAR X}]\!] = \text{LOC}_X \quad \text{(with access sort } L_X)$$

ariables are particular in that they communicate only with their accessors;
his is reflected in the fact that the sort of LOC_X is just $\bar{L}_X$. Procedures
ay, we suppose, contain free variables and call other procedures, so the
orresponding behaviours will have a sort larger than the complement of the
ccess sort.

Let us define

D ::= VAR X | PROC G (VALUE X, RESULT Y) IS C_G

nd add to the syntax of commands

C ::= .... |CALL G(E, Z)

he procedure declaration indicates that G is a one-argument procedure,
aking its argument (by value) into a local variable X; the body of G
command C_G) has free variables X and Y and the result of the pro-
edure is the value in Y on completion. The call passes the value of E
s argument, and assigns the result to variable Z. The access sort of G
s to be $L_G = \{\bar{\alpha}_G, \gamma_G\}$, and we can immediately write the translation of a

procedure call:

$$[\![\text{CALL G (E,Z)}]\!] = [\![E]\!] \text{ result } (\rho x.\bar{\alpha}_G x.\gamma_G z.\bar{\alpha}_Z z.\text{done})$$

We now have to say that the sort of $[\![C]\!]$, when C has free variables $X_1,\ldots,X_k$ and free procedure identifiers $G_1,\ldots,G_m$, is $L_{X_1} \cup\ldots\cup L_{X_k} \cup L_{G_1} \cup\ldots\cup L_{G_m} \cup\{\iota,\bar{o},\bar{\delta}\}$. This will follow from the definition of $[\![D]\!]$ for a procedure declaration. (In fact sort-checking is a good first guide to correct definition, like type-checking in good programming languages and dimension-analysis in school mechanics.)

We can give a first approximation (wrong for at least two reasons) to the translation of procedure declarations:

$$? \; [\![\text{PROC G(VALUE X, RESULT Y) IS } C_G]\!] = g, \text{ where}$$
$$g \Leftarrow (LOC_X | LOC_Y | (\alpha_G x.\bar{\alpha}_X x.[\![C_G]\!] \text{ before } \gamma_Y y.\bar{\gamma}_G y.\text{NIL}))\backslash L_X \backslash L_Y$$

Notice that this has sort $L_G \cup L_C-(L_X \cup L_Y \cup \{\bar{\delta}\})$ where L_C is the sort of C_G; this will make the sort of the block right.

Are the free variables of C_G treated properly? What output do we expect from the following command C_O?

```
BEGIN VAR Z; Z:=3;
   BEGIN PROC G (VALUE X, RESULT Y) IS Y:=Z;
      BEGIN VAR Z;
         CALL G (17, Z);
         OUTPUT Z
      END
   END
END
```

The answer should be "3", since the body of G should use the outer Z. If it used the inner Z the answer would be "no output" since locations cannot be used before they are assigned.

<u>Exercise 9.5</u> If you are interested to see how a mechanical evaluator for P (via CCS) might work, simplify $[\![C_O]\!]$ <u>by first simplifying the translations of subphrases as far as possible</u>, and obtain

$$[\![C_O]\!] \overset{c}{\approx} [\![\text{OUTPUT 3}]\!] \approx \bar{o}3.\text{done}.$$

The first mistake in g above is that it is not much use as a resource, since it dies after one use! Our other resources (registers) restore themselves (with possibly changed content) after use, so we may make g do the same.

Second approximation:

$$? [\![\text{PROC } G(\text{VALUE } X, \text{ RESULT } Y) \text{ IS } C_G]\!] = g, \quad \text{where}$$
$$g \Leftarrow (LOC_X | LOC_Y | (\alpha_G x.\bar{\alpha}_X x.[\![C_g]\!] \text{ before } \gamma_Y y.\bar{\gamma}_G y.g))\backslash L_X\backslash L_Y$$

So the last thing g does is to restore itself. Notice that the restored g is of form $(\ldots)\backslash L_X\backslash L_Y$, so its local variables X,Y are not those of the old g. But you should see how to allow G to have "own" variables which are initialized at declaration and persist from call to call.

Exercise 9.6 Translate the extended declaration

PROC G(VALUE X, RESULT Y) OWN Z:= E is C_G

so that G's "own" variable Z is initialised at declaration to the value of E.

The second mistake in g is that there is no provision for it to call itself recursively. If C_G contains CALL G(-,-) then it will demand a reply to $\bar{\alpha}_G v$ for some value v, and nothing can meet it. What could meet it? The answer is: a fresh resource g for use by C_G. Taking the clue from the translation of blocks (which is the way resources are provided for use), we obtain finally

$$[\![\text{PROC } G(\text{VALUE } X, \text{ RESULT } Y) \text{ IS } C_G]\!] = g, \quad \text{where}$$
$$g \Leftarrow (LOC_X | LOC_Y | (\alpha_G x.\bar{\alpha}_X x.(g|[\![C_G]\!])\backslash L_G \text{ before } \gamma_Y y.\bar{\gamma}_G y.g))\backslash L_X\backslash L_Y$$
$$\text{(with access sort } L_G)$$

Exercise 9.7 If $[\![C_G]\!]$ has sort L_C, check that

$$g: \; L_G \cup L_C - (L_X \cup L_Y \cup \{\bar{\delta}\})$$

yields the same sort for the right hand side of g's definition.

It is rather hard work to evaluate even simple recursive P programs by hand via CCS. What would be the point of evaluating them? Well, the purpose of our translation is to investigate the power of CCS, and also to indicate that properties of languages such as P (as distinct from properties of particular P programs) may thereby be established. But a check on the validity of the translation would be helpful, and could be provided by a mechanical CCS simplifier/evaluator. Peter Mosses has shown how Scott-Strachey semantic specifications expressed in the lambda-calculus can be checked out by a lambda simplifier/evaluator [Mos].

We must now examine a shortcoming of our translation of procedure declarations. Since g only restores itself <u>after</u> returning $(\bar{\gamma}_G y)$ its result, it follows that although there may be concurrent calls of G within the block of the declaration, for example

CALL G(6,Z) PAR CALL G(7,W),

the resulting executions of C_G will not be overlapped in time; one must take priority, while the other waits to use the restored g. (It cannot access the inner g provided for recursive calls of G by itself; that is restricted by $\backslash L_G$.) At first sight, we might hope to allow for concurrent activations of G by making g restore itself directly after receiving its argument:

$$? \ [\![\text{PROC G(VALUE X, RESULT Y) IS } C_G]\!] = g, \text{ where}$$
$$g \Leftarrow \alpha_G x.(g \mid (LOC_X \mid LOC_Y \mid (\bar{\alpha}_X x.(g \mid [\![C_G]\!]) \backslash L_G \text{ before } \gamma_Y y.\bar{\gamma}_G y.NIL) \backslash L_X \backslash L_Y)$$

(Note that we still have guarded recursion). Now the restored g may be activated immediately after the first, and run concurrently with it. But we cannot be sure that the two (or more) g's will return their results $(\bar{\gamma}_G y)$ to the correct calling sequences - each of which is waiting on $\gamma_G z$!

There seems no natural solution to this problem in CCS as it now stands. True, we may generously allow some fixed number of g's to be created, as separate resources, by the declaration. This could be done by

$$? \ [\![\text{PROC G(VALUE X, RESULT Y) IS } C_G]\!] = gs, \text{ where}$$
$$gs \Leftarrow \prod_{1 \le i \le N} g_i, \quad \text{and for each } i$$

$$g_i \Leftarrow \alpha_{G,i} x.(LOC_X \mid LOC_Y \mid (\bar{\alpha}_X x.(gs \mid [\![C_G]\!]) \backslash L_G \text{ before } \gamma_Y y.\bar{\gamma}_{G,i} y.g_i)) \backslash L_X \backslash L$$

with $L_G = \{\bar{\alpha}_{G,i}, \gamma_{G,i}; \ 1 \le i \le N\}$ now.

Notice that each g_i restores itself after completion; only the N distinct g_i can be concurrently active. The calling sequence must also be adjusted:

$$[\![\text{CALL } G(E,Z)]\!] = [\![E]\!] \text{ result } (\rho x.\sum_{1\le i\le N}\bar{\alpha}_{G,i}x.\gamma_{G,i}z.\bar{\alpha}_Z z.\text{done})$$

This solution has one attraction; it may be realistic if we assume a fixed bound N on the number of processors available. But we are looking for solutions at a level of abstraction at which implementation is not yet considered.

Even so, the 'right' solution is suggested by what implementors often do; that is, for each call of G to supply a return link along with the argument. Each activation then knows which return link to use in returning its result. But in CCS this would mean passing labels (or names) as values, which we have excluded.

It is not trivial to give CCS this ability, and yet retain the theory which we have developed, but it may be possible (in exploratory discussions with Mogens Nielsen we have seen some chances). The fact that we have not met this need until now shows that much can be done without name-passing, but its usefulness is certainly not limited to language translations. We must leave the matter open.

Exercise 9.8 Generalise the (correct!) translation of procedure declaration to allow several procedures to be declared mutually recursively (as a single resource) by

PROC G_1 (VALUE X_1, RESULT Y_1) IS C_1
AND - - -
- - - - -
AND G_k (VALUE X_k, RESULT Y_k) IS C_k

9.5 Protection of resources

We finish this chapter with some tentative remarks about mutual exclusion between commands in P which would otherwise run concurrently. There is no doubt that we can, in CCS, represent some methods for providing mutual exclusion, but to provide methods which are robust, flexible and elegant is a very hard problem of high-level language design which is still not fully solved though it has been studied for about ten years.

See for example [Hoa 1,2], [Bri 1]. CCS is unprejudiced, and intentionally so, towards the problem; what it can do is to provide a means for rigorously assessing a proposed solution.

If all we want is to prevent overlapped execution of assignment commands assigning to the same variable, it is easy to adopt the well-known semaphore method. As in §2.4, define

$$\mathrm{SEM}:\{\bar{\pi},\bar{\phi}\} \Leftarrow \bar{\pi}.\bar{\phi}.\mathrm{SEM}$$

$$\mathrm{SEM}_X = \mathrm{SEM}[\pi_X\phi_X/\pi\phi]$$

and redefine

$$\mathrm{LOC}_X = (\alpha x.\mathrm{REG}_X(x))\,|\,\mathrm{SEM}_X$$

The access sort L_X for resource X becomes

$$L_X = \{\bar{\alpha},\gamma,\pi,\phi\}$$

and the only change in translation is to redefine

$$[\![X:=E]\!] = \pi.[\![E]\!] \text{ result } (\rho x.\bar{\alpha}_X x.\phi.\mathrm{done}).$$

Exercise 9.9 Re-work Exercise 9.4 with this new translation, getting .... $\approx[\![$OUTPUT 2$]\!]$ instead of .... $\approx[\![$OUTPUT 1$]\!]$ + $[\![$OUTPUT 2$]\!]$.

An alternative, to allow larger commands to exclude each other, is to adopt the proposal of Hoare in "Towards a theory of parallel programming" (referenced earlier). The idea is to allow the programmer to declare arbitrary abstract resources, by adding a new declaration form

D::= .... |RESOURCE R

(where R is an arbitrary identifier) and a new command form

C::= .... |WITH R DO C

For example, the programmer may associate a particular R with the output device, and adopt the discipline that every OUTPUT command occurs within a "WITH R ..." context; he can thus protect a sequence of OUTPUT commands from interference. In translation, R is just a semaphore, so we specify

$$[\![\mathrm{RESOURCE}\ R\,]\!] = \mathrm{SEM}_R \quad \text{(with access sort } L_R = \{\pi_R,\phi_R\})$$

and

$$[\![\mathrm{WITH}\ R\ \mathrm{DO}\ C]\!] = \pi_R.[\![C]\!] \text{ before } (\phi_R.\mathrm{done})$$

Hoare discusses the virtues and vices of this discipline. In particular, he points out the possiblity of deadly embrace, or deadlock, as in

(WITH R DO WITH R' DO C) PAR (WITH R' DO WITH R DO C')

But he observes that a compile-time check can prevent this; the program must be such that any nesting of "WITH R .... " commands, with distinct R's, must agree with the declaration nesting of the R's. For our translation we must add that, in "WITH R DO C", C must not contain "WITH R ..." for the same R. Also the check must be more sophisticated in presence of procedures, but can still be done by flow-analysis techniques.

Now we can formally state deadlock-freedom for C as follows:

If $[\![C]\!] \stackrel{s}{\Longrightarrow} B$ is a complete derivation (§4.4),

ie $B \sim NIL$, then $s = r\bar{\delta}$ for some r.

(C does not 'die' without signalling completion at $\bar{\delta}$). When the compile-time check is satisfied, it should be possible to prove this property of commands (or a stronger property which implies it) by induction on their structure, though we have not done it. But first we would have to remove a simple source of deadlock - namely the attempt to use an unassigned variable. This can be done by, for example, respecifying

$$[\![VAR\ X]\!] = REG_X(0) \quad (\text{not } LOC_X) .$$

The proof would be a lot easier without procedures.

CHAPTER 10

Determinacy and Confluence

10.1 Discussion

In CCS, non-determinate behaviours (in some sense of determinacy) are the rule rather than the exception. The outcome - or even the capability - of future observations may not be predictable, partly because the order of two interdependent internal communications may affect it, and partly because of the presence of two or more identical guards in a sum of guards (e.g. $\tau.B_1 + \tau.B_2$ or $\alpha.B_1 + \alpha.B_2$) .

Nevertheless, we would probably classify almost all our case-studies as determinate in some sense; the exception is the root-finding algorithm of Chapter 4, where the root found depends upon the relative speeds of concurrent function evaluations.

In this chapter we make precise a notion of Determinacy, and a related concept Confluence, and show that a certain easily characterized subclass of behaviour programs is guaranteed to be determinate. This class also admits a simple proof technique. It is not a trivial class; for example, the Scheduling system of Chapter 3 falls within it, and in §10.5 we complete its correctness proof using the special technique.

In this Chapter we shall for simplicity revert to pure synchronization; that is, no variables or value expressions in guards. The results here probably generalise smoothly to full CCS but we have not studied it.

As a first approximation, one may think it enough to say that B is determinate if, whenever $B \xrightarrow{\lambda} B_1$ and $B \xrightarrow{\lambda} B_2$ for some λ, then B_1 and B_2 are equivalent (e.g. $\sim$ or $\approx$); of course we would again require B_1 and B_2 to be determinate. But this is not enough; for example $B \xrightarrow{\tau} NIL$ may also hold, implying that the capability of a λ-experiment is not determined though the outcome is! This motivates our definition of confluence. We shall treat notions of strong confluence and strong determinacy (so called because they are allied to strong equivalence) in detail first - they will be enough to give us the results we need here - and later we outline a more general notion which is allied to observation equivalence.

10.2 Strong confluence

Our notion of strong confluence will not imply determinacy in the sense of the last section. We separate it from determinacy because, by itself, it implies a property of programs which supports our proof technique. But determinacy will be needed as well when we show that all programs written in a certain derived calculus of CCS are confluent and therefore admit the technique.

The following proposition can be read as a definition of strong confluence, except that it 'defines' the property in terms of itself:

<u>Proposition 10.1</u> The behaviour program A is strongly confluent iff

(i) Whenever $A \overset{\mu}{\to} B$ and $A \overset{\nu}{\to} C$ then <u>either</u> $\mu = \nu$ and $B \sim C$ <u>or</u> there exist D and E such that $B \overset{\nu}{\to} D$, $C \overset{\mu}{\to} E$ and $D \sim E$.

(ii) Whenever $A \overset{\mu}{\to} B$, B is strongly confluent.

<u>Proof:</u> Immediate from the definition to follow. ⊠

We may picture condition (i) as

$$\begin{array}{ccc} & & B \\ & \overset{\mu}{\nearrow} & \\ A & & \\ & \underset{\nu}{\searrow} & \\ & & C \end{array} \qquad \text{implies } \underline{\text{either}}\ \ \mu = \nu \ \ \& \ \ B \sim C \ \ \underline{\text{or}} \qquad \begin{array}{ccc} B & \xrightarrow{\nu} & D \\ & & \wr \\ C & \xrightarrow{\mu} & E \end{array}$$

Such diagrams will be useful in proofs. Note that if $\mu = \nu$ we have two possibilities; the case $B \sim C$ represents intuitively that $A \overset{\mu}{\to} B$ and $A \overset{\mu}{\to} C$ are essentially the "same action". Our definition of determinacy will demand that this <u>must</u> be the case for $\mu \in \Lambda$, but we do not want to demand this for $\mu = \tau$; $A \overset{\tau}{\to} B$ and $A \overset{\tau}{\to} C$ may arise, for example, from two different internal communications.

Now for our formal definition. As usual, we have to resort to a sequence of properties for $k \geq 0$.

<u>Definition</u> A is always <u>strongly 0-confluent</u> .

A is <u>strongly (k+1)-confluent</u> iff

(i) $A \begin{array}{l} \overset{\mu}{\nearrow} B \\ \underset{\nu}{\searrow} C \end{array}$ implies <u>either</u> $\mu = \nu$ and $B \sim C$ <u>or</u> $\begin{array}{ccc} B & \overset{\nu}{\to} & D \\ & & \wr \\ C & \overset{\mu}{\to} & E \end{array}$

for some D and E ;

(ii) $A \overset{\mu}{\to} B$ implies B strongly k-confluent.

A is <u>strongly confluent</u> iff it is strongly k-confluent for all $k \geq 0$.

Let us abbreviate "strongly confluent", "strongly k-confluent" by SC, SC_k respectively. We first want to know that SC is a property of strong equivalence classes, not just of programs.

<u>Proposition</u> 10.2 If A is SC and $A \sim A'$ then A' is SC.

<u>Proof</u> We show by induction on k that if A is SC_k and $A \sim A'$ then A' is SC_k . At $k=0$ there is nothing to prove. Assume at k , and at $k+1$ assume A is SC_{k+1} and $A \sim A'$.

For part (ii) of the definition, if $A' \overset{\mu}{\to} B'$ then by Theorem 5.6 $A \overset{\mu}{\to} B \sim B'$ for some B ; but B is SC_k, hence by inductive hypothesis so is B' .

For part (i), suppose

$$A' \begin{array}{l} \overset{\mu}{\nearrow} B' \\ \underset{\nu}{\searrow} C' \end{array} \quad \text{, yielding for some B,C} \quad \begin{array}{ccccc} & & & & B' \\ & \overset{\mu}{\nearrow} & & & \wr \\ A' & \sim & A & \overset{\mu}{\to} & B \\ & & & \underset{\nu}{\searrow} & C \\ & \underset{\nu}{\searrow} & & & \wr \\ & & & & C' \end{array}$$

Then (since A is SC_{k+1}) <u>either</u> $\mu = \nu$ and $B \sim C$, so $B' \sim C'$, <u>or</u> for some D,E and D',E'

$$\begin{array}{ccc} B' & \overset{\nu}{\longrightarrow} & D' \\ \wr & & \wr \\ B & \overset{\nu}{\longrightarrow} & D \\ & & \wr \\ C & \overset{\mu}{\longrightarrow} & E \\ \wr & & \wr \\ C' & \overset{\mu}{\longrightarrow} & E' \end{array} \quad , \quad \text{so} \quad \begin{array}{ccc} B' & \overset{\nu}{\longrightarrow} & D' \\ & & \wr \\ C' & \overset{\mu}{\longrightarrow} & E' \end{array}$$

⊠

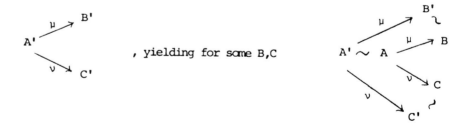

However, SC is not preserved by $\approx$ or $\overset{c}{\approx}$; for example

$$\alpha.\beta.\mathrm{NIL} + \beta.\alpha.\mathrm{NIL} \overset{c}{\approx} \alpha.\beta.\mathrm{NIL} + \beta.\tau.\alpha.\mathrm{NIL}$$

while the first is SC, the second is not. We take up this question later.

For our main property of SC we first need a lemma to do with longer derivations.

<u>Lemma 10.3</u> If A is SC and $A \xrightarrow{\mu} B$, $A \xrightarrow{\mu_1 \cdots \mu_n} C$ then

<u>either</u> $\mu = \mu_i$ (some i) and $B \xrightarrow{\mu_1 \cdots \mu_{i-1}\mu_{i+1} \cdots \mu_n} D$, $D \sim C$, <u>or</u> $B \xrightarrow{\mu_1 \cdots \mu_n} D$, $C \xrightarrow{\mu} E$, $D \sim E$.

<u>Proof</u> By induction on n. For $n = 0$, C is A and take D,E to be B. At $n+1$ we have

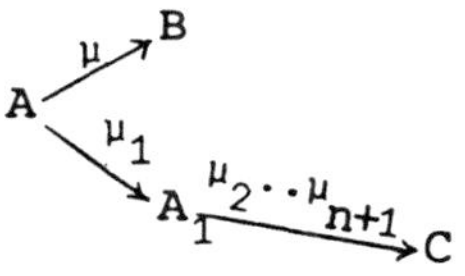

so <u>either</u> $\mu = \mu_1$ and $A_1 \sim B$, whence $B \xrightarrow{\mu_2 \cdots \mu_{n+1}} D \sim C$ by Theorem 5.6, <u>or</u> (first case of inductive hypothesis for A_1) $\mu = \mu_i$ $(i \geq 2)$ and

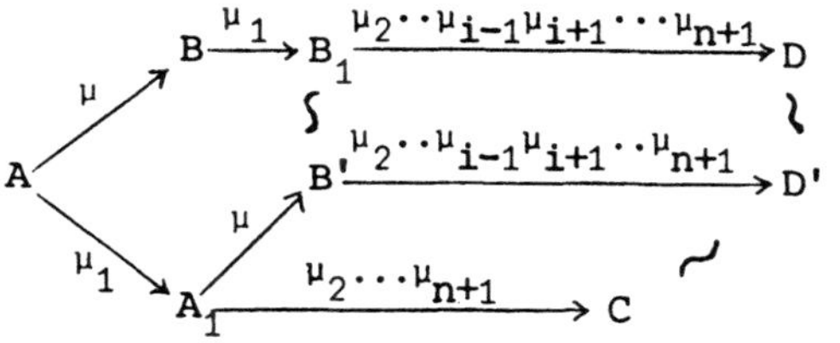

finding first B, B' since A is SC, then D' since A_1 is SC, then D, or (second case of inductive hypothesis)

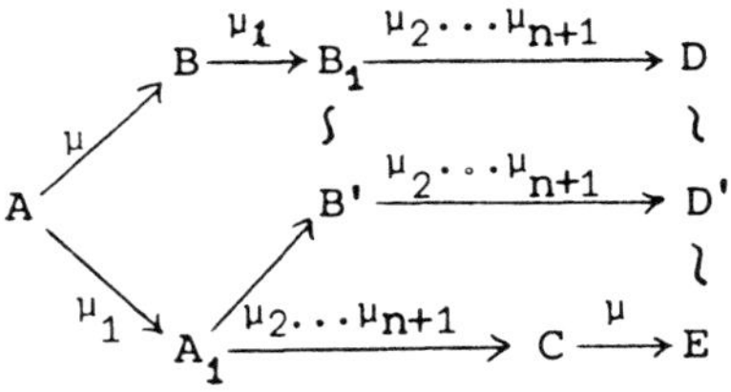

⊠

Now we can deduce our main property as an important special case.

<u>Theorem 10.4</u> (Strong Confluence). If A is SC and $A \xrightarrow{\tau} B$ then $A \approx B$.

<u>Proof</u> We show that if A is SC and $A \xrightarrow{\tau} B$ then $A \approx_k B$, by induction on k. Trivial at $k=0$; assume it at k, and at $k+1$ assume A is SC and $A \xrightarrow{\tau} B$.

(i) If $B \overset{s}{\Longrightarrow} B'$ clearly $A \overset{s}{\Longrightarrow} B'$ also.

(ii) Let $A \overset{s}{\Longrightarrow} A'$. Then from Lemma 10.3 we have, for some B',

either $\begin{array}{c} B \overset{s}{\Longrightarrow} B' \\ \wr \\ A' \end{array}$ or $\begin{array}{c} B \overset{s}{\Longrightarrow} B' \\ \wr \\ A' \xrightarrow{\tau} A'' \end{array}$

In the second case, since A' is SC (Proposition 10.1), $A' \approx_k A''$ by inductive hypothesis; but $\sim$ implies $\approx_k$ (Theorem 7.2) so in either case $A' \approx_k B'$ as required. ⊠

The usefulness of the Strong Confluence Theorem is simply this: a program A may admit many actions, and so may its derivatives, but to find a B such that $A \approx B$ we need only follow an ε-derivation (a sequence of τ-actions) starting from A, provided we know A to be SC.

To follow all other derivations (as, in effect, the Expansion Theorem would do when repeatedly applied to $A, A_1, \ldots$) would often be heavy work - and is unnecessary in this case.

In the next section we illustrate this saving on a toy example, which we assume to be confluent (later it will be seen to be so on general grounds). But we first need to define a class of derived behaviour operations, called composite action.

).3 Composite guards, and the use of confluence

For $\mu_i \in \Lambda \cup \{\tau\}$, $(\mu_1|\cdots|\mu_n)$ is a <u>composite guard</u> $(n \geq 1)$ whose :tions are given as follows, in the style of §5.3 (see Exercise 10.2, id of §10.4, for richer composite guards):

<u>n > 1</u> $(\mu_1|\cdots|\mu_n).B \xrightarrow{\mu_i} (\mu_1|\cdots|\mu_{i-1}|\mu_{i+1}|\cdots|\mu_n).B$

for each i, $1 \leq i \leq n$

<u>n = 1</u> $(\mu_1).B \xrightarrow{\mu_1} B$

:om this it is easy to deduce the following strong equivalences:

<u>:oposition 10.5</u>

1) $(\mu_1).B \sim \mu_1.B$

2) For $n > 1$, $(\mu_1|\cdots|\mu_n).B \sim \sum_{1 \leq i \leq n} \mu_i.(\mu_1|\cdots|\mu_{i-1}|\mu_{i+1}|\cdots|\mu_n).B$

3) For any permutation p of $\{1,\ldots,n\}$, $(\mu_1|\cdots|\mu_n).B \sim (\mu_{p(1)}|\cdots|\mu_{p(n)}).B$

<u>:oof</u> Omitted. ☒

›r example $(\alpha|\beta|\gamma).B \sim \alpha.(\beta|\gamma).B + \beta.(\alpha|\gamma).B + \gamma.(\alpha|\beta).B \sim (\beta|\gamma|\alpha).B$; : just means that α,β,γ can be done in any order. Note that we do not equire $\mu_1,\ldots,\mu_n$ to be distinct.

In some proofs it is convenient to define $(\mu_1|\cdots|\mu_n).A$ to be A, ıen $n = 0$.

We now want to examine the toy system built from the cycler of

S

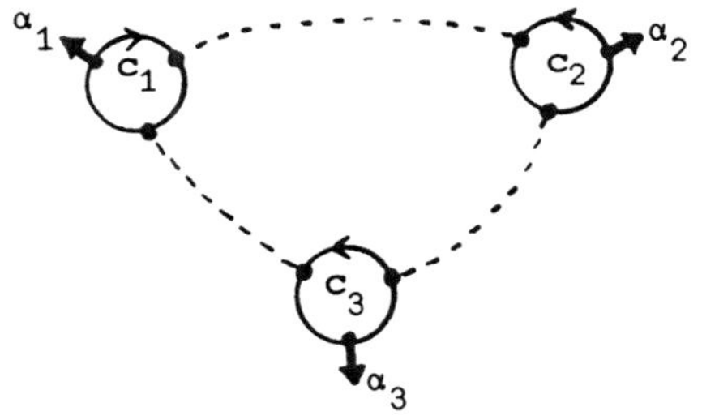

xercise 2.7; notice that c_1 is cycling clockwise, while c_2 and c_3 re cycling anticlockwise. Before going further you might try to guess ts behaviour (as the author did, for five minutes, and got it wrong).

We have

$c_1 \Leftarrow \alpha_1.\beta.\delta.c_1$
$c_2 \Leftarrow \alpha_2.\bar{\beta}.\gamma.c_2$
$c_3 \Leftarrow \alpha_3.\bar{\gamma}.\bar{\delta}.c_3$

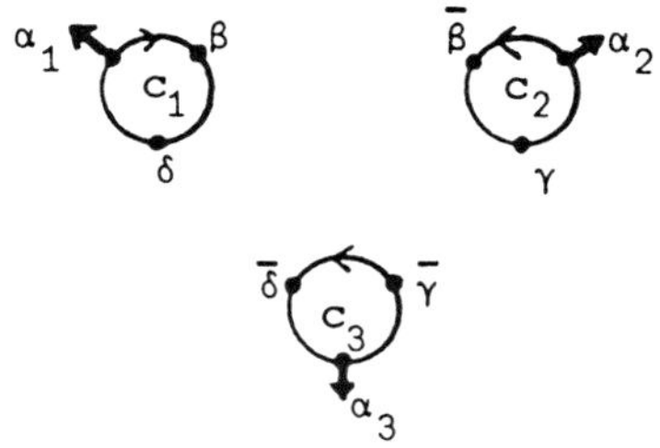

and

S is $(c_1|c_2|c_3)\backslash A$. $(A = \{\beta,\gamma,\delta\})$

We assume S strongly confluent. Now by expansion

$S \sim \alpha_1.S_{23} + \alpha_2.S_{13} + \alpha_3.S_{12}$

where S_{23} is $(\beta.\delta.c_1|c_2|c_3)\backslash A$,

S_{13} is $(c_1|\bar{\beta}.\gamma.c_2|c_3)\backslash A$

and S_{12} is $(c_1|c_2|\bar{\gamma}.\bar{\delta}.c_3)\backslash A$.

By expansion again,

$S_{23} \sim \alpha_2.S_3 + \alpha_3.S_2$

where S_3 is $(\beta.\delta.c_1|\bar{\beta}.\gamma.c_2|c_3)\backslash A$

and S_2 is $(\beta.\delta.c_1|c_2|\bar{\gamma}.\bar{\delta}.c_3)\backslash A$,

$S_{13} \sim \alpha_1.S_3 + \alpha_3.S_1$

where S_1 is $(c_1|\bar{\beta}.\gamma.c_2|\bar{\gamma}.\bar{\delta}.c_3)\backslash A$,

and $S_{12} \sim \alpha_1.S_2 + \alpha_2.S_1$.

Now we need to consider S_0

where S_0 is $(\beta.\delta.c_1|\bar{\beta}.\gamma.c_2|\bar{\beta}.\bar{\gamma}.c_3)\backslash A$,

and we find

$$S_0 \xrightarrow{\tau} (\delta.c_1|\gamma.c_2|\bar{\gamma}.\bar{\delta}.c_3)\backslash A$$
$$\xrightarrow{\tau} (\delta.c_1|c_2|\bar{\delta}.c_3)\backslash A$$
$$\xrightarrow{\tau} S \qquad (\dagger)$$

whence by confluence $S_0 \approx S$. Also

$S_1 \sim \alpha_1.S_0$ (by Expansion) $\approx \alpha_1.S$,

$S_2 \sim \alpha_2.S_0 \approx \alpha_2.S$

while for S_3 we have something different:

$$S_3 \xrightarrow{\tau} (\delta.c_1|\gamma.c_2|c_3)\backslash A$$
$$\sim \alpha_3.(\delta.c_1|\gamma.c_2|\bar{\gamma}.\bar{\delta}.c_3)\backslash A \quad \text{by Expansion}$$
$$\approx \alpha_3.S \quad \text{by the same derivation as for } S_0 \text{ above,}$$

ence by confluence $S_3 \approx \alpha_3.S$.

finally we get

$$S_{12} \overset{c}{\approx} (\alpha_1|\alpha_2).S \;, \quad S_{13} \overset{c}{\approx} (\alpha_1|\alpha_3).S \;, \quad S_{23} \overset{c}{\approx} (\alpha_2|\alpha_3).S$$

d at last

$$S \overset{c}{\approx} (\alpha_1|\alpha_2|\alpha_3).S$$

ich specifies our system. It was only at (†) that we were able to nore other actions in following a ε-derivation, but such opportunities ll abound in even slightly bigger systems.

Here, we used composite actions only to abbreviate expressions which obtained. Later, we will see that composite guarding preserves confluence.

e final remark: in the above calculation we were careful only to assume rong confluence of S, its derivatives, and expressions strongly equi- alent to them. All this is justified by Propositions 10.1 and 10.2, but could well have wished to assume confluence of an expression which is ly <u>observation equivalent</u> to something confluent. As we said earlier, servation equivalence does not preserve <u>strong</u> confluence; but it does reserve a weaker form as we shall see, and fortunately Theorem 10.4 applies lso to the weaker form - so all is well.

<u>xercise 10.1</u> Use confluence to find the behaviour of other systems with the same shape as S, or as Exercise 2.7(i), but with different cycling directions and/or different starting states (initial capabilities).

Is the disjoiner d of Exercise 2.7 strongly confluent? What about the behaviour s in Exercise 2.7(ii)?

10.4 Strong determinacy; Confluent Determinate CCS

The natural definition of determinacy is as follows:

Definition Let $\lambda \in \Lambda$, and let A be a program. Then A is strongly λ-determinate (λ-SD) iff for all k A is strongly λ-k-determinate (λ-SD_k), where:

Every A is λ-SD_0;

A is λ-SD_{k+1} iff

(i) $A \overset{\lambda}{\rightarrow} B$, $A \overset{\lambda}{\rightarrow} C$ implies $B \sim C$;

(ii) $A \overset{\mu}{\rightarrow} B$ implies B is λ-SD_k.

Definition A is strongly k-determinate (SD_k) iff it is λ-SD_k for all $\lambda \in \Lambda$. A is strongly determinate (SD) iff it is SD_k for all k.

λ-determinacy for particular λ may have some use, but we will only consider determinacy for all λ.

Proposition 10.6

A is SD iff

(i) $A \overset{\lambda}{\rightarrow} B$, $A \overset{\lambda}{\rightarrow} C$ implies $B \sim C$;

(ii) $A \overset{\mu}{\rightarrow} B$ implies B is SD.

Proof Immediate. ⊠

As usual, we have had to make an inductive definition and then prove a more usable property. We also have that SD is a property of strong equivalence classes:

Proposition 10.7 If $A \sim A'$ and A is SD, then so is A'.

Proof Analogous to Proposition 10.2 but simpler. ⊠

We use the abbreviation SCD (SCD_k) for "strongly (k-)confluent and strongly (k-)determinate". We look for behaviour operations which preserve SCD, and first eliminate some which do not.

Clearly both $\alpha.NIL$ and $\alpha.\beta.NIL$ are SCD, but

$$\alpha.NIL|\alpha.\beta.NIL \sim \alpha.(\alpha.\beta.NIL) + \alpha.(\alpha|\beta).NIL$$

is not SD, since $\alpha.\beta.NIL \not\sim (\alpha|\beta).NIL$. We shall have to forbid $B_1|B_2$ except when $B_1:L_1$, $B_2:L_2$ and $L_1 \cap L_2 = \emptyset$. But this is not enough; $\bar{\alpha}.NIL$ and $\alpha.\beta.NIL$ are SCD, but

$$\bar{\alpha}.NIL|\alpha.\beta.NIL \sim \tau.\beta.NIL + \bar{\alpha}.(\alpha.\beta.NIL) + \ldots..$$

is not SC, since $\beta.NIL \xrightarrow{\bar{\alpha}} B$ is impossible. The problem here is that the $\bar{\alpha}$-action of $\bar{\alpha}.NIL$ may be observed either by $\alpha.\beta.NIL$ or externally. In effect (thinking of pictures) we shall have to prevent the sharing of ports, i.e. one port supporting two links.

In summary, we will forbid $B_1|B_2$, but allow $B_1||B_2$ when $B_1:L_1$, $B_2:L_2$, $L_1 \cap L_2 = \emptyset$; we may call this operation <u>rd-composition</u> (rd = "restricted disjoint").

(Note: we have mostly avoided the operation $||$, and indeed its definition needs some care. Precisely, it is given by $B_1||B_2 = (B_1|B_2)\backslash A$ where $A = \text{names}\ (L(B_1) \cap \overline{L(B_2)})$; we can get a different result if we take $A = \text{names}\ (L_1 \cap \bar{L}_2)$ for arbitrary sorts L_1, L_2 for which $B_1:L_1$ and $B_2:L_2$. Strictly therefore, in each use of $||$ we should make explicit the names which are restricted; but in most cases these will be implied by the sorts of the argument expressions.)

Also we will forbid $B_1 + B_2$ (see remark in §10.1) but allow $(\mu_1|\ldots|\mu_n).B$, composite guarding, which includes (simple) guarding as a special case.

We denote by DCCS the derived calculus whose operations are: <u>Inaction</u>(NIL), <u>Composite Action</u>, <u>rd-Composition</u>, <u>Restriction</u> and <u>Relabelling</u>; we now show that every DCCS program is SCD. (Skip to §10.5 if you are not interested in the proof.)

<u>Proposition 10.8</u> Inaction, Restriction and Relabelling preserve both the properties SC_k and SD_k, for all k.

<u>Proof</u> Clearly NIL is SCD_k. Let us just prove that if A is SC_k, so is $A\backslash\alpha$; the remainder are equally simple. For the inductive step on k, suppose A is SC_{k+1} and

$$A\backslash\alpha \xrightarrow{\mu} B\backslash\alpha,\quad A\backslash\alpha \xrightarrow{\nu} C\backslash\alpha \qquad \text{so} \qquad A \xrightarrow{\mu} B,\quad A \xrightarrow{\nu} C$$

Then <u>either</u> $\mu = \nu$ and $B \sim C$, whence $B\backslash\alpha \sim C\backslash\alpha$ also, <u>or</u> for some D and E, since $\mu, \nu \notin \{\alpha, \bar{\alpha}\}$,

$$\begin{array}{c} B \xrightarrow{\nu} D \\ \wr \\ C \xrightarrow{\mu} E \end{array} \text{, so also} \qquad \begin{array}{c} B\backslash\alpha \xrightarrow{\nu} D\backslash\alpha \\ \wr \\ C\backslash\alpha \xrightarrow{\mu} E\backslash\alpha \end{array}$$

(We have of course used that $\sim$ is a congruence, Theorem 5.4).
Also if $A\backslash\alpha \xrightarrow{\mu} B\backslash\alpha$ then $A \xrightarrow{\mu} B$, so B is SC_k, whence also (by induction) $B\backslash\alpha$ is SC_k. ☒

For Composite Action we can prove more (which we need in handling recursion later), namely that an n-component guard raises the level of SC and SD by n:

<u>Proposition 10.9</u> If A is SC_k (respectively SD_k) then $(\mu_1|\ldots|\mu_n).A$ is SC_{k+n} (respectively SD_{k+n}).

<u>Proof</u> By induction on n, for fixed k. For $n=0$ there is nothing to prove, since $(\mu_1|\ldots|\mu_n).A$ is just A in this case. Now let A' be $(\mu_1|\ldots|\mu_{n+1}).A$, and let us show that A' is SC_{k+n+1}.

Assume

$$A' \begin{array}{l} \xrightarrow{\mu} B' \\ \xrightarrow{\nu} C' \end{array}$$

Then $\mu,\nu \in \{\mu_1,\ldots,\mu_{n+1}\}$. <u>Either</u> $\mu=\nu$, $= \mu_{n+1}$ say, and B', C' are both $(\mu_1|\ldots|\mu_n).A$ up to a permutation of the guard, whence $B' \sim C'$ by Proposition 10.5(3), <u>or</u> $\mu=\mu_n$, $\nu=\mu_{n+1}$ say, and then

$$A' \begin{array}{l} \xrightarrow{\mu} B' \xrightarrow{\nu} \\ \xrightarrow{\nu} C' \xrightarrow{\mu} \end{array} (\mu_1|\ldots|\mu_{n-1}).A$$

Also, if $A' \xrightarrow{\mu} B'$ then $\mu = \mu_{n+1}$ say, and B' is $(\mu_1|\ldots|\mu_n).A$ which is SC_{k+n} by inductive hypothesis. Hence A' is SC_{k+n+1}. We leave the SD part to the reader. ☒

rollary 10.10 If A is SC_k (resp. SD_k) and $n \geq 1$, then $(\mu_1|\ldots|\mu_n).A$ is SC_{k+1} (resp. SD_{k+1}).

roof Immediate, since SC_{k+n} implies SC_{k+1} if $n \geq 1$. ⊠

Thus far, the operations preserve SC and SD separately. We n only show that rd-Composition preserves them together.

roposition 10.11 If A_1 and A_2 are SCD_k, with $A_1:L_1, A_2:L_2$ and $\cap\, L_2 = \emptyset$, then $A_1 \| A_2$ is SCD_k.

roof Take the inductive step; assume A_1, A_2 are SCD_{k+1} and show first that $A_1 \| A_2$ is SC_{k+1}. Suppose

$$A_1 \| A_2 \xrightarrow{\mu} B \qquad A_1 \| A_2 \xrightarrow{\nu} C$$

here are essentially four cases:

(i) B is $B_1 \| A_2$, C is $A_1 \| C_2$ (an A_1 action and an A_2 action), and

$$\begin{array}{l} A_1 \xrightarrow{\mu} B_1 \\ A_2 \xrightarrow{\nu} C_2 \end{array} \quad , \text{ yielding} \quad \begin{array}{l} B_1 \| A_2 \xrightarrow{\nu} B_1 \| C_2 \\ A_1 \| C_2 \xrightarrow{\mu} B_1 \| C_2 \end{array}$$

(ii) B is $B_1 \| A_2$, C is $C_1 \| A_2$ (two A_1 actions), and

$$A_1 \xrightarrow{\mu} B_1 \qquad A_1 \xrightarrow{\nu} C_1$$

Then either $\mu = \nu$ and $B_1 \sim C_1$, whence also $B_1 \| A_2 \sim C_1 \| A_2$, or

$$\begin{array}{l} B_1 \xrightarrow{\nu} D_1 \\ \qquad\quad \wr \\ C_1 \xrightarrow{\mu} E_1 \end{array} \quad , \text{ whence also} \quad \begin{array}{l} B_1 \| A_2 \xrightarrow{\nu} D_1 \| A_2 \\ \qquad\qquad\qquad \wr \\ C_1 \| A_2 \xrightarrow{\mu} E_1 \| A_2 \end{array}$$

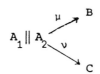

(iii) B is $B_1 \| B_2$, $\mu = \tau$, C is $C_1 \| A_2$ (a communication and an A_1 action), and

$$A_1 \begin{array}{l} \overset{\lambda}{\nearrow} B_1 \\ \underset{\nu}{\searrow} C_1 \end{array} \quad \text{and} \quad A_2 \xrightarrow{\bar{\lambda}} B_2 \qquad (\lambda \in L_1 \cap \bar{L}_2)$$

But then $\nu \neq \lambda$, since $A_1 \| A_2 \xrightarrow{\lambda} C$ is impossible.
Hence

$$\begin{array}{l} B_1 \xrightarrow{\nu} D_1 \\ \qquad\ \ \wr \\ C_1 \xrightarrow{\lambda} E_1 \end{array} \quad \text{, whence also} \quad \begin{array}{l} B_1 \| B_2 \xrightarrow{\nu} D_1 \| B_2 \\ \qquad\qquad\quad \wr \\ C_1 \| A_2 \xrightarrow{\tau} E_1 \| B_2 \end{array}$$

(iv) B is $B_1 \| B_2$, C is $C_1 \| C_2$, $\mu = \nu = \tau$ (two communications), and

$$A_1 \begin{array}{l} \overset{\lambda}{\nearrow} B_1 \\ \underset{\lambda'}{\searrow} C_1 \end{array} \qquad A_2 \begin{array}{l} \overset{\bar{\lambda}}{\nearrow} B_2 \\ \underset{\bar{\lambda}'}{\searrow} C_2 \end{array} \qquad (\lambda, \lambda' \in L_1 \cap \bar{L}_2)$$

If $\lambda = \lambda'$ then $\bar{\lambda} = \bar{\lambda}'$ also, and since A_1, A_2 are SD_{k+1} we must have $B_1 \sim C_1$, $B_2 \sim C_2$, whence also $B_1 \| B_2 \sim C_1 \| C_2$.
Otherwise

$$\begin{array}{l} B_1 \xrightarrow{\lambda'} D_1 \\ \qquad\ \ \wr \\ C_1 \xrightarrow{\lambda} E_1 \end{array} \quad \text{and} \quad \begin{array}{l} B_2 \xrightarrow{\bar{\lambda}'} D_2 \\ \qquad\ \ \wr \\ C_2 \xrightarrow{\bar{\lambda}} E_2 \end{array} \text{, whence} \quad \begin{array}{l} B_1 \| B_2 \xrightarrow{\tau} D_1 \| D_2 \\ \qquad\qquad\quad \wr \\ C_1 \| C_2 \xrightarrow{\tau} E_1 \| E_2 \end{array}$$

Only in the fourth case did we need determinacy of A_1, A_2.
To complete the SC part : if $A_1 \| A_2 \xrightarrow{\mu} B_1 \| B_2$ then, for $i = 1,2$ B_i is either A_i or a μ- or λ-derivative of A_i, hence is SC_k and SD_k, so SCD_k, so by induction $B_1 \| B_2$ is also SCD_k.

For the SD part it only remains to show that

$$A_1 \| A_2 \begin{array}{l} \overset{\lambda}{\nearrow} B \\ \underset{\lambda}{\searrow} C \end{array} \quad \text{implies} \quad B \sim C \qquad (\lambda \in \Lambda).$$

Now either both actions are from A_1 or both from A_2, since $L_1 \cap L_2 = \emptyset$ (our first use of disjointness). In the first case

$A_1 \xrightarrow{\lambda} B_1$, $A_1 \xrightarrow{\lambda} C_1$, whence $B_1 \sim C_1$, whence B(i.e. $B_1 \| A_2$) $\sim C$(i.e. $C_1 \| A_2$).

Similarly in the second case. ☒

It remains to show that definition by recursion in DCCS guarantees hat the behaviour identifiers are SCD.

<u>rop. 10.12</u> Every behaviour identifier b in DCCS is SCD_k for all k.

<u>roof</u>. By induction on k. By guarded well-definedness, (§ 5.4), the definition $b_0 \Leftarrow B_{b_0}$ may be expanded (by substituting B_b for any b where necessary) until every behaviour identifier is guarded. Formally, we apply König's lemma to find

$$b_0 \sim B'_{b_0}$$

containing no b unguarded. Assuming then that every b is SCD_k, we deduce that B'_{b_0} is SCD_{k+1} from Props 10.8, 10.11 and Cor 10.10 - the latter being crucial in raising k to $k+1$. It follows that b_0 - and similarly each other behaviour identifier - is SCD_{k+1}. ☒

<u>xercise 10.2</u> We can also allow guard sequences in composite guards, e.g. $(\alpha.\beta)|\gamma$ or even $(\alpha.(\beta|\gamma))|\delta$. These still preserve SCD. Prove the analogue of Prop 10.9 and Cor 10.10 for composite guards defined as follows:

(i) μ is a composite guard

(ii) If $g_1,\ldots,g_n$ are composite guards $(n \geq 1)$, so are $(g_1.\cdots.g_n)$ and $(g_1|\cdots|g_n)$.

10.5 Proof in DCCS; the scheduler again

We are interested in systems definable in DCCS. The toy system of §10.3 is an example; each c_i there is defined in DCCS, and the system S is also definable in DCCS by

$$c_1 \| c_2 \| c_3$$

Of course we were able to use the form $S \sim (c_1|c_2|c_3)\backslash A$ since $\sim$ preserves SCD, and also $S \sim \alpha_1.S_{23} + \alpha_2.S_{13} + \alpha_3.S_{12}$; neither of these are DCCS expressions, but the faithfulness of $\sim$ to SCD justifies their use in the proof.

Let us return to the scheduler problem of §3.1 ;
we had

$$\boxed{c \Leftarrow \gamma.\bar{\alpha}.(\bar{\beta}|\delta).c}$$

and defining $\boxed{c_i \Leftarrow c[\alpha_i\beta_i\gamma_i\bar{\gamma}_{i+1}/\alpha\beta\gamma\delta]}$ we get

$$c_i \sim \gamma_i.\bar{\alpha}_i.(\bar{\beta}_i|\bar{\gamma}_{i+1}).c_i \qquad (*)$$

We also had

$$\mathrm{Sch} \Leftarrow (s|c_1|\ldots.|c_n)\backslash\gamma_1\ldots\backslash\gamma_n$$

and the second part of our specification demanded

$$\mathrm{Sch} \,\|\, (\prod_{j\neq 1}\alpha_j^{\omega} \mid \prod_{j\neq 1}\beta_j^{\omega}) \approx (\bar{\alpha}_1\bar{\beta}_1)^{\omega} \qquad (1)$$

Now - getting rid of the start button - we have

$$\mathrm{Sch} \approx \bar{\alpha}_1.(\bar{\beta}_1|\bar{\gamma}_2).c_1 \| c_2 \| \ldots \| c_n$$

Now we may define, for $2 \le j \le n$,

$$\boxed{c'_j \Leftarrow c_j \| \alpha_j^{\omega} \| \beta_j^{\omega}}$$

whence easily

$$c'_j \sim \gamma_j.\tau.(\tau|\bar{\gamma}_{j+1}).c'_j \qquad (*)$$

We shall show, then, that

$$\mathrm{Sch}_1 \approx \bar{\alpha}_1.\bar{\beta}_1.\mathrm{Sch}_1 \qquad (2)$$

(compare equation (2) in §3.4, and note the remarks there)
where

$$\boxed{\mathrm{Sch}_1 \Leftarrow \bar{\alpha}_1.(\bar{\beta}_1|\bar{\gamma}_2).c_1 \| c'_2 \| \ldots \| c'_n}$$

Clearly $Sch_1 \approx$ the left side of equation (1) above. Notice that all our definitions - in boxes above - are in DCCS. Since SCD is a property of $\sim$ equivalence classes, we can use the equivalences (*) freely.

$$Sch_1 \sim \bar{\alpha}_1.((\bar{\beta}_1|\bar{\gamma}_2).c_1 \| c_2' \| \ldots. \| c_n')$$

and

$$(\bar{\beta}_1|\bar{\gamma}_2).c_1 \| c_2' \| \ldots \| c_n'$$

$$\xrightarrow{\tau^3} \bar{\beta}_1.c_1 \| \bar{\gamma}_3.c_2 \| c_3' \| \ldots. \| c_n'$$

$$\stackrel{\varepsilon}{\Longrightarrow} \bar{\beta}_1.c_1 \| c_2' \| c_3' \| \ldots. \| c_{n-1}' \| \bar{\gamma}_1.c_n' \qquad (+)$$

$$\sim \bar{\beta}_1.(c_1 \| c_2' \| \ldots. \| c'_{n-1} \| \bar{\gamma}_1.c_n')$$

while $c_1 \| c_2' \| \ldots \| c_{n-1}' \| \bar{\gamma}_1.c_n'$

$$\xrightarrow{\tau} \bar{\alpha}_1.(\bar{\beta}_1|\bar{\gamma}_2).c_1 \| c_2' \| \ldots \| c_n' \sim Sch_1$$

Putting this together, using Theorem 10.4 and known properties of $\approx$, we get $Sch_1 \approx \bar{\alpha}_1.\bar{\beta}_1.Sch$ as required.

The crucial part was the long $\stackrel{\varepsilon}{\Longrightarrow}$ derivation (+) in which the $\bar{\beta}_1$ action could be persistently ignored; without SCD we would have had to deal with this action by absorption, as we did for the first part of the scheduler specification in §3.4. Thus SCD in effect guarantees absorption.

One point is worth noting. From $c_j' \sim \gamma_j.\tau.(\tau|\bar{\gamma}_{j+1}).c_j'$ we can easily get $c_j' \approx \gamma_j.\bar{\gamma}_{j+1}.c_j'$, and this transformation would slightly clarify our proof. But we don't know that SCD is preserved by $\approx$ (in fact we know it is <u>not</u>, in general). Our proofs will therefore be less delicate when we have a weaker property OCD which <u>is</u> preserved by $\approx$, and which also allows a version of Theorem 10.4. We now turn to this question.

Observation Confluence and Determinacy

How should we arrive at a property OCD, weaker than SCD but supporting our proof method (based on Theorem 10.4) and preserved by $\approx$? For determinacy, we would probably look at

$$\begin{array}{l} A \xrightarrow{\lambda} B \\ A \xrightarrow{\lambda} C \end{array} \qquad \text{implies} \qquad B \approx C$$

as a possibility. But the use of $\xrightarrow{\lambda}$ will prevent preservation of this property by $\approx$; you will see this if you try diagrams as in Prop. 10.2. So we might try

$$\begin{array}{l} A \overset{\lambda}{\Longrightarrow} B \\ A \overset{\lambda}{\Longrightarrow} C \end{array} \qquad \text{implies} \qquad B \approx C$$

This is closer to what we will adopt, but notice that it already entails a sort of confluence, for if $B \xrightarrow{\tau} B'$ then we would have $B' \approx C$ also, whence $B \approx B'$ (this is because $A \overset{\lambda}{\Rightarrow} B'$ also holds).

Since we want to harmonize with our definition of $\approx$ we do wish to use $\Rightarrow$ rather than $\rightarrow$; if we cannot separate determinacy from confluence then a definition which covers both seems necessary. We should also deal with $\overset{s}{\Rightarrow}$ $(s \in \Lambda^*)$ rather than just $\overset{\lambda}{\Rightarrow}$ $(\lambda \in \Lambda)$.

What should confluence say about

$$\begin{array}{l} A \overset{r}{\Longrightarrow} B \\ A \overset{s}{\Longrightarrow} C \end{array} \quad , \qquad r,s \in \Lambda^* \ ?$$

It should imply some commutativity of observations, in so far as r and s differ; B should admit an absservation which is in some sense the <u>excess</u> of s over r , written s/r , and C should admit r/s , in such a way that the two results are suitably related:

$$\begin{array}{l} A \overset{r}{\Longrightarrow} B \\ A \overset{s}{\Longrightarrow} C \end{array} \qquad \text{implies} \qquad \begin{array}{c} B \overset{s/r}{\Longrightarrow} D \\ \wr\wr \\ C \overset{r/s}{\Longrightarrow} E \end{array}$$

we shall need to adjust "$\approx$" slightly, but first we define r/s . Intuitivel we get it by working through r from left to right, deleting in r and in s any symbol which occurs in (what remains of) s . Thus r/s is unchanged by a permutation of s , but depends upon the order of r .

<u>Definition</u> For $r, s \in \Lambda^*$, r/s, <u>the excess of r over s</u>, is given recursively by

$$\varepsilon/s = \varepsilon$$
$$(\lambda.r)/s = \begin{cases} \lambda.(r/s) & \text{if } \lambda \text{ is not in } s \\ r/(s/\lambda) & \text{otherwise} . \end{cases}$$

<u>Examples</u>:

r	s	r/s	s/r
$\alpha\beta\gamma$	$\beta\gamma\alpha$	ε	ε
$\alpha\beta\alpha$	$\alpha\gamma$	$\beta\alpha$	γ
$\alpha\beta\alpha$	$\beta\alpha\gamma\beta$	α	$\gamma\beta$

We list some of the properties of "/" without proof (we write r <u>perm</u> s to mean r is a permutation of s):

(i) If r <u>perm</u> s then $r/s = s/r = \varepsilon$.

(ii) If s <u>perm</u> s' then $r/s = r/s'$,
s/r <u>perm</u> s'/r.

(iii) If r and s have no member in common then
$r/s = r$, $s/r = s$.

(iv) If r <u>perm</u> ss', then r/s <u>perm</u> s' and $s/r = \varepsilon$.

(v) $r.(s/r)$ <u>perm</u> $s.(r/s)$.

(vi) $r/s_1s_2 = (r/s_1)/s_2$, $r_1r_2/s = (r_1/s).(r_2/(s/r_1))$.

There are many others, some needed in proving the propositions below, but we will not give those proofs here.

We now define OCD by a sequence $\{OCD_k \; ; \; k \geq 0\}$:

<u>Definition</u>. A is always OCD_0.

A is OCD_{k+1} iff

(i) $A \overset{r}{\Longrightarrow} B$, $A \overset{s}{\Longrightarrow} C$ implies $B \overset{s/r}{\Longrightarrow} D$, $C \overset{r/s}{\Longrightarrow} E$, $D \approx_k E$ for some D,E ;

(ii) $A \overset{r}{\Longrightarrow} B$ implies B is OCD_k

A is OCD iff it is OCD_k for all $k \geq 0$.

Note the use of $\approx_k$ rather than $\approx$; this is essential in showing that $\approx$ preserves OCD.

Thus if A is OCD we have for each k, for example:

$$\begin{array}{l} A \overset{r}{\Longrightarrow} B \\ A \overset{r}{\Longrightarrow} C \end{array} \quad \text{implies} \quad \begin{array}{l} B \overset{\varepsilon}{\Longrightarrow} D \\ \qquad\ \ \wr\wr_k \\ C \overset{\varepsilon}{\Longrightarrow} E \end{array} \quad \text{(determinacy)} \ ;$$

$$\begin{array}{l} A \overset{\alpha\beta}{\Longrightarrow} B \\ A \overset{\beta\alpha}{\Longrightarrow} C \end{array} \quad \text{implies} \quad \begin{array}{l} B \overset{\varepsilon}{\Longrightarrow} D \\ \qquad\ \ \wr\wr_k \\ C \overset{\varepsilon}{\Longrightarrow} E \end{array} \ ;$$

$$\begin{array}{l} A \overset{\varepsilon}{\Longrightarrow} B \\ A \overset{s}{\Longrightarrow} C \end{array} \quad \text{implies} \quad \begin{array}{l} B \overset{s}{\Longrightarrow} D \\ \qquad\ \ \wr\wr_k \\ C \overset{\varepsilon}{\Longrightarrow} E \end{array} \ ;$$

$$\begin{array}{l} A \overset{r}{\Longrightarrow} B \\ A \overset{rs}{\Longrightarrow} C \end{array} \quad \text{implies} \quad \begin{array}{l} B \overset{s}{\Longrightarrow} D \\ \qquad\ \ \wr\wr_k \\ C \overset{\varepsilon}{\Longrightarrow} E \end{array} \ .$$

The following results hold:

<u>Proposition 10.13</u> If A is OCD and $A \approx A'$ then A' is OCD. ⊠

[<u>Exercise 10.3.</u> Prove this by showing that if A is OCD_k and $A \approx_{2k} A'$ then A' is OCD_k .

Theorem 10.14 (Confluence) If A is OCD and $A \overset{\varepsilon}{\Longrightarrow} B$ then $A \approx B$.

<u>Proof</u> We show it for $\approx_k$ by induction on k . For the inductive step, assume A is OCD and $A \overset{\varepsilon}{\Longrightarrow} B$.

(i) If $B \overset{s}{\Longrightarrow} B'$, then clearly $A \overset{s}{\Longrightarrow} B'$ also.

(ii) If $A \overset{s}{\Longrightarrow} A'$ then, because A is OCD,

$$\begin{array}{l} B \overset{s}{\Longrightarrow} B' \\ \qquad\ \ \wr\wr_k \\ A' \overset{\varepsilon}{\Longrightarrow} C \end{array} \qquad \text{for some } B', C$$

But A' is OCD, so by induction $A' \approx_k C$, whence $A' \approx_k B'$ as required.

<u>Proposition 10.15</u> If A is SCD then it is OCD. ⊠

From this we immediately know that DCCS, and anything $\approx$ to a DCCS progr is OCD. Although these facts do not imply it immediately, we also have

<u>Proposition 10.16</u> The operations of DCCS all preserve the property OCD. ⊠

Two remarks should be made. First, we do not know of any derived ılculus of CCS whose programs are all OCD but not all SCD. It would be ery interesting to find one, particularly if it contained systems ıich are intuitively determinate in some sense, like earlier case-studies ı these notes, but cannot be expressed in DCCS. First of course we would ınt to extend the present notions, and DCCS, to allow value-passing.

Second, the reader may wonder why we introduced SCD at all, since D has the property which we used in proofs and preserves $\approx$; OCD ıs the advantage that it is a property of behaviours ($\overset{c}{\approx}$ congruence classes), ot only of programs. The reason is partly technical; the crucial property SCD (Cor 10.10), which provided for recursively defined behaviours in CS, cannot be established for OCD. Also of course the stronger notion y yield stronger methods.

In conclusion: we have found a derived calculus of CCS which possesses ı interesting property, and it is possible that other derived calculi may found with useful properties. For confluence and determinacy, there is strong connection - still to be explored - with notions in Petri's Net ıeory, particularly the notions of (absence of) Conflict and Confusion ıd the subclass of nets called Marked Graphs [CoH]. Other authors have plored confluence in various settings. The origin of the idea appears be the Church-Rosser theorem for the λ-calculus; Church-Rosser properties e discussed by Rosen [Ros] . Huet [Hue] studied conditions under which rm-rewriting systems are confluent; the principal difference here is that ır rewriting relations $\xrightarrow{\mu}$ and $\overset{s}{\Rightarrow}$ are indexed by labels and sequences. eller [Kel] introduces a confluence notion into parallel computation; is rewriting relations are indexed, but his definition of confluence does ot exploit the indexing.

The author's impression is that confluence is a deep notion which (as ith most deep notions) manifests itself very differently in different ormal or mathematical settings. We have not invented it, but only found t some new clothes.

CHAPTER 11

Conclusion

11.1 What has been achieved?

We hope to have shown that our calculus is based on few and simple ideas, that it allows us to describe succinctly and to manipulate a wide variety of computing agents, that it offers rich and various proof techniques, that it underlies and explains some concurrent programming concepts, and that it allows the precise formulation of questions which remain to be answered (e.g. which equivalence relation to employ). It also appears to have some intrinsic mathematical interest. Thus we claim to have achieved, to some extent, the aims of articulacy and conceptual unity expressed in Chapter 0.

In the next few sections we examine CCS critically (though briefly) in one or two respects; in doing so some suggestions for further work arise very clearly. In the final section we propose some other directions for the future.

11.2 Is CCS a programming language?

It is not universally agreed what qualifications justify the title "programming language". Let us try to examine CCS critically with respect to some possible qualifications.

First, we have not said how to implement it on a computer (with one or many processors). Implementation of concurrent programs raises a host of difficult questions. To start with, such a program is often (at least in our case) non-determinate; should its 'implementation' be able to follow any possible execution, by having the power to toss a coin from time to time or by using a machine whose parts run at unpredictable relative speeds? Or is it more correct to talk of, not a single implementation, but a set of implementations for each program, each implementation being determinate?

Again, would one allow an implementation which is, if not sequential, conducted under some centralised control? This would be rather unsatisfactory since the calculus is designed to express heterarchy among concurrently active components. But since it can express systems which generate unboundedly many such components, it is natural to expect an implementation to administer (not necessarily in a hierarchic manner) the allocation of a fixed number of processors in executing the components.

An implementation problem arises, even with CCS programs with a fixed number of concurrent components, and even if there are enough processors to go round. In the general case where the components are arbitrarily linked and where each one may have at each moment an arbitrary set of communication capabilities, our primitive notion of synchronised communication does not admit direct realisation by hardware (at least by current techniques) as far as the author knows. Jerry Schwarz [Sch] has exposed the difficulty and proposed a solution, which can indeed become simple in special cases but is not so in general. So CCS does not (yet) have the property that its primitives have primitive realisations. We claim rather to have found a communication primitive which allows other disciplines of communication (e.g. by shared variables, or by bounded or unbounded buffers) to be defined, and which can be handled mathematically. There is no a priori reason that any such primitive should also be simple to realise. But we may compare the primitives of the λ-calculus (functional abstraction and application), or of combinatory logic (the combinators and combination); ten years ago these may have been thought to require very indirect realisation, even via software, but they are now being realised directly by hardware.

Let us look at another qualification usually expected of a practical programming language. It should not only have a powerful and not too redundent set of constructs, but should also encourage disciplined and lucid programming. This can mean that its constructs are conceptually rather non-primitive; consider the sophisticated array manipulations of ALGOL 68, or - closer to concurrency - the monitors of Hoare. On the other hand a calculus, as distinct from a programming language, should contain only a small set of conceptually primitive constructs (it will be hard to theorize about it otherwise), and should remain largely impartial with respect to design decisions which aim at 'good' programming. Then the calculus can serve as a basis for defining practical languages, or for building practical hardware configurations. Of course one cannot distinguish sharply between the aims of conceptual parsimony and practical utility, but it is fairly certain that a language for writing good large programs will itself be too large to serve as a theoretical tool, and its design may well be motivated by current implementation techniques; when these change it can grow obsolete.

Returning to the λ-calculus as a prime example, it is now widely accepted as a medium which can be used to define and discuss sequential algorithms, and richer languages for them. Although CCS is not as small and simple, it is intended as a step towards such a medium for concurrent systems. We also hope to have shown that at least some concurrent systems can be expressed lucidly in CCS; perhaps this is because it is not yet small enough!

11.3 The question of fairness

In terms of CCS we may state a property, which is arguably a property of real systems and should therefore be reflected in a model: if an agent persistently offers an experiment, and if an observer persistently attempts it, then it will eventually succeed. A model which reflects this property is sometimes called <u>fair</u>. Is CCS fair?

Consider the program

$B = \tau^{\omega}|\lambda.\mathrm{NIL}$, where τ^{ω} may be defined by $b \Leftarrow \tau.b$.

The only actions of B are

$$B \xrightarrow{\lambda} \tau^{\omega}|\ \mathrm{NIL} \quad \text{and} \quad B \xrightarrow{\tau} B \ .$$

So B has no ε-derivative which does not offer a λ-experiment; this may plausibly be taken to mean that B persistently offers the experiment.

Now if we consider only the derivations of B, the infinite derivation $B \xrightarrow{\tau^{\omega}}$ suggests that the experiment is not bound to succeed even if attempted by an observer; hence we may choose to infer that CCS is not fair.

On the other hand if we consider observation equivalence, we can easily deduce

$$B \approx \lambda.\mathrm{NIL}$$

and we argued in Chapter 1 that if an agent offers an experiment and has no alternative action - as here λ.NIL has no alternative to its offer of an λ-experiment - then an observer's attempt at the experiment is bound to succeed. It therefore seems that the insensitivity of ≈ to infinite unobservable action makes CCS fair, at least for this one example. This is slightly strengthened by noticing that the agents

$$B_1 = \lambda.\mathrm{NIL} + \tau^{\omega}, \quad B_2 = \lambda.\mathrm{NIL} + \tau(\lambda.\mathrm{NIL} + \tau^{\omega}), \ \ldots$$

ich do not persistently offer a λ-experiment, are not equivalent to B hough all equivalent to each other).

Indeed, we may tentatively formalise "B persistently offers λ" r arbitrary B as follows:

finition B must λ iff $B \overset{\varepsilon}{\Longrightarrow} B'$ implies $\exists B''.B' \overset{\lambda}{\Longrightarrow} B''$.

en it is easy to prove that

$$B \approx C \text{ implies } \forall\lambda.(B \text{ must } \lambda \Longleftrightarrow C \text{ must } \lambda)$$

owing that, under this definition, observation equivalence respects e persistence or non-persistence of offers.

But this is very far from a demonstration that CCS is fair; for ample, there are alternatives to the above definition, and a much re detailed investigation seems necessary to decide which is correct. en if we could conclude that CCS is fair, with the present notion of servation equivalence, the fact remains that other equivalences (see e remarks in §7.2) which respect the presence of infinite unobservable tion - and are therefore unfair in view of the above discussion - may ve other factors in their favour. We must leave the question open.

Other authors have focussed more directly on the fairness issue. ueli [Pnu 1, 2], for example, shows how "eventually" (closely allied fairness, as seen from the first paragraph of this section) can be presented in a temporal logic. It would be interesting to combine ch a treatment with our algebraic methods.

1.4 The notion of behaviour

This work has been concerned throughout with expressing behaviour. e have tried not to prejudge what a behaviour is, but rather regard it s a congruence by considering which expressions can be distinguished by servation. At first we hoped this approach would lead us to one obviously est congruence relation, and entitle us to say that - within our chosen de of expression - we have defined behaviour. This has not transpired; he discussion in §7.2 shows that there is still latitude for choice in he definition of observation equivalence, and some (though not all) of he choices induce different congruences.

However, we have provided a setting in which the latitude for choice s not embarrassingly great, and in which the consequences of each choice can be examined. It is not improbable that a best choice will thus emerge. Furthermore, although the calculus itself cannot claim to be canonical since alternatives exist for the basic operations and their derivational meaning, the same approach to behaviour can be taken for many alternatives.

Our methods should be contrasted with what has often been done in providing a denotational semantics for programming languages, following the work of Scott and Strachey [SS]. The method - a very fruitful one - is to define outright one or several semantic domains, built from simple domains by such standard means as Cartesian product, function space construction and (for nondeterminism) a powerdomain construction [Plo 1, Smy]; then the semantic interpretation of phrases in these domains is specified by induction on phrase structure. The approach has given immense insight, and yet it was found that the match between denotational and operational meaning was sometimes imperfect; this mismatch was first exposed by Plotkin for a typed λ-calculus [Plo 2]. We found a mismatch again for the model of concurrent processes presented in [MM]. There is no reason to expect, a priori, that an explicitly presented denotational model will match the operational meaning; the latter should serve as a criterion for the correct denotational model, not vice versa (see also §0.4). Of course, it would be satisfying to find an explicit presentation of a model which does meet the criterion; this may entail extending our repertoire of domains and domain constructions, as found in [HP 1] where so-called nondeterministic domains and a tensor product is used.

We can summarise our approach, then, as an attempt to calculate with behaviours without knowing what they are explicitly; the calculations are justified by operational meaning, and may help towards a better understanding - even an explicit formulation - of a domain of behaviours.

11.5 Directions for further work

(i) In Chapter 9 we explained a simple high-level language in terms of CCS. It will be interesting to see how far such languages can be so explained, and how CCS may help in their design. For example, in that chapter we exposed an apparent deficiency of the calculus, which could be removed if we allowed labels to be passed as values in communication. What effect would such an extension have on our theory? And is the extension really necessary, or can we find a way of simulating label-passing with CCS as it stands? (An analogy is that the λ-calculus does not take the notions of memory and assignment as primitive, but can simulate them.)

(ii) Although hardware devices can be described abstractly as in §8.2, it is not clear how to extend the calculus to deal with detailed timing considerations, or to bring it into harmony with existing description methods which deal with timing. We have some grounds for hope here; for example, Luca Cardelli [Car] has recently constructed an algebra of analog processes (whose communication signals are time functions) and has shown it to be a Flow Algebra [Mil 2] that is, it satisfies the laws presented in Theorem 5.5. However, Flow Algebra deals only with our static operations (Composition, Restriction, Relabelling) and it is the dynamic operations (Action, Summation) which are more committed to the idea of discreteness and synchronisation in communication. I am not competent to judge whether it is desirable, from the engineering point of view, to build hardware components which realize these dynamic operations. An alternative may be to try to find a continuous version of CCS, but how to do it is unclear.

(iii) In Chapters 9 and 10 we were able to find two interesting derived calculi. In particular DCCS, determinate CCS, has certain simple properties which facilitate proof. (Since Chapter 10 was written, Michael Sanderson has with little difficulty extended DCCS to allow value-passing.) It is important to isolate other subclasses of behaviour, characterised by intuitively simple properties, and to find for any such subclass a derived calculus which can express only its members. Of particular interest, for example, would be a calculus of deadlock-free behaviours. Again, it would be illuminating to find that certain known models correspond to derived calculi; possible cases are Kahn/MacQueen networks of processes [KMQ], and the Data Flow model of Dennis et al [DFL].

(iv) As far as proof methods for CCS are concerned, we appear only to have made a beginning. On the theoretical side, we should look for complete axiomatizations for subcalculi, where these are possible; the results in [HM] and [HP 2] go some way towards this.

On the more practical side, completeness (which may not be possible for the full calculus anyway) is less important than a repertoire powerful and manageable techniques. In our examples we have found a few useful techniques; in particular we found it useful to work not just with congruence ($\stackrel{c}{\approx}$) but with equivalence ($\approx$) also, and this immediately suggests that other predicates of behaviour may be used with advantage. Further, we often wish to show that an agent meets an incomplete specification, i.e. one which does not determine a unique behaviour; this was illustrated by the examples of Chapters 3 and 8. In these examples the incomplete specification could be expressed within the terms of CCS, and we would like to discover how far this is possible in general, and whether - when possible - it is natural.

(v) More particularly, concerning proof techniques, the question of recursive definitions and induction principles needs further study. For our definition of observation equivalence and congruence we are able to identify a class of recursive definitions which possess unique solutions (up to $\approx$ or $\stackrel{c}{\approx}$); see Exercise 7.7. We believe this class can be considerably widened. It was this uniqueness which allowed us to do certain proofs, e.g. the scheduler proof in Chapter 3, without appealing to any induction principle. But as we remarked at the end of §7.5, we believe that the Computation Induction principle of Scott will apply in the presence of a finer version of observation equivalence. The strength of this principle is that it works without assuming <u>unique</u> solutions of recursive definitions; it allows us to deduce properties of <u>least</u> solutions with respect to a partial ordering of behaviours. But it remains to be seen how important the principle will be in practice; moreover, since the finer observation equivalence appears to be unfair (in the sense of §11.3) there is a delicate and difficult problem in relating proof theory to the conceptual correctness of the model.

We are not discouraged by the emergence of this problem. On the contrary, we believe it to be intrinsic to concurrent computing, not merely a defect of our approach, and are rather pleased to see it emerge in a sharp form.

(vi) Finally, and fundamentally, however successful we may become in working within CCS, its primitive constructs deserve re-examination. Are they the smallest possible set? Are other constructs needed to express a richer class of behaviours? How can we relate Petri Net Theory to the ideas of observation and synchronized communication? By repeatedly returning to such basic questions we may hope to get closer to an underlying theory for distributed computation.

APPENDIX

Properties of congruence and equivalence

Direct equivalence	$\equiv$	... §5.6
Strong congruence	$\sim$	... §5.7
Observation equivalence	$\approx$	... §7.2
Observation congruence	$\overset{c}{\approx}$	... §7.3

$B \equiv C$ implies $B \sim C$ implies $B \overset{c}{\approx} C$ implies $B \approx C$ ... Ex 5.2, Cor 7.

Observation congruence "$\overset{c}{\approx}$" is also denoted by equality "=", though many laws (as their names indicate) hold for strong congruence "$\sim$" or even direct equivalence "$\equiv$". Except where indicated, the laws are those of Theorems 5.3 and 5.5 generalised by Theorem 5.7 .

Summation

Sum $\equiv$
(1) $B_1 + B_2 = B_2 + B_1$
(2) $B_1 + (B_2 + B_3) = (B_1 + B_2) + B_3$
(3) $B + NIL = B$
(4) $B + B = B$

Action

Act $\equiv$ $\alpha\tilde{x}.B = \alpha\tilde{y}.B\{\tilde{y}/\tilde{x}\}$
where $\tilde{y}$ is a vector of distinct variables not in B .

Composition

Com $\equiv$ Let B and C be sums of guards. Then

$$\begin{aligned} B|C = &\textstyle\sum\{g.(B'|C);\ \ g.B' \text{ a summand of } B\} \\ &+ \textstyle\sum\{g.(B|C');\ \ g.C' \text{ a summand of } C\} \\ &+ \textstyle\sum\{\tau.(B'\{\tilde{E}/\tilde{x}\}|C');\ \ \alpha\tilde{x}.B' \text{ a summand of } B \text{ and } \bar{\alpha}\tilde{E}.C' \text{ a summand of } C\} \\ &+ \textstyle\sum\{\tau.(B'|C'\{\tilde{E}/\tilde{x}\});\ \ \bar{\alpha}\tilde{E}.B' \text{ a summand of } B \text{ and } \alpha\tilde{x}.C' \text{ a summand of } C\} \end{aligned}$$

provided that in the first (second) summand no free variable of C(B) is bound by g.

Com ~ (1) $B_1|B_2 = B_2|B_1$

(2) $B_1(B_2|B_3) = (B_1|B_2)|B_3$

(3) $B|NIL = B$

estriction

Res ≡ (1) $NIL\backslash\beta = NIL$

(2) $(B_1 + B_2)\backslash\beta = B_1\backslash\beta + B_2\backslash\beta$

(3) $(g.B)\backslash\beta = \begin{cases} NIL \text{ if } \beta=name(g) \\ g.(B\backslash\beta) \text{ otherwise} \end{cases}$

Res ~ (1) $B\backslash\alpha = B$ $(B{:}L,\ \alpha\notin names\ (L))$

(2) $B\backslash\alpha\backslash\beta = B\backslash\beta\backslash\alpha$

(3) $(B_1|B_2)\backslash\alpha = B_1\backslash\alpha|B_2\backslash\alpha$

$(B_1{:}L_1, B_2{:}L_2, \ \alpha\notin names\ (L_1\cap\bar{L}_2))$

elabelling

Rel ≡ (1) $NIL[S] = NIL$

(2) $(B_1 + B_2)[S] = B_1[S] + B_2[S]$

(3) $(g.B)[S] = S(g).(B[S])$

Rel ~ (1) $B[I] = B$ $(I{:}L \rightarrow L$ the identity mapping)

(2) $B[S] = B[S']$ $(B{:}L$ and $S{\restriction}L = S'{\restriction}L)$

(3) $B[S][S'] = B[S'{\circ}S]$

(4) $B[S]\backslash\beta = B\backslash\alpha[S]$ $(\beta = name\ (S(\alpha)))$

(5) $(B_1|B_2)[S] = B_1[S]|B_2[S]$

Identifier

Ide ≡ Let $b(\tilde{x}) \Leftarrow B_b$; then

$b(\tilde{E}) = B_b\{\tilde{E}/\tilde{x}\}$

Conditional

Con ≡ (1) If true then B_1 else $B_2 = B_1$

(2) if false then B_1 else $B_2 = B_2$

Unobservable action τ

(1) $g.\tau.B = g.B$

(2) $B + \tau.B = \tau.B$ ... Theorem 7.13

(3) $g.(B + \tau.C) + g.C = g.(B + \tau.C)$

(4) $B + \tau.(B + C) = \tau.(B + C)$ ... Cor. 7.14

Observation Equivalence

(1) $B \approx \tau.B$ ... Prop. 7.1

(2) $\approx$ is preserved by all operations except + ... Theorem 7.3

(3) $B \approx C$ implies $B = C$ when B,C stable ... Prop. 7.11

(4) $B \approx C$ implies $g.B = g.C$ ... Prop. 7.12

Expansion

... Theorem 5.8

Let $B = (B_1|\ldots|B_m)\backslash A$, where each B_i is a sum of guards. Then

$$B = \sum\{g.((B_1|\ldots|B_i'|\ldots|B_m)\backslash A);\ g.B_i' \text{ a summand of } B_i,\ \text{name}(g) \notin A\}$$
$$+ \sum\{\tau.((B_1|\ldots|B_i'\{\tilde{E}/\tilde{x}\}|\ldots|B_j'|\ldots|B_m)\backslash A);\ \alpha\tilde{x}.B_i' \text{ a summand of } B_i,\ \bar{\alpha}\tilde{E}.B_j' \text{ a summand of } B_j,\ i \neq j\}$$

provided that in the first term no free variable in $B_k (k \neq i)$ is bound by g.

eferences

(In these references, LNCSn stands for Lecture Notes in Computer Science, Vol n, Springer Verlag.)

Bri1] P. Brinch Hansen, Operating Systems Principles, Prentice Hall, 1973.

Bri2] P. Brinch Hansen, "Distributed processes; a concurrent programming concept", Comm. ACM 21, 11, 1978.

CaH] R. Campbell and A. Habermann, "The specification of process synchronization by Path Expressions", LNCS 16, 1974.

Car] L. Cardelli, "Analog Processes", To appear in Proc 9th MFCS, Poland, 1980.

CoH] F. Commoner and A. Holt, "Marked directed graphs", JCSS 5, 1971.

DFL] J. Dennis, J. Fosseen and J. Linderman, "Data flow schemas", LNCS 5, 1974.

Dij] E. Dijkstra, "Guarded commands, nondeterminacy and formal derivation of programs", Comm. ACM 18, 8, 1975.

EBJ] P. van Emde Boas and T. Janssen, "The impact of Frege's principle of compositionality for the semantics of programming and natural languages", Report 79-07, Dept. of Mathematics, University of Amsterdam, 1979.

GLT] H.J. Genrich, K. Lautenbach and P.S. Thiagarajan, "An overview of Net Theory", Proc. Advanced Course on General Net Theory of Processes and Systems, to appear in LNCS, 1980.

HAL] C. Hewitt, G. Attardi and H. Liebermann, "Specifying and proving properties of guardians for distributed systems", LNCS 70, 1979.

HM] M. Hennessy and R. Milner, "On observing nondeterminism and concurrency", to be presented at 8th ICALP at Amsterdam, and appear in LNCS, 1980.

Hoa1] C.A.R. Hoare, "Towards a theory of parallel programming", in Operating Systems Techniques, Academic Press, 1972.

Hoa2] C.A.R. Hoare, "Monitors: an operating system structuring concept", Comm. ACM 17, 10, 1974.

Hoa3] C.A.R. Hoare, "Communicating Sequential Processes", Comm. ACM 21, 8, 1978.

[HP1] M. Hennessy and G. Plotkin, "Full abstraction for a simple parallel programming language", Proc 8th MFCS, Czechoslovakia, LNCS 74, 1979.

[HP2] M. Hennessy and G. Plotkin, "A term model for CCS", to appear in Proc 9th MFCS, Poland, 1980.

[Hue] G. Huet, 'Confluent reductions: abstract properties and applications to term-rewriting systems", Report No. 250, IRIA Laboria, Paris 1977.

[Kel] R. Keller, "A fundamental theorem of asynchronous parallel computation", Parallel Processing, ed. T.Y. Feng, Springer, 1975.

[KMQ] G. Kahn and D. MacQueen, "Coroutines and networks of parallel processes", Proc. IFIP Congress, North Holland, 1977.

[Kun] H.T. Kung, "Synchronized and asynchronous algorithms" in Algorithms and Complexity, ed J.F. Traub, Academic Press, 1976.

[Mil1] R. Milner, "Processes; a mathematical model of computing agents", Proc Logic Colloquium '73, ed. Rose and Shepherdson, North Holland, 1973.

[Mil2] R. Milner, "Flowgraphs and flow algebras", J. ACM 26, 4, 1979.

[Mil3] R. Milner, "Synthesis of communicating behaviour", Proc 7th MFCS, Poland, LNCS 64, 1978.

[Mil4] R. Milner, "Algebras for communicating systems", Report CSR-25-78, Computer Science Dept., Edinburgh University, 1978.

[Mil5] R. Milner, "An algebraic theory of synchronization", LNCS 67, 1979.

[Mln] G. Milne, "A mathematical model of concurrent computation", Ph.D. Thesis, Computer Science Dept, University of Edinburgh, 1978

[MM] G. Milne and R. Milner, "Concurrent processes and their syntax", J. ACM, 26, 2, 1979.

[Mos] P. Mosses, "SIS, Semantic Implementation System", DAIMI Report MD-33, Aarhus University, 1979.

[MQ] D. MacQueen, "Models for distributed computing", Report No. 351, IRIA-Laboria, Paris, 1979.

[Mül] T. Müldner, "On synchronizing tools for parallel programs", Report 357, Inst. of Computer Science, Polish Academy of Science, Warsaw, 1979.

[MWW] A Maggiolo-Schettini, H. Wedde and J. Winkowski, "Modelling a Solution for a control problem in distributed systems by restrictions, LNCS 70, 1979.

[Pet] C.A. Petri, "Introduction to General Net Theory", Proc. Advanced Course on General Net Theory of Processes and Systems, to appear in LNCS, 1980.

[Plo1] G. Plotkin, "A powerdomain construction", SIAM J. Comp 5, 1976.

[Plo2] G. Plotkin, "LCF considered as a programming language", TCS 5, 3, 1977.

[Pnu1] A. Pnueli, "The temporal logic of programs", 19th Annual Symp. on Foundations of Computer Science, Providence R.I., 1977.

[Pnu2] A. Pnueli, "The temporal semantics of concurrent programs", LNCS 70, 1979.

[Ros] B. Rosen, "Tree manipulation systems and Church-Rosser Theorems", J. ACM 20, 1, 1973.

[Sch] J. Schwarz, "Distributed synchronization of processor communication", Internal Report, Dept. of Artificial Intelligence, University of Edinburgh, 1978.

[Smy] M. Smyth, "Powerdomains", JCSS 16, 1978.

[SS] D. Scott and C. Strachey, "Towards a mathematical semantics for computer languages", Proc. Symp. on Computers and Automata, Microwave Res. Inst. Symposia Series, Vol 21, Polytechnic Inst. of Brooklyn, 1972.

[Wad] W. Wadge, "An extensional treatment of dataflow deadlock", LNCS 70, 1979.

[Wir] N. Wirth, "MODULA: A language for modular multiprogramming", Report 18, ETH Zurich, 1976.

: Interactive Systems. Proceedings 1976. Edited by A. Blaser Hackl. VI, 380 pages. 1976.

: A. C. Hartmann, A Concurrent Pascal Compiler for Miniters. VI, 119 pages. 1977.

: B. S. Garbow, Matrix Eigensystem Routines – Eispack Extension. VIII, 343 pages. 1977.

. Automata, Languages and Programming. Fourth Colloquium, sity of Turku, July 1977. Edited by A. Salomaa and M. Steinby. pages. 1977.

: Mathematical Foundations of Computer Science. Proceed-77. Edited by J. Gruska. XII, 608 pages. 1977.

: Design and Implementation of Programming Languages. dings 1976. Edited by J. H. Williams and D. A. Fisher. X, ges. 1977.

: A. Gerbier, Mes premières constructions de programmes. 3 pages. 1977.

: Fundamentals of Computation Theory. Proceedings 1977. by M. Karpiński. XII, 542 pages. 1977.

: Portability of Numerical Software. Proceedings 1976. Edited Cowell. VIII, 539 pages. 1977.

: M. J. O'Donnell, Computing in Systems Described by Equa-IV, 111 pages. 1977.

: E. Hill, Jr., A Comparative Study of Very Large Data Bases. pages. 1978.

: Operating Systems, An Advanced Course. Edited by R. Bayer, Graham, and G. Seegmüller. X, 593 pages. 1978.

: The Vienna Development Method: The Meta-Language. by D. Bjørner and C. B. Jones. XVIII, 382 pages. 1978.

: Automata, Languages and Programming. Proceedings 1978. by G. Ausiello and C. Böhm. VIII, 508 pages. 1978.

: Natural Language Communication with Computers. Edited nard Bolc. VI, 292 pages. 1978.

: Mathematical Foundations of Computer Science. Proceed-978. Edited by J. Winkowski. X, 551 pages. 1978.

5: Information Systems Methodology, Proceedings, 1978. by G. Bracchi and P. C. Lockemann. XII, 696 pages. 1978.

: N. D. Jones and S. S. Muchnick, TEMPO: A Unified Treat-f Binding Time and Parameter Passing Concepts in Pro-ing Languages. IX, 118 pages. 1978.

: Theoretical Computer Science, 4th GI Conference, Aachen, 1979. Edited by K. Weihrauch. VII, 324 pages. 1979.

: D. Harel, First-Order Dynamic Logic. X, 133 pages. 1979.

: Program Construction. International Summer School. Edited Bauer and M. Broy. VII, 651 pages. 1979.

. Semantics of Concurrent Computation. Proceedings 1979. by G. Kahn. VI, 368 pages. 1979.

Automata, Languages and Programming. Proceedings 1979. by H. A. Maurer. IX, 684 pages. 1979.

: Symbolic and Algebraic Computation. Proceedings 1979. by E. W. Ng. XV, 557 pages. 1979.

3: Graph-Grammars and Their Application to Computer e and Biology. Proceedings 1978. Edited by V. Claus, H. Ehrig Rozenberg. VII, 477 pages. 1979.

: Mathematical Foundations of Computer Science. Proceed-979. Edited by J. Bečvář. IX, 580 pages. 1979.

5: Mathematical Studies of Information Processing. Pro-gs 1978. Edited by E. K. Blum, M. Paul and S. Takasu. VIII, ages. 1979.

: Codes for Boundary-Value Problems in Ordinary Differential ons. Proceedings 1978. Edited by B. Childs et al. VIII, 388 1979.

7: G. V. Bochmann, Architecture of Distributed Computer s. VIII, 238 pages. 1979.

Vol. 78: M. Gordon, R. Milner and C. Wadsworth, Edinburgh LCF. VIII, 159 pages. 1979.

Vol. 79: Language Design and Programming Methodology. Proceedings, 1979. Edited by J. Tobias. IX, 255 pages. 1980.

Vol. 80: Pictorial Information Systems. Edited by S. K. Chang and K. S. Fu. IX, 445 pages. 1980.

Vol. 81: Data Base Techniques for Pictorial Applications. Proceedings, 1979. Edited by A. Blaser. XI, 599 pages. 1980.

Vol. 82: J. G. Sanderson, A Relational Theory of Computing. VI, 147 pages. 1980.

Vol. 83: International Symposium Programming. Proceedings, 1980. Edited by B. Robinet. VII, 341 pages. 1980.

Vol. 84: Net Theory and Applications. Proceedings, 1979. Edited by W. Brauer. XIII, 537 Seiten. 1980.

Vol. 85: Automata, Languages and Programming. Proceedings, 1980. Edited by J. de Bakker and J. van Leeuwen. VIII, 671 pages. 1980.

Vol. 86: Abstract Software Specifications. Proceedings, 1979. Edited by D. Bjørner. XIII, 567 pages. 1980

Vol. 87: 5th Conference on Automated Deduction. Proceedings, 1980. Edited by W. Bibel and R. Kowalski. VII, 385 pages. 1980.

Vol. 88: Mathematical Foundations of Computer Science 1980. Proceedings, 1980. Edited by P. Dembiński. VIII, 723 pages. 1980.

Vol. 89: Computer Aided Design - Modelling, Systems Engineering, CAD-Systems. Proceedings, 1980. Edited by J. Encarnacao. XIV, 461 pages. 1980.

Vol. 90: D. M. Sandford, Using Sophisticated Models in Resolution Theorem Proving.
XI, 239 pages. 1980

Vol. 91: D. Wood, Grammar and L Forms: An Introduction. IX, 314 pages. 1980.

Vol. 92: R. Milner, A Calculus of Communication Systems. VI, 171 pages. 1980.

Printed in the United States
119024LV00002B/18/A

9 783540 10235